MEDIA ETHICS
A GUIDE FOR PROFESSIONAL CONDUCT

MEDIA ETHICS
A GUIDE FOR PROFESSIONAL CONDUCT

5TH EDITION

Revised by Fred Brown, editor, and members of the
Society of Professional Journalists' Ethics Committee

Copyright © 2020 by Society of Professional Journalists Foundation and Society of Professional Journalists

All rights reserved. No part of this book may be reproduced or transmitted in any form or by any means, electric or mechanical including photocopying, recording or by any information storage and retrieval system, without written permission of the copyright owners.

Printed in the United States of America

ISBN: 978-0-578-63170-7
eISBN: 978-0-578-63354-1

Library of Congress Control Number: 2020900083

Media Ethics: A Guide for Professional Conduct / Revised by Fred Brown, editor, and members of the SPJ Ethics Committee —
5th edition

Revised edition of: Journalism Ethics: A Casebook of Professional Conduct for News Media / Revised by Fred Brown, editor, and the SPJ Ethics Committee — 4th edition
ISBN: 978-1-933338-80-4

Cover: Billy O'Keefe
Design: Cindy Kelley

Published by Society of Professional Journalists
3909 N. Meridian St, Suite 200
Indianapolis, IN 46208
317/927-8000
spj.org

Dedicated to the memory of

John Ensslin and Mike Farrell

In August 2019, as the final touches were being put on this edition, the Society of Professional Journalists lost two of its most revered members.

John Ensslin, 65, was SPJ's national president from 2011 to 2012, and was a tireless innovator and contributor to the organization.

Mike Farrell, 70, served on SPJ's s FOI and Ethics committees, adding expertise and wisdom to the drafting of the 2014 Code of Ethics.

Both were gentlemen — and gentle men — who combined a fierce passion for accurate, assertive and responsible journalism with a civil demeanor and a lively sense of humor.

They were taken from us too soon, and are sorely missed.

TABLE OF CONTENTS

INTRODUCTION vi

CHAPTER ONE: Ethical Thinking: History and Definitions 1

JOURNALISM ORGANIZATIONS' CODES OF ETHICS 8
    Ethical Decision-Making: Procedures 27

CHAPTER TWO: The Role of the Journalist 31

CHAPTER THREE: Codes of Ethics and Beyond 39
    The 2014 SPJ Code 41
    What Other Codes Say: General Principles 45

CHAPTER FOUR: Guidelines and Rules: Ethics and the Law 51

CHAPTER FIVE: To Tell the Truth: Accuracy and Fairness 59
    Accuracy Checklist 60
    Accuracy and Social Media 60
        Case Study: Cooperating with Government 62
        Case Study: A Congressman's Past 63
        Case Study: Satire as Journalism 67
        Case Study: The BTK Killer and the Eagle 70
        Case Study: A Suspect 'Confession' 71
        Case Study: Pre-publication Review 72
        Case Study: The Media's Foul Ball 74
        Case Study: A Confrontational Confirmation 75
    What the Codes Say: Truth and Accuracy 79

CHAPTER SIX: Deception 85
Deception Checklist 86
Case Study: Who's the 'Predator'? 87
Case Study: The Masquerading Mortician 89
Case Study: ABC and Food Lion 91
What the Codes Say: Using Deception 95

CHAPTER SEVEN: Minimize Harm 97
Fairness Checklist 99
Case Study: Moral Decisions in a Massacre 100
Case Study: TV Doctors in Haiti 102
Case Study: Admiral Boorda Suicide 104
Case Study: Publishing Drunk Drivers' Photographs 106
Case Study: Naming Victims of Sex Crimes 109
Case Study: When the Crime Is Incest 112
Case Study: Turning Down a Political Ad 117
What the Codes Say: Minimizing Harm 120

CHAPTER EIGHT: Diversity 123
Putting Diversity to Work in Your News Organization 124
Guidelines for Racial Identification 124
Case Study: When Sources Won't Talk 126
Case Study: Prejudiced and Persistent 128
Case Study: The 'Art' of Darkness 131
Case Study: Using the 'Holocaust' Metaphor 133
What the Codes Say: Diversity 136

CHAPTER NINE: Conflicts of Interest 139
Conflict of Interest Checklist 140
Indifference vs Impartiality 141
Case Study: The Embedded Reporter 143
Case Study: Reigning on the Parade 144
Case Study: Controversy over a Concert 146
Case Study: Writing Checks, Getting Exclusives 147
Case Study: Expensive Home Movies 151
Case Study: 'A Rude, Terrible Person' 153
Case Study: Journalists on the Political Stage 156
Case Study: The Press Can Be Prickly 158
What the Codes Say: Conflicts of Interest 160

CHAPTER TEN: Photojournalism 167
Photojournalism Checklist 167
Case Study: Illegitimate Image 169
Case Study: Too Graphic? 171
Case Study: 'An Indelible Photo' 173
What the Codes Say: Video, Photo and Other Images 176

CHAPTER ELEVEN: Privacy 177
Privacy Checklist 178
Case Study: A Rape on Campus Or Not 179
Case Study: Covering, or Covering Up, Suicide? 182
Case Study: 'Naming' a Dilemma 185
Case Study: A Controversial Apology 188
What the Codes Say: Privacy 193

CHAPTER TWELVE: Source/Reporter Relationships 195
Relationships Checklist 196
Case Study: A Self-/Serving Leak 197
Case Study: Keeping a Promise to a Source 199
Case Study: Deep Throat, and His Motive 200
Case Study: The Dilemma of Anonymity 202
What the Codes Say: Source-Reporter Relationships 205

CHAPTER THIRTEEN: Being Accountable and Transparent 207
Celebrity Coverage: When Is It Time to Say Enough? 209
Case Study: Aaarrghh! Pirates! (And the Press) 211
Case Study: You Don't Know Jack 213
Case Study: The Times and Jayson Blair 215
Case Study: And the Winner Is 217
Case Study: CIA Crack Contra-versy 220
Case Study: Nasty Swamp Creatures 223
What the Codes Say: Accountability and Transparency 226

APPENDIX: The Code through the Years 233

ACKNOWLEDGEMENTS 242

BIBLIOGRAPHY 245

INDEX 251

Introduction

This ethics handbook and collection of ethics cases appears for the first time in online form as well as in print. It comes at a time of rapid change and challenges in the world of journalism and communications. It is still organized as if it were only a printed book, but in its online format, it's intended to be more accessible (and less expensive). The Society of Professional Journalists' ethics casebook went through three print editions with the title *Doing Ethics*. The fourth edition, printed in 2011, was called *Journalism Ethics: A Casebook of Professional Conduct for News Media*. The first three editions were primarily the work of three faculty members associated with the Poynter Institute, a journalism training and research center in St. Petersburg, Florida. Much of the material, and the wisdom, contributed by Jay Black, Robert Steele and Ralph Barney remains a part of this fifth edition. This edition and the one before it have been group efforts by the members of the Ethics Committee of the Society of Professional Journalists, edited by Fred Brown, a former chairman of the committee and former national president of SPJ.

There's another difference in this fifth edition. It's broader in scope, intended to deal not only with all the various fields of journalism, and the growing number of technologies available for delivering information, but also to cover other forms of communication. As traditional journalism shrinks, journalists may find themselves drawn to, or compelled to pursue, other options. Whether they do or not, it's worth knowing how other fields in the information game express their own ethics. All of them place very high value on integrity, accuracy and accountability. But professions with clients, including public relations, also place a very high value on loyalty and advocacy. Since these other professions and journalists are constantly interacting with each other — and since a number of institutions of higher education are requiring all their communications students to have a grounding in media ethics — this casebook also attempts to offer a roadmap for ethical, responsible relationships among those who advocate and those who observe and report.

The book's principal focus, though, remains journalism in its broadest sense: the gathering, organizing and interpreting of information for delivery to a wider audience. Traditional journalism has been challenged as never before by rapidly evolving technologies and regrettably relaxed standards. Technology has brought us 24/7 news on cable television, smart phones with cameras and video capability and a staggering number of individual websites where seekers of information — or affirmation — can find everything from kittens playing pianos to people being stoned to death.

With so many media outlets competing for attention, there's a temptation to emphasize quantity over quality, speed over accuracy, to not be quite so strict about what meets long-established standards for broadcast or publication. Reporters are expected to post, to tweet, to react instantly, to be ready at all times to produce factoids and snippets that will distract and attract, even if only briefly, the attention of the darting fish swimming in a sea of available information.

> A roadmap for ethical, responsible relationships among those who advocate and those who observe and report.

Managers at news outlets promise they will no longer "lecture" to their audiences; now it's time to have a "conversation." But journalists may be trying too hard to be accommodating, and this will inevitably diminish the traditional media's voice of authority. This is not a good outcome. Mainstream media will survive only if they insist on providing accurate, reliable and fair information. Let others give readers what they want to see. The ethical journalist's information is to give them information they need to make sound decisions — information that may challenge assumptions rather than simply affirm preconceptions. That sense of responsibility is what separates an ethical journalist from a slapdash polemicist.

This handbook will help journalists reinforce that sense of responsibility, and students to develop that sense. The case studies are both recent and classic, providing contemporary and timeless examples of the dilemmas facing those who communicate information.

The book includes a template for analyzing ethics dilemmas. Some of the examples are outlined in that format. Others are left for students and their instructors to organize and analyze as they choose. In addition to cases that can be analyzed from a strategic communications perspective, the book also includes a chapter explaining how ethical obligations may differ from legal requirements.

The book is organized around the Society of Professional Journalists' Code of Ethics, an industry standard most recently updated in September 2014. Unlike media employers' codes of ethics, the SPJ code is entirely voluntary. It has no enforcement provisions. It provides a framework for evaluating ethical behavior, emphasizing the need to ask the right questions. Most ethical questions do not have a single, simple answer. Different people evaluating the same situation may very well arrive at different, defensible decisions. As a voluntary compact, the code has no enforcement provision. Accountability for journalists, we believe, is best regulated through other journalists' sensitivity to, and disclosure of, unethical behavior. Disclosure, not sanction, is the journalists' enforcement tool.

The 2014 version of the code contains very few changes from the previous version, adopted in 1996. During the revision committee's work, a two-year period, 2013-2014, inspired and directed by then-Ethics Committee chair Kevin Smith, some academics, journalists and others who think deeply about media ethics expressed an opinion that the drastically changed landscape of information delivery systems required a thorough reexamination of media ethics. The need for change was implicit, although the possible specifics of change were not so clearly expressed.

For example, there was a strong argument that transparency — the disclosure of the reporter's (or communicator's) real and perceived conflicts of interest — was a more realistic approach than strict avoidance of potential conflicts of interest. In the end, the SPJ code revision committee decided that transparency was, indeed, critical. But it didn't accept that it was no longer necessary to try to avoid conflicts of interest.

The revision committee's bottom-line philosophy is that there are abiding principles of ethical, responsible journalism that don't change when the technology of information delivery systems changes. The committee's answer to the rapidly-changing nature of media "platforms" was to eliminate, as much as possible, references to specific technologies. It was the committee's hope that this would indefinitely extend the code's shelf life, and make the code as abiding as the principles it espouses.

One final note about an editorial crotchet: The editor of this work has finally come to the acceptance of "media" as a singular noun, taking a singular verb, but only when the word is used to describe the profession as a collective. He still shudders at the use of "mediums" as a plural, believing that mediums are attempting to speak to the dead, while media should strive to speak to the living.

Additional Resources:

The Society of Professional Journalists Ethics Committee continually offers new ethics-related educational materials, including case studies, through its website (www.spj.org). Related content on the Web also includes occasional blog posts that students, their professors and working professionals can access for online discussions.

CHAPTER ONE:

Ethical Thinking: History and Definitions

It is certainly possible to be an ethical person without knowing any of the history or terminology of moral reasoning. The most exemplary ethical people are not necessarily PhDs who have spent years studying philosophers, but those who have excellent instincts about what's right and wrong. Still, it can be useful to have at least some grounding in the evolution of thought that has led us to where we are today.

And where we are is not a particularly good place to be. As communicators — journalists and other professionals who collect, collate, organize and provide information to the public — we may not always practice the best ethics. Journalism, in particular, finds itself spending an increasing and regrettable amount of time identifying and apologizing for its ethical lapses. And yet, this increased sensitivity and attention to ethics is a hopeful sign. At least all of this self-criticism serves to illustrate that responsible journalists, and other communicators, do have standards and moral codes, and that they find deviation from those standards unacceptable.

> The best way to arrive at an ethical decision is to ask the right questions.

We are surrounded by ethical questions in our daily lives. Consider: Do I have an ethical obligation to report my roommate's underage drinking to campus authorities? What is the proper relationship between a reporter and a source? When is it permissible to use deception in collecting information for a story? Should I cross a striking clerical union's picket line to attend class? When does a woman's right to control her own destiny trump her unborn child's right to life? What do I do if I think a colleague is fabricating information in his reporting? What do I do if a reporter wants free tickets to an event my agency is promoting?

Some of these ethical dilemmas are easier to answer than others. Most of us probably know what we would do, and maybe even could explain *why* we would do what we do.

But it helps to know the fundamentals of moral theory so that we can compare our thinking with others who have established long-lasting ethical principles.

In the most basic terms, the best way to arrive at an ethical decision is to **ask the right questions**. If you can do that, and if your answers to those questions make sense to you — and if you can then explain your reasoning sensibly to other people — you've done what you needed to do to reach a sound, defensible ethical decision. That's true even if someone else, given the same set of circumstances, might arrive at the opposite decision and consider it just as defensible.

Along the way to reasoning through a problem, it helps to know the terminology. For instance, there is a subtle but significant difference between morals and ethics. *Morals* comprise a system of beliefs. *Ethics* is a way to employ those beliefs in the process of *reasoning*. One *acts* ethically from a moral *foundation*.

Jay Black and Jennings Bryant described the difference concisely in their *Introduction to Media Communications* (from the Fourth Edition, Brown and Benchmark, 1995, pp. 540-541):

> Ask a layperson what he or she means by ethics or morality, and you're likely to hear that these subjects deal with the nature of human values and moral conscience, of choosing and following the "right" rather than the "wrong," and of understanding and applying standards that have been set down by a group, association or community. These definitions are useful for openers, but our fuller understanding of the issues ... might be better based on some of the insights and definitions posed by philosophers over the ages.
>
> *Ethics* is based on the Greek word *ethos*, meaning character, or what a good person is or does in order to have a good character. In general, ethics deals with the philosophical foundations of decision making, of choosing among the good and bad options that one faces. *Morality*, on the other hand, comes from the Latin *mores*, and refers to the way or manner in which people behave. Thus, *morality* has come to mean socially approved customs, or the *practice* or application of ethics. (One easy way to remember the distinction, according to a philosopher with a sense of humor, is to think of ethics as behavior that occurs above the neck, and morality as behavior that occurs below the neck!)
>
> Ethics, in short, may be seen as being concerned with that which holds society together or provides the stability and security essential to the living of human life. Ethics as a branch of philosophy involves thinking about morality, moral problems and moral judgments. It deals with "owes" and "oughts"; what obligations we owe or to responsibilities we have toward our fellow humans; what we "should do" to make the world a better place. It is unlike law, which is a bottom-line, minimalistic enterprise that tells us what we *can* do or what we *can* get away with. When we describe the practicing of ethics, of putting these ideas to work, we are talking about "doing ethics."

Understanding the context of moral reasoning

Meta-ethics is the study of the very nature of ethics. It deals with the meaning of abstractions such as "good" or "justice." It distinguishes between true ethical problems and simple matters of taste, for example. It's nonjudgmental; a field of inquiry, not a decision-making process. What do words with a moral connotation mean? Words such as "good," "evil," "wrong," "fair"? And how do we know how to answer these questions? In other words, it goes to the root of any discussion of moral reasoning.

> We are surrounded by ethical questions in our daily lives.

Normative ethics comes next in this three-part continuum and is concerned with developing rules and principles for moral conduct as well as general theories of ethics. It's based on society's fundamental *norms* for good behavior (thus *normative*) and has a great deal to do with duty. An example of normative ethics would be: Don't lie even to get a good story.

Applied ethics is the problem-solving step. It provides road maps, using the rules of normative ethics as a guide. It shows how to arrive at a defensible solution to an ethical problem. It's what students study in ethics classes.

Why study ethics?

The goals of studying ethics are to:
1. Stimulate your moral thinking and awareness of the consequences of behavior so that you can…
2. Recognize ethical issues and anticipate possible dilemmas.
3. Develop your analytical skills through case studies and classroom discussions and role-playing.
4. Enhance your sense of moral obligation and personal responsibility.
5. Learn to respect other points of view and tolerate disagreement.

Sources of our values

Our innate moral values, the places from which we begin to develop personal standards, come from several sources:
- Our **parents**, or the people who nurtured us in their homes as we were developing into adults, are probably our most important examples. We tend to behave the way they behaved, giving us a sense of right and wrong, offering rewards and punishment.
- **Peer groups** exert enormous pressure to conform. We encounter them at work, in schools, churches, social networks and among our neighbors. Peer groups are particularly influential during the adolescent years. This enormous pressure can drive us away from the best moral choices, but also can be a force for good.
- **Role models** are like that, too — sometimes good, sometimes not so good. A coach, a teacher, an editor or a senior executive can be a good role model;

a Hollywood celebrity with repeated unsuccessful encounters with drug rehabilitation can be the worst sort of example to follow.
- **Institutions** also give us values. Journalism as an institution has a different set of values than, say, religion. Journalists are always questioning, skeptical, often negative. Religion is based on faith. Communicators in other disciplines, while expected to show loyalty to the causes they promote, and thus to be more positive, still have a more pragmatic approach and to rely less on faith than on more tangible goals.

A brief history

The study of ethics can be traced back 2,500 years to Socrates, who traveled throughout Greece asking questions. He wanted the people he engaged in these conversations to think about why they were doing what they were doing, and to probe deeper and more broadly about concepts such as goodness and justice. The Socratic method, the constant testing of ideas through a progressive series of questions and answers, is essential to ethical decision-making,

Socrates (circa 470-399 B.C.E.) is not credited with developing any particular philosophical system, but his method, the "Socratic dialogue," is the foundation for the way of thinking that led to everything else. He believed that anyone, given time to think and question, could gain insight into universally accepted rules of moral conduct.

His protégé and disciple, **Plato** (circa 428-348 B.C.E.), expanded on Socrates' delving into the nature of such universal moral values as goodness and justice. He argued that justice is achieved through *wisdom*, consisting of a person's experience and knowledge of the world; *moderation* of thought and behavior in striving to reach sound ethical decisions; and *courage* in living up to and defending those decisions. He believed that "good" was an enduring value, and that a moral person may sometimes have to defy current standards of what's moral in order to achieve a higher, more abiding, good.

Aristotle (384-322 B.C.E.), who studied under Plato for many years, is given credit for developing the clearest articulation of *virtue ethics*, which is the overarching concept and logical evolution of the thinking of the three ancient Greek philosophers. The idea is that a virtuous person will do the right thing primarily because he or she is of good character, someone whose instincts trend toward universal ideas of justice.

Using Moral Theory

In the broadest of terms — and, remember, this short introduction oversimplifies in an attempt to merely acquaint you with the basics — moral theories are of three types:
- **Deontological**, or duty-based, in which the moral agent's motives are more important than the outcome.
- **Teleological**, which emphasizes the consequences of one's actions, and
- **Virtue ethics**, focusing more on good character than on moral behavior. Let's begin there, because, as a late stage in ethical evolution, it has broad application in most situations involving a moral choice.

Virtue Ethics

Aristotle's **golden mean** theory holds that virtue, in most cases, is somewhere between the extremes. The ideal falls between doing nothing and doing too much; between overachieving and underachieving; between excess and neediness. In contemporary journalism, the golden mean most often comes down to finding a balance between telling the truth and minimizing harm. Telling the truth can cause great discomfort to some people, adding to the grief of the bereaved, even ruining the careers of public officials or business executives.

Minimizing harm doesn't mean avoiding the truth because it might hurt, but it does at least require that moral people understand what the consequences of their actions might be. The "golden mean" might also be defined as the middle path that achieves the best balance among possible outcomes. It's rarely a 50-50 balance, though, and some things are always wrong. "The very names of some things imply evil," Aristotle himself wrote, "—for example, the emotions of spite, shamelessness and envy, and such actions as adultery, theft and murder."

The golden mean is rather like the *golden rule*, which is a fundamental creed of the **Judeo-Christian** ethic. "Love thy neighbor as thyself," it says. Remember that everyone — rich or poor, famous or forgotten — is just as deserving of respect and fair treatment as you are. Treat them all the way you would want to be treated. Historically, it's the next significant development of moral theory after Aristotle's enduring work. It is equally as enduring and perhaps even easier to comprehend.

Deontology — duty-based ethics

Perhaps a harsher version of the golden rule is Immanuel Kant's **categorical imperative**. Kant (1724-1804) was one of the most important figures of the 18th Century intellectual movement known as the Enlightenment. His imperative holds that an ethical person should never do anything that he or she would not want to see applied as a universal standard of behavior. Or in Kant's own words: "So act, that the rule on which thou actest would admit of being adopted as a law by all rational beings." Or, as he explained it elsewhere, "Act only according to that maxim whereby you can, at the same time, will that it should become a universal law." *[1785, Grounding for the Metaphysics of Morals].*

Kant's categorical imperative is an absolute. It's less forgiving than the Golden Rule. It holds that any proposition that defines a certain position — whether it's what one must always do or what one must never do — is always necessary. Propositions that include words like "never" or "always" ("never plagiarize" or "always tell the truth") can be considered categorical imperatives — unconditional, absolute requirements.

While the Judeo-Christian ethic elevates the dignity of all as an end in itself, Kant believed in following standards of behavior simply because they are good standards, not because of the consequences. He puts duty above all. A thinker more attuned to *teleology*, believing the ends justify the means, would argue that Robin Hood was a good, ethical person because he stole from the rich only to give to the poor. A deontologist such as Kant would say Robin Hood was wrong to steal, never mind what he did with the loot.

Several teleological theories

Utilitarianism holds that the best ethical decision is that which produces the greatest good for the greatest number. It is one of the major systems of ethics, and is important to journalists, who often argue that what they have reported is for the greater good of society. Kant would ask if your intentions were good; if you were pursuing a cause that is just. The proponents of utilitarianism, chief among them Jeremy Bentham (1748-1832) and John Stuart Mill (1806-1873), would ask how many people are going to benefit from your actions. Today's practitioners would add that you should not to forget the animals, either, or the planet.

Mill, the most prominent figure in this school of thought, believed that the only good reason for attempting to stop someone from doing what he wants to do was to prevent harm to other people — the "harm principle," he called it. If someone is acting out of ignorance or a lack of awareness of what the consequence to himself and others might be, the ethical observer has ample justification to intervene. For example, it would be ethical to try to warn another person against going into a dangerous neighborhood. But such situations would be rare, he felt; most people would know of the dangers.

Utilitarianism is also called the Happiness Theory. As Mill wrote in *Utilitarianism*, published in 1863: "The utilitarian morality does recognise in human beings the power of sacrificing their own greatest good for the good of others. It only refuses to admit that the sacrifice is itself a good. A sacrifice which does not increase, or tend to increase, the sum total of happiness, it considers as wasted. The only self-renunciation which it applauds, is devotion to the happiness, or to some of the means of happiness, of others; either of mankind collectively, or of individuals within the limits imposed by the collective interests of mankind."

This happiness of which Mill speaks "is not the agent's own happiness, but that of all concerned." And yet, necessarily, individuals begin from a position of considering their own happiness, how to improve their lot in life. If an individual can achieve that self-improvement without causing harm to others in that pursuit, it's the purest expression of true freedom, Mill maintained.

Relativism is the anti-Kant school of thought that arose in the late 19th and early 20th centuries. If Kant was an absolutist, focusing on duty, thinkers such as Bertrand Russell (1872-1970) and John Dewey (1859-1952) were moral libertarians. Essentially, they said the moral thing to do depends on one's point of view: You decide what's right for you; I'll decide what's right for me. They will not pass judgment on the decisions of others. Critics say it can lead to anarchy, a way to justify whatever you feel like doing.

And one's point of view relies principally on that person's cultural environment. So what an individual regards as ethical depends on custom and the individual's ability to justify that behavior in the language and mores of that cultural environment. It does not attempt to judge a culture by establishing some ultimate standards of right and wrong.

Dewey, a towering figure in establishing standards for American education, held that ethics evolved over time, as circumstances change. He would not be particularly friendly to the idea of abiding, eternal ethical principles. What one culture regards as ethical may not be regarded as a best practice in another culture.

Egalitarianism embodies the idea that all individuals deserve equal treatment; minorities, and minority viewpoints, should be given exactly the same consideration as the majority — at least at the beginning of one's consideration of an ethical dilemma. Philosopher John Rawls (1921-2002) said this "original position" should occur behind a "veil of ignorance" in which one sets aside any prejudices he or she may have established from parents, peer groups or institutions.

Ideally, everyone affected by the decision would enjoy an equal outcome; there should be no double standards. Rawls does concede, however, that there can be morally defensible reasons for an outcome that hurts some more than others. This is something journalists have to think about all the time — yes, minimize the harm that might come from your news coverage, but recognize that you can't totally avoid it. Or, as the Stanford Encyclopedia of Philosophy explains it, "choosing the alternative that renders the best of the worst possible outcomes."

Professional Associations' Codes of Ethics

Society of Professional Journalists
(adopted September 2014)

Preamble

Members of the Society of Professional Journalists believe that public enlightenment is the forerunner of justice and the foundation of democracy. Ethical Journalism strives to ensure the free exchange of information that is accurate, fair and thorough. An ethical journalist acts with integrity.

The Society declares these four principles as the foundation of ethical journalism and encourages their use in its practice by all people in all media.

Seek Truth and Report It

Ethical journalism should be accurate and fair. Journalists should be honest and courageous in gathering, reporting and interpreting information.

Journalists should:

- Take responsibility for the accuracy of their work. Verify information before releasing it. Use original sources whenever possible.
- Remember that neither speed nor format excuses inaccuracy.
- Provide context. Take special care not to misrepresent or oversimplify in promoting, previewing or summarizing a story.
- Gather, update and correct information throughout the life of a news story.
- Be cautious when making promises, but keep the promises they make.
- Identify sources clearly. The public is entitled to as much information as possible to judge the reliability and motivations of sources.
- Consider sources' motives before promising anonymity. Reserve anonymity for sources who may face danger, retribution or other harm, and have information that cannot be obtained elsewhere. Explain why anonymity was granted.
- Diligently seek subjects of news coverage to allow them to respond to criticism or allegations of wrongdoing.
- Avoid undercover or other surreptitious methods of gathering information unless traditional, open methods will not yield information vital to the public.
- Be vigilant and courageous about holding those with power accountable. Give voice to the voiceless.
- Support the open and civil exchange of views, even views they find repugnant.
- Recognize a special obligation to serve as watchdogs over public affairs and government. Seek to ensure that the public's business is conducted in the open, and that public records are open to all.

- Provide access to source material when it is relevant and appropriate.
- Boldly tell the story of the diversity and magnitude of the human experience. Seek sources whose voices we seldom hear.
- Avoid stereotyping. Journalists should examine the ways their values and experiences may shape their reporting.
- Label advocacy and commentary.
- Never deliberately distort facts or context, including visual information. Clearly label illustrations and re-enactments.
- Never plagiarize. Always attribute.

Minimize Harm

Ethical journalism treats sources, subjects, colleagues and members of the public as human beings deserving of respect.

Journalists should:

- Balance the public's need for information against potential harm or discomfort. Pursuit of the news is not a license for arrogance or undue obtrusiveness.
- Show compassion for those who may be affected by news coverage. Use heightened sensitivity when dealing with juveniles, victims of sex crimes, and sources or subjects who are inexperienced or unable to give consent. Consider cultural differences in approach and treatment.
- Recognize that legal access to information differs from an ethical justification to publish or broadcast.
- Realize that private people have a greater right to control information about themselves than do public officials and others who seek power, influence or attention. Weigh the consequences of publishing or broadcasting personal information.
- Avoid pandering to lurid curiosity, even if others do.
- Balance a suspect's right to a fair trial with the public's right to know. Consider the implications of identifying criminal suspects before they face legal charges.
- Consider the long-term implications of the extended reach and permanence of publication. Provide updated and more complete information as appropriate.

Act Independently

The highest and primary obligation of ethical journalism is to serve the public.

Journalists should:

- Avoid conflicts of interest, real or perceived. Disclose unavoidable conflicts.
- Refuse gifts, favors, fees, free travel and special treatment, and avoid political and other outside activities that may compromise integrity or impartiality, or may damage credibility.

- Be wary of sources offering information for favors or money; do not pay for access to news. Identify content provided by outside sources, whether paid or not.
- Deny favored treatment to advertisers, donors or any other special interests and resist internal and external pressure to influence coverage.
- Distinguish news from advertising and shun hybrids that blur the lines between the two. Prominently label sponsored content.

Be Accountable and Transparent

Ethical journalism means taking responsibility for one's work and explaining one's decisions to the public.

Journalists should:

- Explain ethical choices and processes to audiences. Encourage a civil dialogue with the public about journalistic practices, coverage and news content.
- Respond quickly to questions about accuracy, clarity and fairness.
- Acknowledge mistakes and correct them promptly and prominently. Explain corrections and clarifications carefully and clearly.
- Expose unethical conduct in journalism, including within their organizations.
- Abide by the same high standards they expect of others.

The SPJ Code of Ethics is a statement of abiding principles supported by additional explanations and position papers (at spj.org) that address changing journalistic practices. It is not a set of rules, rather a guide that encourages all who engage in journalism to take responsibility for the information they provide, regardless of medium. The code should be read as a whole; individual principles should not be taken out of context. It is not, nor can it be under the First Amendment, legally enforceable.

Radio Television Digital News Association
(adopted June 2015)

Guiding Principles:

Journalism's obligation is to the public. Journalism places the public's interests ahead of commercial, political and personal interests. Journalism empowers viewers, listeners and readers to make more informed decisions for themselves; it does not tell people what to believe or how to feel.

Ethical decision-making should occur at every step of the journalistic process, including story selection, news-gathering, production, presentation and delivery. Practitioners of ethical journalism seek diverse and even opposing opinions in order to reach better conclusions that can be clearly explained and effectively defended or, when appropriate, revisited and revised.

Ethical decision-making — like writing, photography, design, or anchoring — requires skills that improve with study, diligence and practice.

The RTDNA Code of Ethics does not dictate what journalists should do in every ethical predicament; rather it offers resources to help journalists make better ethical decisions — on and off the job — for themselves and for the communities they serve.

Journalism is distinguished from other forms of content by these guiding principles:

Truth and accuracy above all

- The facts *should* get in the way of a good story. Journalism requires more than merely reporting remarks, claims or comments. Journalism verifies, provides relevant context, tells the rest of the story and acknowledges the absence of important additional information.
- For every story of significance, there are always more than two sides. While they may not all fit into every account, responsible reporting is clear about what it omits, as well as what it includes.
- Scarce resources, deadline pressure and relentless competition do not excuse cutting corners factually or oversimplifying complex issues.
- "Trending," "going viral" or "exploding on social media" may increase urgency, but these phenomena only heighten the need for strict standards of accuracy.
- Facts change over time. Responsible reporting includes updating stories and amending archival versions to make them more accurate and to avoid misinforming those who, through search, stumble upon outdated material.
- Deception in newsgathering, including surreptitious recording, conflicts with journalism's commitment to truth. Similarly, anonymity of sources deprives the audience of important, relevant information. Staging, dramatization and other

alterations — even when labeled as such — can confuse or fool viewers, listeners and readers. These tactics are justified only when stories of great significance cannot be adequately told without distortion, and when any creative liberties taken are clearly explained.
- Journalism challenges assumptions, rejects stereotypes and illuminates — even where it cannot eliminate — ignorance.

Independence and transparency

- Editorial independence may be a more ambitious goal today than ever before. Media companies, even if not-for-profit, have commercial, competitive and other interests — both internal and external — from which the journalists they employ cannot be entirely shielded. Still, independence from influences that conflict with public interest remains an essential ideal of journalism. Transparency provides the public with the means to assess credibility and to determine who deserves trust.
- Acknowledging sponsor-provided content, commercial concerns or political relationships is essential, but transparency alone is not adequate. It does not entitle journalists to lower their standards of fairness or truth.
- Disclosure, while critical, does not justify the exclusion of perspectives and information that are important to the audience's understanding of issues.
- Journalism's proud tradition of holding the powerful accountable provides no exception for powerful journalists or the powerful organization that employ them. To profit from reporting on the activities of others while operating in secrecy is hypocrisy.
- Effectively explaining editorial decisions and processes does not mean making excuses. Transparency requires reflection, reconsideration and honest openness to the possibility that an action, however well intended, was wrong.
- Ethical journalism requires owning errors, correcting them promptly and giving corrections as much prominence as the error itself had.
- Commercial endorsements are incompatible with journalism because they compromise credibility. In journalism, content is gathered, selected and produced in the best interest of viewers, listeners and readers — not in the interests of somebody who paid to have a product or position promoted and associated with a familiar face, voice or name.
- Similarly, political activity and active advocacy can undercut the real or perceived independence of those who practice journalism. Journalists do not give up the rights of citizenship, but their public exercise of those rights can call into question their impartiality.
- The acceptance of gifts or special treatment of any kind not available to the general public creates conflicts of interest and erodes independence. This does not include the access to events or areas traditionally granted to working journalists in order to facilitate their coverage. It does include "professional courtesy" admission, discounts and "freebies" provided to journalists by those who might someday be the subject of coverage. Such goods and services are often

offered as enticements to report favorably on the giver or rewards for doing so; even where that is not the intent, it is the reasonable perception of a justifiably suspicious public.
- Commercial and political activities, as well as the acceptance of gifts or special treatment, cause harm even when the journalists involved are "off duty" or "on their own time."
- Attribution is essential. It adds important information that helps the audience evaluate content and it acknowledges those who contribute to coverage. Using someone else's work without attribution or permission is plagiarism.

Accountability for consequences

- Journalism accepts responsibility, articulates its reasons and opens its processes to public scrutiny.
- Journalism provides enormous benefits to self-governing societies. In the process, it can create inconvenience, discomfort and even distress. Minimizing harm, particularly to vulnerable individuals, should be a consideration in every editorial and ethical decision.
- Responsible reporting means considering the consequences of both the newsgathering — even if the information is never made public — and of the material's potential dissemination. Certain stakeholders deserve special consideration; these include children, victims, vulnerable adults and other inexperienced with American media.
- Preserving privacy and protecting the right to a fair trial are not the primary mission of journalism; still, these critical concerns deserve consideration and to be balanced against the importance or urgency of reporting.
- The right to broadcast, publish or otherwise share information does not mean it is always right to do so. However, journalism's obligation is to pursue truth and report, not withhold it. Shying away from difficult cases is not necessarily more ethical than taking on the challenge of reporting them. Leaving tough or sensitive stories to non-journalists can be a disservice to the public.

Online News Association Code of Ethics

The Online News Association in 2013-14 developed a tool to help online journalists customize their own codes of ethics. Some journalism instructors do this, too, asking their students to set down in writing the basic principles they will strive to follow as they go forward in their careers. The Society of Professional Journalists doesn't reject this approach, and in fact would encourage journalists to think more deeply about what they should do as individuals to act responsibly. But SPJ also believes there are certain broad principles that are abiding and don't change as the delivery media become more technologically diverse. And in fact, ONA accepts abiding principles, too. Here's what ONA says about its "build your own code" program:

A customized ethics code for every organization

The "Build Your Own Ethics Code" project grew out of an open workshop at the Online News Association annual conference in Atlanta in October 2013, where journalists expressed a need for codes that fit the world we live in and report on, and the tools we use.

Aimed at helping news organizations, small startups and individual bloggers create codes of ethics for our digital times, the project has involved the work of more than 20 journalists and journalism educators over two years. The project has also been crowdsourced for comments, bringing suggestions from all over the world.

We started with the recognition that the journalism profession encompasses ever more people, philosophies and technologies. There are many definitions these days of a "journalist," making it more important than ever for journalists to be clear about who they are and what they stand for.

Our "Build Your Own Ethics Code" project recognizes that no single ethics code can reflect the needs of everyone in our widely varied profession. We believe the best hope for convincing all journalists to adopt and live by an ethics code is to give them ownership and flexibility in creating one.

After laying out the fundamentals we believe should apply to all journalists (e.g. tell the truth, don't plagiarize, promptly correct errors), this project offers a set of specific "building blocks" that let you customize the remainder of the code.

Once you've worked through the site, you should have a comprehensive, personalized statement of how you see journalism ethics — a code that can be publicly posted and lived by.

Even if you don't create a full code from this website, we hope that looking through it will spark discussions of the most important ethical issues for your organization. We also encourage you to look beyond our building blocks to the sources we consulted in the course of this project and to the much wider range of codes throughout the world of journalism.

We know that given the political and financial pressures many news organizations face — along with ethical challenges that are often difficult to anticipate — complying perfectly with any ethics code is not easy. Still, we believe it's important to have a code as a guiding star. Even if journalists feel forced to violate their code, a code often makes it clear that they're being asked to act contrary to their principles. In cases like this, some collective bargaining agreements recognize a "clause of conscience" that allows journalists to leave their jobs with some form of compensation if they feel their organizations' ethical principles are being violated.

Writing and posting an ethics code doesn't solve every issue. Whatever you proclaim about your beliefs, the ultimate test remains how you behave over time and the reliability of what you report.

In whatever way you end up using this project, we hope you'll find our work useful. We encourage you to help us continue improving this project.

Thomas Kent
Leader, ONA ethics code project and standards editor, The Associated Press

In April 2016, though, the Online News Association did announce some standards it felt should be more generally applicable to gathering news and information from social media. Here it is:

ONA Social Newsgathering Ethics Code

The ONA Social Newsgathering Ethics Code is a document that is intended to gather the support of news and journalism organizations of all sizes around the globe to endorse a set of standards and practices relating to the gathering and use of content created by members of the public.

The below organizations, groups, companies and individuals endorse and support these standards as best practices for the industry and acknowledge that integration of each element into their own operations would be desirable. This code may also be used to form the basis of a new UGC [user-generated content] ethics code by any individual or organization.

If your news organization wants to be listed as a supporter of the code, please send an email with your organization's name to socialnewsgathering@journalists.org.

The standards and practices are as follows:

- Endeavoring to verify the authenticity of user-generated content before publishing or distributing it, holding it to standards that are equal or equivalent to those maintained for content acquired through other means.
- Being transparent with the audience about the verification status of UGC.
- Considering the emotional state and safety of contributors.
- Considering the risk inherent in asking a contributor to produce and deliver UGC, including whether it incentivizes others to take unnecessary risks.
- Considering technical measures to ensure anonymity of sources when required.
- Seeking informed consent for the use of UGC through direct communication with the individual who created it.
- Being transparent about how content will be used and distributed to other platforms.
- Giving due credit to the owner of the content providing that consideration has been given to potential consequences, including their physical, mental and reputational well-being.
- Endeavoring to inform and equip journalists to confront the dangers of engaging with sources through social media networks and the digital footprint they leave behind.
- Supporting and assisting journalists who are confronted with graphic or otherwise disturbing content. Maintaining an organizational culture that enables journalists to seek help or speak out when they need to protect their mental health.

Public Relations Society of America Code of Ethics

This casebook is produced by the nation's leading journalism membership organization, so its focus inevitably is on the ethics of conveying information to the public in an impartial, fair and balanced manner. But journalism is not the only field of communications that insists on honesty, accuracy and accountability. Some journalists may find it odd that public relations professionals stress these same principles in their code of ethics. But they do. There are differences, though. The Public Relations Society of America (PRSA) Code of Ethics lists advocacy as its first principle — not something that would show up prominently, if at all, in a journalists' code of ethics. And there's an emphasis on loyalty, too, a concept that is only implicit in the SPJ or RTDNA codes' discussion of confidentiality and duty to the public. Loyalty does show up in some employers' codes of ethics. Today, with traditional journalism jobs in decline and ethics education often pooling all types of communication majors in a single class, it's worthwhile to consider how various communications professions interact, and how their guiding principles compare to one another.

PRSA Code of Ethics: Preamble

This Code applies to PRSA members. The Code is designed to be a useful guide for PRSA members as they carry out their ethical responsibilities. This document is designed to anticipate and accommodate, by precedent, ethical challenges that may arise. The scenarios outlined in the Code provision are actual examples of misconduct. More will be added as experience with the Code occurs.

The Public Relations Society of America (PRSA) is committed to ethical practices. The level of public trust PRSA members seek, as we serve the public good, means we have taken on a special obligation to operate ethically.

The value of member reputation depends upon the ethical conduct of everyone affiliated with the Public Relations Society of America. Each of us sets an example for each other — as well as other professionals - by our pursuit of excellence with powerful standards of performance, professionalism, and ethical conduct.

Emphasis on enforcement of the Code has been eliminated. But the PRSA Board of Directors retains the right to bar from membership or expel from the Society any individual who has been or is sanctioned by a government agency or convicted in a court of law of an action that fails to comply with the Code.

Ethical practice is the most important obligation of a PRSA member. We view the Member Code of Ethics as a model for other professions, organizations, and professionals.

PRSA Member Statement of Professional Values

This statement presents the core values of PRSA members and, more broadly, of the public relations profession. These values provide the foundation for the Member Code of Ethics and set the industry standard for the professional practice of public relations. These values are the fundamental beliefs that guide our behaviors and decision-making process. We believe our professional values are vital to the integrity of the profession as a whole.

ADVOCACY

We serve the public interest by acting as responsible advocates for those we represent. We provide a voice in the marketplace of ideas, facts, and viewpoints to aid informed public debate.

HONESTY

We adhere to the highest standards of accuracy and truth in advancing the interests of those we represent and in communicating with the public.

EXPERTISE

We acquire and responsibly use specialized knowledge and experience. We advance the profession through continued professional development, research, and education. We build mutual understanding, credibility, and relationships among a wide array of institutions and audiences.

INDEPENDENCE

We provide objective counsel to those we represent. We are accountable for our actions.

LOYALTY

We are faithful to those we represent, while honoring our obligation to serve the public interest.

FAIRNESS

We deal fairly with clients, employers, competitors, peers, vendors, the media, and the general public. We respect all opinions and support the right of free expression.

PRSA Code Provisions of Conduct

FREE FLOW OF INFORMATION

Core Principle: Protecting and advancing the free flow of accurate and truthful information is essential to serving the public interest and contributing to informed decision-making in a democratic society.

Intent:
- To maintain the integrity of relationships with the media, government officials, and the public.
- To aid informed decision-making.

Guidelines:
A member shall:
- Preserve the integrity of the process of communication.
- Be honest and accurate in all communications.
- Act promptly to correct erroneous communications for which the practitioner is responsible.
- Preserve the free flow of unprejudiced information when giving or receiving gifts by ensuring that gifts are nominal, legal, and infrequent.

Examples of Improper Conduct Under this Provision:
- A member representing a ski manufacturer gives a pair of expensive racing skis to a sports magazine columnist, to influence the columnist to write favorable articles about the product.
- A member entertains a government official beyond legal limits and/or in violation of government reporting requirements.

COMPETITION

Core Principle: Promoting healthy and fair competition among professionals preserves an ethical climate while fostering a robust business environment.

Intent:
- To promote respect and fair competition among public relations professionals.
- To serve the public interest by providing the widest choice of practitioner options.

Guidelines:
A member shall:
- Follow ethical hiring practices designed to respect free and open competition without deliberately undermining a competitor.
- Preserve intellectual property rights in the marketplace.

Examples of Improper Conduct Under This Provision:
- A member employed by a "client organization" shares helpful information with a counseling firm that is competing with others for the organization's business.
- A member spreads malicious and unfounded rumors about a competitor in order to alienate the competitor's clients and employees in a ploy to recruit people and business.

DISCLOSURE OF INFORMATION

Core Principle: Open communication fosters informed decision-making in a democratic society.

Intent:
To build trust with the public by revealing all information needed for responsible decision-making.

Guidelines:
A member shall:
- Be honest and accurate in all communications.
- Act promptly to correct erroneous communications for which the member is responsible.
- Investigate the truthfulness and accuracy of information released on behalf of those represented.
- Reveal the sponsors for causes and interests represented.
- Disclose financial interest (such as stock ownership) in a client's organization.
- Avoid deceptive practices.

Examples of Improper Conduct Under this Provision:
- Front groups: A member implements "grass roots" campaigns or letter-writing campaigns to legislators on behalf of undisclosed interest groups.
- Lying by omission: A practitioner for a corporation knowingly fails to release financial information, giving a misleading impression of the corporation's performance.
- A member discovers inaccurate information disseminated via a website or media kit and does not correct the information.
- A member deceives the public by employing people to pose as volunteers to speak at public hearings and participate in "grass roots" campaigns.

SAFEGUARDING CONFIDENCES

Core Principle: Client trust requires appropriate protection of confidential and private information.

Intent:
To protect the privacy rights of clients, organizations, and individuals by safeguarding confidential information.

Guidelines:
- A member shall: Safeguard the confidences and privacy rights of present, former, and prospective clients and employees.
- Protect privileged, confidential, or insider information gained from a client or organization.
- Immediately advise an appropriate authority if a member discovers that confidential information is being divulged by an employee of a client company or organization.

Examples of Improper Conduct Under This Provision:
- A member changes jobs, takes confidential information, and uses that information in the new position to the detriment of the former employer.
- A member intentionally leaks proprietary information to the detriment of some other party.

CONFLICTS OF INTEREST

Core Principle: Avoiding real, potential or perceived conflicts of interest builds the trust of clients, employers, and the publics.

Intent:
- To earn trust and mutual respect with clients or employers.
- To build trust with the public by avoiding or ending situations that put one's personal or professional interests in conflict with society's interests.

Guidelines:
A member shall:
- Act in the best interests of the client or employer, even subordinating the member's personal interests.
- Avoid actions and circumstances that may appear to compromise good business judgment or create a conflict between personal and professional interests.
- Disclose promptly any existing or potential conflict of interest to affected clients or organizations.
- Encourage clients and customers to determine if a conflict exists after notifying all affected parties.

Examples of Improper Conduct Under This Provision:
- The member fails to disclose that he or she has a strong financial interest in a client's chief competitor.
- The member represents a "competitor company" or a "conflicting interest" without informing a prospective client.

ENHANCING THE PROFESSION

Core Principle: Public relations professionals work constantly to strengthen the public's trust in the profession.

Intent:
- To build respect and credibility with the public for the profession of public relations.
- To improve, adapt and expand professional practices.

Guidelines:
A member shall:
- Acknowledge that there is an obligation to protect and enhance the profession.
- Keep informed and educated about practices in the profession to ensure ethical conduct.
- Actively pursue personal professional development.
- Decline representation of clients or organizations that urge or require actions contrary to this Code.
- Accurately define what public relations activities can accomplish.
- Counsel subordinates in proper ethical decision-making.
- Require that subordinates adhere to the ethical requirements of the Code.
- Report practices that fail to comply with the Code, whether committed by PRSA members or not, to the appropriate authority.

Examples of Improper Conduct Under This Provision:
- A PRSA member declares publicly that a product the client sells is safe, without disclosing evidence to the contrary.
- A member initially assigns some questionable client work to a non-member practitioner to avoid the ethical obligation of PRSA membership.

PRSA Member Code of Ethics Pledge

I pledge:

To conduct myself professionally, with truth, accuracy, fairness, and responsibility to the public; To improve my individual competence and advance the knowledge and proficiency of the profession through continuing research and education;

And to adhere to the articles of the Member Code of Ethics 2000 for the practice of public relations as adopted by the governing Assembly of the Public Relations Society of America.

I understand and accept that there is a consequence for misconduct, up to and including membership revocation.

And, I understand that those who have been or are sanctioned by a government agency or convicted in a court of law of an action that fails to comply with the Code may be barred from membership or expelled from the Society.

_____

Signature

_____

Date

National Press Photographers Association

Preamble

The National Press Photographers Association, a professional society that promotes the highest standards in visual journalism, acknowledges concern for every person's need both to be fully informed about public events and to be recognized as part of the world in which we live.

Visual journalists operate as trustees of the public. Our primary role is to report visually on the significant events and varied viewpoints in our common world. Our primary goal is the faithful and comprehensive depiction of the subject at hand. As visual journalists, we have the responsibility to document society and to preserve its history through images.

Photographic and video images can reveal great truths, expose wrongdoing and neglect, inspire hope and understanding and connect people around the globe through the language of visual understanding. Photographs can also cause great harm if they are callously intrusive or are manipulated.

This code is intended to promote the highest quality in all forms of visual journalism and to strengthen public confidence in the profession. It is also meant to serve as an educational tool both for those who practice and for those who appreciate photojournalism. To that end, The National Press Photographers Association sets forth the following.

Code of Ethics

Visual journalists and those who manage visual news productions are accountable for upholding the following standards in their daily work:

1. Be accurate and comprehensive in the representation of subjects.
2. Resist being manipulated by staged photo opportunities.
3. Be complete and provide context when photographing or recording subjects. Avoid stereotyping individuals and groups. Recognize and work to avoid presenting one's own biases in the work.
4. Treat all subjects with respect and dignity. Give special consideration to vulnerable subjects and compassion to victims of crime or tragedy. Intrude on private moments of grief only when the public has an overriding and justifiable need to see.
5. While photographing subjects, do not intentionally contribute to, alter, or seek to alter or influence events.
6. Editing should maintain the integrity of the photographic images' content and context. Do not manipulate images or add or alter sound in any way that can mislead viewers or misrepresent subjects.

7. Do not pay sources or subjects or reward them materially for information or participation.
8. Do not accept gifts, favors, or compensation from those who might seek to influence coverage.
9. Do not intentionally sabotage the efforts of other journalists.

Ideally, visual journalists should:
1. Strive to ensure that the public's business is conducted in public. Defend the rights of access for all journalists.
2. Think proactively, as a student of psychology, sociology, politics and art to develop a unique vision and presentation. Work with a voracious appetite for current events and contemporary visual media.
3. Strive for total and unrestricted access to subjects, recommend alternatives to shallow or rushed opportunities, seek a diversity of viewpoints, and work to show unpopular or unnoticed points of view.
4. Avoid political, civic and business involvements or other employment that compromise or give the appearance of compromising one's own journalistic independence.
5. Strive to be unobtrusive and humble in dealing with subjects.
6. Respect the integrity of the photographic moment.
7. Strive by example and influence to maintain the spirit and high standards expressed in this code. When confronted with situations in which the proper action is not clear, seek the counsel of those who exhibit the highest standards of the profession. Visual journalists should continuously study their craft and the ethics that guide it.

Public Radio News Directors Incorporated

Code of Ethics

Public Radio News Directors Inc. is committed to the highest standards of journalistic ethics and excellence. We must stand apart from pressures of politics and commerce as we inform and engage our listeners. We seek truth, and report with fairness and integrity.

Independence and integrity are the foundations of our service, which we maintain through these principles:

TRUTH

- Journalism is the rigorous pursuit of truth. Its practice requires fairness, accuracy, and balance.
- We strive to be comprehensive. We seek diverse points of view and voices to tell the stories of our communities.

FAIRNESS

- Fairness is at the core of all good journalism.
- We gather and report the news in context, with clarity and compassion.
- We treat our sources and the public with decency and respect.
- Our reporting is thorough, timely and avoids speculation.

INTEGRITY

- The public's faith in our service rests on our integrity as journalists.
- Editorial independence is required to ensure the integrity of our work.
- We identify the differences between reporting and opinion.
- We guard against conflicts of interest — real and perceived — that could compromise the credibility and independence of our reporting.
- We are accountable when conflicts occur. We disclose any unavoidable conflicts of interest.

• BALDO © 2010 Baldo Partnership. Dist. By ANDREWS MCMEEL SYNDICATION. Reprinted with permission. All rights reserved.

Ethical Decision-Making: Procedures

In today's saturated media environment, with so many technologies competing for information-seekers' attention, successful media need a loyal base audience. Credibility is crucial to retaining those readers and viewers, and an ethical decision-making process is key to credibility.

Ideally, ethical questions should be discussed in groups of people. Much of ethical decision-making involves a back-and-forth testing of ideas. A lot of it is just good instinct. Newsrooms should have more ethical discussions, and those discussions would benefit from some input from outside the newsroom as well.

Discussions about ethical challenges are essential, as well, in fields of communication other than journalism. The method outlined here can be applied there, too, and several of the case studies on this site present issues involving public relations professionals or others who practice advocacy communications.

The process outlined below is based on several models, including those developed by Bernard Gert of Dartmouth College and Louis Alvin Day of Louisiana State University. The important thing is to identify all pertinent facts and then — especially — to ask the right questions.

Most of the case studies in this collection use this model. Others do not. Instructors may want to use those scenarios that do not follow this template to test their students' abilities to identify the elements of an ethical dilemma. The exercise that follows is based on a decision that was made by a Danish newspaper in 2006, and the furor that ensued. It has elements of both journalistic integrity and a public relations response.

WHAT: Describe the situation. Assemble all relevant facts, list all the angles. In other words, do the reporting. Put the ethical dilemma in the form of a question; write it down, to be sure it makes sense.

For example, if you were considering the furor over publication of caricatures of the Prophet Muhammad, you'd want to assemble all pertinent facts about:
- The original motivation for publication.
- Why it took so long after their initial appearance for the images to cause such a violent reaction.

- Differences of opinion in the Islamic community, including over whether any depiction of the Prophet is considered blasphemy.

Think of all the questions you can, and try to answer them. Boil it down to one basic question. Perhaps this one:

QUESTION: Do we publish the cartoons or not?

WHO: *The principals (people) who will make the decision and those who will be affected by it. First, decide who is responsible for the decision. The managing editor? News director? Does this go all the way to the top? Then list the major stakeholders, ranging from the subjects of the story to the general public. Remember that not everyone will be affected to the same degree by what you decide to do.*

The decision-maker here most likely would be at least at the managing editor level at a newspaper; perhaps the news director at a television station.

The stakeholders include the local Islamic community, Muslims around the world, people in places that might be targeted by riots, your newspaper or TV station and its reputation for truth-telling and fairness, and readers and viewers — who have an interest in seeing what is driving such outrage. You may be able to think of others whose interest in the outcome of your decision should be considered.

WHY: These are principles (standards) you will use in deciding what to do. In most cases, it comes down to a balance between telling the truth and minimizing possible harms. Identify these and other moral responsibilities. The best decision is the one that does the greatest good for the greatest number of stakeholders.

There are several principles at issue in the case of the caricatures. Is it freedom of expression? Or is it unnecessary provocation? Is there an acceptable middle ground between showing the blunt truth and minimizing the harm of insult?

Consider the principles that may have motivated the principals, and then consider your options. At the extremes, they could range from publishing all 12 cartoons on the front page, or to show them with riot scenes on your newscast, to the other extreme of simply describing a couple of them. Or you could provide a link to a Web site where they could be viewed.

HOW: This is your decision: How do you achieve the outcome you've identified as the best? How do you answer the question you raised in the first step? Again, if you write it down, you will have a better idea of whether it makes sense. Also, write down your rationale, and consider making your decision-making part of your coverage. Articulating your reasoning will help you answer the questions you're bound to get.

For example, you might begin simply by saying, "We decided to publish only one cartoon because ..." In this case, different media made different decisions. Whatever the decision, it's important to have a serious discussion and a good reason for it.

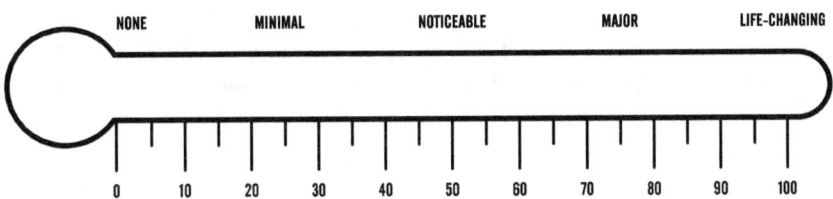

The Stake-O-Meter

In attempting to arrive at an ethical decision, it's important to identify as many individuals, groups, businesses and institutions as you can that might be affected by your decision. It's important, too, to realize that not all of them are affected equally.

Think of this "Stake-O-Meter" as a Celsius thermometer. Some individuals with a minimum investment in the outcome will barely be affected by your story; others with a maximum involvement may reach the boiling point of stress.

That concept may run counter to the ideal of Egalitarianism, which holds that all individuals deserve equal treatment. But it runs closer to reality.

The consequences of your publishing a story about official misfeasance, for example, will be the most severe for the official implicated — somewhere toward 90-100 on the scale above. Others in that official's department, as well as contractors, clients, etc., would not be quite as impacted by the story, but still might fall at 60-70 or thereabouts.

In most stories, the general public's stake in the outcome — the impact on your readers and viewers — is not all that great. It might be around 30-40 if the official's misconduct affected a public project or misused large amounts of tax dollars. If the unsavory activity were instead an interoffice exchange of suggestive emails, say, the public's investment in the outcome of the story would be very low, down toward 10-20. It's an interesting story, but not particularly important.

As the publisher or broadcaster of the story, you have a stake, too. If the story has a major impact on improving public policy, for example, your reputation will soar. If it strikes the public as unfair, poorly researched and insufficiently supported by the facts, your reputation can suffer. In either case, your "stake" in the story is a fairly weighty one.

Consider the Case Study: "A Congressman's Past," on page 63. Three weeks before the 2004 election, *The* (Portland) *Oregonian* published a story about a sexual assault complaint filed against U.S. Rep. David Wu while he and the alleged victim were students at Stanford University, 28 years earlier. Neither the woman involved, nor Wu, wanted to talk about it; the newspaper assembled its 3,000-word story from other sources.

Clearly, Wu is the stakeholder who faces the most severe consequences from the story. And the woman involved, even though she was not named, is at the high end of the scale, too. But in this case, so is the newspaper. As the newspaper's public editor wrote, "Reader after reader raised questions about fairness, relevancy and timing" of the article.

It's important to caution that it's possible to put too much weight on the consequences for one individual. Typically, the numbers of people affected increase as the impact of the consequences decreases, with the largest number — the general public — often the least seriously affected.

Thus, the ethical principle of Utilitarianism, that the best decision is that which produces the greatest good for the greatest number, should enter into your reasoning, too.

CHAPTER TWO:

The Role of the Journalist

With startling regularity, journalists and newsrooms find themselves vigorously discussing whether to run stories they know will cause a storm of discussion on talk shows and in the streets.

Debates rage over publishing unproven accusations of sexual improprieties against powerful figures (including several examples in the political world), or naming alleged rape victims (as in the Kobe Bryant case), or juvenile offenders.

Questions swirl around whether public accusations of improprieties or other behavior that invade the privacy of a celebrity or a public figure should be plucked from tabloid newspapers and blogs and given wider distribution in the "mainstream" press.

The questions may not be whether such stories should be published, but how well journalists reason and explain decisions that cause obvious and grievous harm to an individual, even a public official.

> News people increasingly are perplexed about how to handle problems that until recently seemed black and white.

Television talk shows inevitably pit defenders of publication against critics of the press. Unfortunately, the critics most often carry the day, correctly pointing to the harm. This happens largely because journalists and their defenders find it difficult to spell out clearly and convincingly why the media often have a moral obligation to publish such stories.

Rights versus Obligations

Defenders tend to speak of the *right* rather than the moral *obligation* to publish such material. It is as if insistent assertions of the right to publish would somehow turn away attacks and public outrage. The *right* to publish, granted by the First Amendment to the U.S. Constitution and confirmed by judicial decisions, is widely documented and discussed in civics classes and history lectures. But the *obligation* to distribute information, which resides in the soul of a journalistic ethic, is rarely discussed. It is the *why* of this process that demands articulation, so that the public can understand and appreciate the journalist's motives for telling so much.

Journalists are often denounced and ridiculed for invoking First Amendment rights in their demands for access to sensitive information. They are bitterly criticized as they invade privacy in pursuit of information. The citizens' sense of justice often demands that journalists act differently. Journalists are accused of selfishly claiming special privileges for themselves while victimizing others, particularly in privacy invasions. Often, the strongest critics in such cases are those who feel threatened by media disclosures or practices, those who have a vested interest in passive media. These public people often try to convince the rest of the public, often successfully, that journalists are jackals. The grieving families of the victims and people prematurely, and wrongly, identified as criminal suspects would agree.

The force and durability of the accusations cause the industry to smart. Journalists are jostled into introspection, asking whether traditional rules still apply and, in a complex world, what they *should* do to serve a critical society.

- Does ethics require publication or temporary withholding of names of suspects or other public figures named in police reports?
- Is it obligatory or optional to expose extramarital escapades and drug experimentation of political candidates, or are other issues more important and useful in the election process?
- What moral obligation requires a reporter to keep sources confidential, and when may those sources ethically be "burned"?
- Is it a moral obligation of journalists to detect and warn about impending disasters, and when is it acceptable to declare a consensus on such matters as the causes and effects of global warming?
- How can journalists balance their obligations to tell the truth, remain independent and minimize harm during — and after — such extraordinary crises as the September 11, 2001, terrorist attacks in New York City and Washington, D.C.?

News people increasingly are perplexed about how to handle problems that until recently seemed black and white.

Until the first Gulf War, combat had never been viewed live by both sides on a single commercial television outlet. Cable News Network kept the world informed, blow by blow. In other wars, the military generally has controlled the communications systems. Direct portable satellite transmission and cellular telephones allowed many journalists to bypass that control in the gulf.

When rape and sexual attacks never got to court without evidence of a brutal assault, torn clothing, bruises, and evidence of resistance, the procedures for news coverage were clearly prescribed. In today's society, ambiguities between accused and accuser make old coverage policies seem inadequate.

What moral burden rested on the *Seattle Times*, for example, to find provable truths before it published allegations of sexual harassment against a sitting U.S. senator, Brock Adams, particularly when a similar accusation had been investigated and dismissed by a government agency? By the same token, what allowed Oregon media, when confronted with repeated complaints about Sen. Robert Packwood's proclivities, to keep silent as he ran for re-election and largely deprived the state of his representation for two years while he tried to defend himself?

Can journalists argue that they ought not be expected to be so expert in finance that they could detect approaching financial disaster, such as the collapse of the dot-com boom or the 2009 recession, months or years before disaster struck?

When thousands of Los Angeles buildings were torched during riots that erupted after the controversial Rodney King verdict in 1992, what moral rules directed helicopter-borne camera operators to broadcast live picture showing where dangers lay or where there were no police? Such coverage provided sensitive information to two disparate groups — frightened citizens and marauders.

> The journalist's social role is critical, but often is not appreciated by the public and is poorly explained by the profession.

The journalist's mission can be complicated, too, by public relations practitioners who make favorable information abundantly available while obscuring the trail to unfavorable information.

As these dilemmas arise, often requiring decisions on deadline, journalists must search beyond the dogma of news values and tradition for help. A critical tool in the search is a greater understanding of the ethical role a journalist plays in making the wheels of society turn, and in keeping those wheels on.

Journalism is Different

The journalist's social role is critical, but often is not appreciated by the public and is poorly explained by the profession. While most journalists talk about protections the Constitution and the courts offer the practice of journalism, few explain to critics and the public **why** society protects journalists. What are the foundations of the First Amendment and favorable court interpretations? *Seattle Times* executive editor Michael Fancher described the painstaking procedures *Times* staffers followed in assuring fairness in the case of former Sen. Brock Adams, accused of sexual improprieties by several women, yet Fancher still cited "traditional standards" to be met for publication. Recall for a moment the traditional standards for deciding what is news, standards you first learned in journalism school or on the job: conflict, novelty, prominence, proximity, impact, timeliness, etc. These traditional standards may be suitable for defining routine news coverage, but they have no ethical or philosophical foundation. In short, these definitions of newsworthiness are amoral. Relying upon them to defend yourself against an accusation of questionable ethics can't satisfy an intelligent critic. In fairness to the *Seattle Times*, we must add that its editorial staff did go beyond these minimalistic standards; many other journalists, however, never get that far.

Unlike other professionals who have institutionally defined social roles and ethics, journalists have been left to their own devices in working out their social roles and in determining their ethics, and then in justifying those roles and ethics to the public.

Surgeons, in contrast, enjoy a clear mandate. It is unthinkable that most of us would pick up a knife and cut on a friend. Yet the surgeon has that specific moral charge: Inflict some pain and shed some blood, but be sure to bring more benefit than trauma to the patients. Thus the surgeon has a role bestowed and protected by society: Shed blood for a greater good. Likewise, a military commander has a role that morally justifies sending people to their deaths and inflicting death on an enemy, presumably for a greater good.

While it is generally accepted that surgeons have a moral right to shed blood, and generals in certain circumstances may morally end the lives of human beings they do not know, it is more difficult to define the journalist's role.

Journalists are not licensed, as are surgeons, nor are they hired, legitimized, and controlled by government, as are generals. Thus individual journalists and the profession as a whole must work out their own role definitions according to (1) their perceptions of what society needs, and (2) an ethical recognition that Constitutional protection must not knowingly be socially destructive. Because it would be silly for society to protect a class of people who are hastening its destruction, it must be assumed that journalists bear a strong moral obligation to avoid conscious social damage.

> Because information helps ensure informed consent, the principle of open communication has a unique standing in American society

A substantial amount of unjustifiable social damage can be avoided if journalists satisfy themselves that what they publish, however controversial it may be, has a high probability of being the truth. While truth is sometimes difficult to identify, the journalist nevertheless should generally err in favor of disclosure, rather than withhold information in cases in which probability of truth is high.

In a society that protects people who speak or write, any person (literate or illiterate, learned or ignorant, socialized or rebellious, passive or outraged) may become a journalist without standards imposed either by government or professional groups. Even regulation by society at large in the form of intimidating public opinion, while often formidable, is difficult to enforce because of the Bill of Rights. First Amendment protection slows suppression, even by the compelling power of public opinion, until society considers and discusses restrictions.

A big problem for journalists as they compare their duties with those of the surgeon and the general is that their discussions all too often begin by citing law rather than explaining the moral obligations that journalists are attempting to fulfill. Defenders talk of the *right* to publish, rather than the *reason* they publish. There is a tendency by journalists to wrongly assume the public understands the rationale behind First Amendment protections. Just as the public now questions basic assumptions about the environment and natural resources, so journalists are being pressed to answer basic questions about their function.

Journalists distribute information, a traditional role that often puts the journalist at odds with individuals and power brokers who want to keep power by controlling information.

The democratic principle supporting quality journalism has been expressed by philosopher Carl Friedrich. He wrote that since everyone is fallible in making decisions, society needs the collective judgments of many fallible people to produce valid social decisions and solve social problems. The journalist is the central figure in improving the odds that good decisions will be made. He or she provides key information that will assist the populace in giving informed consent to public proposals. Constantly opposing the journalists, for good reasons of their own, are those with competing strong ideas about how the world should turn out, and a corresponding commitment to promote their own agendas. Discouraging journalists from distributing contrary information is a common way true believers attempt to advance causes.

Because information helps ensure informed consent, the principle of open communication has a unique standing in American society. In that context, ethical reasoning requires a considerably different approach than is common in professional ethics. The First Amendment and subsequent court rulings give journalists unparalleled freedom to inform the fallible without government interference.

The conscientious journalist needs to deal with the moral question of social contract. In this case, it is a question of a journalists' contracts with an audience: What contract is created between me and my reader or viewer when that person buys my newspaper or spends time watching a newscast to which I contribute?

In a democratic society, the audience is expected to process a much broader range of information than in other cultures.

So, when we speak of journalism ethics, then, we speak not of regulated behavior, the phenomenon most familiar to us as we look at the activities of doctors, lawyers, plumbers and others who follow professional codes. In journalism, we speak of the far more important concepts of "reasoned" and "principled" behavior. Journalists must decide for themselves, rather than having others decide for them, what information they will distribute, and what form that information will take. Even professional groups, without authority to keep journalists from practicing their craft, may not tell the journalist how to perform.

Most discussions of professional ethics imply the existence of documented restrictions on ethical behavior as a means to protect society. Such restrictions are expected to be universally accepted and mandatory. However, a free society specifically rejects most speech and press restrictions. Therefore, mandatory standards for journalism are rightly unenforceable and unworkable. Judicial interpretations of the First Amendment consistently resist pressure to insist that journalists be licensed. Thus, anybody can be a journalist without fear of being prohibited from practicing the craft (or being depressed or ex-communicated, if you would).

This absence of professional discipline makes journalistic codes, including the SPJ Code of Ethics, more advisory than mandatory. That is in sharp contrast to the enforceable codes of the legal and medical professions, and a source of concern to those who see a need to "control" anyone who possesses the kind of power the media are perceived to have. But it also means that journalists, individually and collectively, have a greater need for an articulated sense of ethics than do the more regulated professions.

Principle and Reason

There are several propositions journalists should be aware of as they participate in principled and reasoned decision-making. These propositions, abbreviated here, are expanded in other ethics publications, but they provide a starting place for someone working to understand the journalistic role.

First, society is committed to the possibility of the free flow of information as a means of (a) informing the population so its members may (b) make informed decisions which (c) combine with thousands or millions of other decisions to (d) contribute to the strength of society or determine how society will treat its individual members.

Second, the journalistic mission is often obscured because information control is related to power. Distribution of information is a redistribution of power. Thus, because the traditional function of the journalist is the distribution of information, the journalist is often at odds with individuals and entities wishing to retain power by controlling or withholding information.

Distribution of information can be a mixed bag. All information may help someone while at the same time harming others. Disclosure about nursing home abuses my benefit patients by improving care. However, it also reduces the power of nursing home operators, placed in a public spotlight, to control their own operations. Nursing home disclosures may also cause anxiety and even guilt feelings in families who comfortably assume family members in *all* nursing homes are receiving competent, caring treatment.

Surgeons cut people open, and generals commit lives to combat. Both life-and-death or pain-inflicting functions have strong public support. Journalists do their job by taking power from groups bent on retaining or accumulating it. They then redistribute power to the public by disseminating information. Brock Adams had the power to run again for the Senate, but the *Seattle Times* story gave the public information that diminished his power. The citizens of the state of Washington, with more information, gained the power to decide if Brock Adams should continue to hold public office.

The journalist is likely to be immersed in a variety of differing loyalties and ties that affect the pure gathering and distribution of information: the desire to win fame and fortune; biases for or against social institutions or individuals; conceptions about what a journalist or investigative reporter is, or does, etc. Such pressures may blunt the journalist's moral judgment, producing faulty journalistic decisions. The public then suffers from distorted information. Despite the journalists' service to audiences, those largely defenseless and unorganized groups seldom express themselves. They contrast with special interest groups which, because they tend to be extremely vocal, create an impression of a public opinion outpouring. This book is concerned with giving voice to the voiceless, those who have minimal leverage or position in society. The voiceless can then air their views, along with the views of more vocal special interests, to produce legitimate public opinion, which in turn can be understood and enhanced by the news media. Communications media thus fulfill their basic functions of communicating — making experiences common or sharing information — and mediating — coming between and pulling together various interest groups.

A society that trusts the media to keep it informed has mixed feelings about those media. Minimizing harm while trying to keep audiences fully informed requires that journalists formulate justification mechanisms to defend publishing decisions. Those defenses must go beyond mere restatements of traditional journalistic rights or unquestioned institutional norms. They need to be articulated journalistic obligations.

Conclusion

In using this handbook, then, one must recognize the paramount importance of distributing information to a democratic society. Once that role is understood as a primary obligation, journalists can use moral reasoning and can follow principles, rather than routine and tradition, in making ethical decisions. Those decisions should support journalists' obligation to distribute necessary information fully — to tell the truth — while avoiding unnecessary harm and holding themselves accountable.

The remainder of this examination of ethics is devoted to guiding journalists (and other communicators) through a decision- making process that will protect society by supporting the full disclosure of information and giving voice to the voiceless, while protecting innocent people from needless harm.

CHAPTER THREE:

Codes of Ethics and Beyond

Ever since the first journalist began assembling the first information for the first news story, people have been concerned about journalism ethics. Millions of words have been spoken, and thousands of pages written, about identifying and resolving the tough calls journalists face while gathering and reporting the news.

However, for all the work that has been put into ethics through the years, the job is nowhere near finished. In the words of Philip Meyer, author of *Ethical Journalism*, journalists are still ethically confused. As a profession, journalism has come a long way in its ability to identify ethical issues and dilemmas. However, journalists have a long way to go before knowing how to resolve those problems carefully and systematically. They have heightened their sensitivity far more than they have expanded their decision-making skills.

Much of the credit and a fair share of the blame for this confusing state of affairs can be laid at the feet of those who invoke codes of ethics as the panacea. At best, the codes have helped define many of the problems and have kept the profession alert to its responsibilities to gather and report news thoroughly and accurately and to remain vigilant toward governmental and other forces that would usurp the media's independence. At worst, codes have short-circuited journalists' ability to act as independent decision-makers.

Pros and Cons of Codes

One of the prerequisites of a profession is to have its own code of ethics. Codes of ethics are supposed to act as the conscience of the professional, of the organization, of the enterprise. A code of ethics falls somewhere between societal and personal values on the one hand and law on the other. A code is neither as subjective as personal beliefs and opinions, nor as rigid and enforceable as the law.

The strength of an ethics code is a function not only of its various principles and mandates, but of its legitimacy and power in the eyes of those for whom it is written. The code will be obeyed because individuals willingly subject themselves to ethical standards above and beyond their own personal beliefs or because the code has specific provisions for enforcement, which they fear should they violate it.

Even the best codes have built-in limitations. Codes of ethics identify useful lists of sins, and to some extent outline truly noble behavior. They are of some use to newcomers who need a road map that points out troublesome ethical intersections, sharp corners, and the biggest potholes. They also have some public relations value to an industry that tries to convince the public of its seriousness about ethics. But codes cannot delineate all the territory likely to be encountered, and they aren't much help when negotiating the vast foggy terrain through which journalists travel daily. As a result of these natural limitations to codes, many journalists erroneously conclude that there are no useful guidelines, that each ethical decision is made *ad hoc* or independently of all other decisions.

The goal of this examination of ethics is like the goals of moral philosophers throughout history: to help individuals and groups make ethical decisions that are morally defensible, and to base those decisions on justification processes that hold true from situation to situation, person to person, time to time. The authors of *Journalism Ethics* (now *Media Ethics*) hoped to help students and practitioners of the art of communication systematically work through ethical dilemmas because of an articulated ethical mission, a dedication to *doing the right thing for the right reasons*. To accomplish such a complex goal requires more than a code.

Bruce W. Sanford, then counsel to the nation's oldest and largest journalism organization, the Society of Professional Journalists, wrote, "History teaches that the most effective way to promote ethical behavior is through discussion and information, not enforcement."

In an article in the Associated Press Managing Editors publication *Ethics Codes: Sunrise or Sunset?* Sanford quotes Geoffrey Hazard, who makes a good case for relying on a process of examination and discussion rather than a list of dos and don'ts:

> Ethical principles can be established only as a result of deliberation and argumentation. These principles are not the kind of thing that can be settled by fiat, agreement or by authority. To assume that they can is to confuse ethics with lawmaking, rule-making, policy-making and other kinds of decision-making.

For years, SPJ members have debated the pros and cons of enforcement procedures for their code. Some maintained that a professional organization without the means and willingness to censure code violations is undeserving of the public trust. Others insisted that the constitutionally protected enterprise of journalism had fought too hard and long for freedom from outside control, and journalism should not impose any more control over itself than absolutely necessary. Still others argued that to enforce the code would invite litigation financially devastating to the Society and establish precedents that would serve the purposes of those seeking a universal standard of conduct enforceable in court. And others claimed that the wording of the Society's code combines lofty idealistic statements and minimal standards of performance in such a way as to render the code unenforceable in the first place.

In 1987, SPJ deleted from its code of ethics a clause requiring journalists to "actively censure" code violators. In its place, the Society promised a strong education program that stressed ethics and encouraged journalists to adhere to the code's honorable ideals.

Preeminent among these ideals was the desire "to preserve and strengthen the bond of mutual trust and respect among American journalists and the American people." That bond is based on both credibility and ethics, the former being the profession's image, the latter its substance.

The code as revised in 1987 also called on journalists in print and broadcasting to frame individual and institutional codes of ethics. However, in their fear that having clearly articulated standards would play into the hands of lawyers, some journalists appeared to back away from the hard but necessary work of spelling out precisely what they believe is ethically proper. As time has gone on, however, and as journalists have become more sensitive to ethical problems, more and more journalists have been drafting or revising their newsrooms' codes or policy manuals.

The 2014 SPJ Code

Codes of ethics, like muscles, brains and old house pets, wither and atrophy unless they are exercised occasionally. The SPJ code is no exception.

SPJ has had a written code since 1926, very early in its history. (It had been founded in 1909 as Sigma Delta Chi, a fraternity also known as SDX.) It borrowed the American Society of Newspaper Editors' canons of journalism, which served SDX until it drafted its own code in 1973, in the aftermath of Watergate. The 1973 code, unanimously approved by delegates to the organization's national convention, was amended several times in the ensuing years. The 1987 amendment, as noted earlier, dropped the "censure" clause and replaced it with an "education" clause.

A decade of changing technologies, changing managements, changing marketplaces, changing roles, changing reputations and changing dilemmas suggested to the Society of Professional Journalists that it was time once again to change its code of ethics. A two-year effort that involved thousands of SPJ members from hundreds of professional and student chapters, and the work of the several committees and subcommittees, resulted in adoption of a totally new code in 1996. It was framed around a set of three guiding principles proposed in earlier editions of this handbook, then entitled *Doing Ethics in Journalism*: to seek truth, to minimize harm, and to remain independent. A fourth principle was added in light of numerous discussions, and an increasingly apparent public concern, that journalists should hold themselves publicly accountable. The fourth principle is not an enforcement clause *per se*, but it is as close to one as SPJ has had since 1987.

> The revision committee attempted to make the code applicable to a broader range of people who practice journalism — not necessarily just those who consider themselves professional journalists.

The debate over enforcement is an ongoing discussion in SPJ. And so is the discussion about updating the code of ethics to reflect the rapidly evolving nature of information delivery systems. There was a revision of the SPJ Code of Ethics over a two-year period beginning in 2013. Some members of SPJ's ethics committee believed it was well past time to change the code's language to reflect the challenges presented by a growing internet presence and the emergence of "citizen journalists." Others maintained that the principles remain the same; only the technology of delivering information changes. Some wanted a longer, more specific code. Some wanted to elevate transparency as a principle ahead of independence — in other words, if a journalist is open about his or her potential conflicts of interest, that's more important than attempting to avoid any potential conflict that might taint coverage.

In the end, the committee that worked on revising the code, led by ethics committee chairman Kevin Smith, adopted a conservative position, holding that the principles of good journalism should not change when the technology changes. Rather than going into more detail about the challenges presented by evolving communication platforms, the revision committee decided to eliminate references to specific technologies, hoping to make the code simpler and shorter. It recognized the importance of being transparent about one's potential conflicts, but continued to maintain that it's better to avoid conflicts whenever possible.

What follows is a brief explanation of the revised code, adopted in September 2014, and how it differs from the SPJ Code of Ethics that was adopted in 1996.

The Preamble

The four sentences constituting the preamble to the SPJ code of ethics proclaim, in lofty language, what it is that professional journalists stand for:

> Members of the Society of Professional Journalists believe that public enlightenment is the forerunner of justice and the foundation of democracy. Ethical journalism strives to ensure the free exchange of information that is accurate, fair and thorough. An ethical journalist acts with integrity.
>
> The Society declares these four principles as the foundation of ethical journalism and encourages their use in practice by all people in all media.

This preamble sets the stage for the set of four fundamental guiding principles (truth, harm, independence and accountability), and more specific lists of the profession's generally accepted standards of practice. It is worth emphasizing that the guiding principles are abstract and idealistic, but the standards of practice that follow those major principles are more specific. Unlike many codes, however, both components tend to be framed in the affirmative ("Thou shalt") rather than the negative ("Thou shalt not"). This was a deliberate choice on the part of the code writers, believing as they did that more professional, ethical behavior will result from conscientious application of principles than from blind obedience to minimalist rules.

Principles and Questions

Members of the SPJ Ethics Committee, bolstered by thoughtful observers of journalism and by work across the spectrum of ethical decision-making, believe it is possible to help journalists weigh the ingredients of a good ethical decision without compromising deadlines. The following four principles (and subsequent checklists of 10 questions, plus the decision-making template described earlier) are intended to help journalists work their way through an ethical dilemma.

These are not "fault" standards that can be trotted out by libel lawyers seeking to discover some bottom line of propriety below which journalists may have fallen. Rather, they are proactive models for clear thinking, drawn from interviews with several hundred working journalists, the contents of more than 100 news media codes of ethics and policy statements, and the insights of many philosophers and news media critics. The object is to help journalists recognize ethical dilemmas when they arise, to explore the complexities of decision-making, to resist moralizing and to recognize the limits of blind obedience to customs and codes. Throughout this examination of ethics in communication, we will see how these principles and questions play out in the decision-making process.

Guiding Principles for Journalism

Seek Truth and Report It. Ethical journalism should be accurate and fair. Journalists should be honest and courageous in gathering, reporting and interpreting information.

Minimize Harm. Ethical journalism treats sources, subjects, colleagues and members of the public as human beings deserving of respect.

Act Independently. The highest and primary obligation of ethical journalism is to serve the public.

Be Accountable and Transparent. Ethical journalism means taking responsibility for one's work and explaining one's decisions to the public.

These principles in the 2014 version of the SPJ Code of Ethics are almost exactly the same as they were in the 1996 version. One subtle, yet significant difference, is that the 2014 code more often addresses "journalism" rather than "journalists." That was part of the revision committee's effort to make the code applicable to a broader range of people who practice journalism — not necessarily just those who consider themselves professional journalists.

This book explores how each of these four principles plays out in the world of journalism, and other forms of communication. It is important to note that the four guiding principles are intended to work in tandem, and not in isolation. To put it another way, any given ethical dilemma entails a balancing act between or among two or more of the principles.

For instance, how can journalists seek and report truth without disrupting the status quo and causing a certain amount of harm? And how can journalists act independently while being held accountable? The tendency to polarize these two sets of principles is very tempting indeed. But there is a better way.

Journalists frequently maintain that they are justified in causing harm during the gathering and reporting of information that the general public needs to know. Be that as it may, the choice should not be either/or. A good choice probably rests somewhere along a continuum: How much harm is necessary in order to tell how much important truth? (Do you name a rape victim or identify a sexual predator, citing community interest? Is it necessary to photograph a badly disfigured youth who happens to be in the midst of an unpleasant lawsuit?)

All else being equal, journalism's first objective is to seek out and report truth. Ethical journalists do not revert to minimizing harm as the first step when doing journalism, but as a second step. The harm principle is not invoked as a means of blunting criticism, or currying favor, or avoiding having to do substantial truth-telling. All too often journalists "wimp out" when better journalism — and more civic good — would have resulted from putting truth-telling and minimizing harm in their proper contexts.

Likewise, a balance between independence and accountability must be sought. Journalists, bolstered by the First Amendment and a history of favorable court rulings, are cantankerously independent. Traditionalists in the craft worry about face-licking journalism. They don't think the recent public journalism movement is healthy, because they see it as a lessening of journalism's hard-fought independence. Sharing trade secrets and airing dirty laundry (the ombudsman movement, news councils, etc.) could chip away at the nascent profession's mystique, because such exercises in public accountability allow the barbarians to cross the moat.

On closer examination, it is perfectly reasonable for journalists to maintain enough independence to remain free from external and internal pressures that dilute the truth-telling enterprise, while simultaneously recognizing that as professional journalists we are accountable to our readers, listeners, viewers and each other.

It's time to reframe the thought process. We can accomplish this by avoiding the either-or polarization of ethical decision-making. Instead, picture journalism on a set of horizontal and vertical axes.

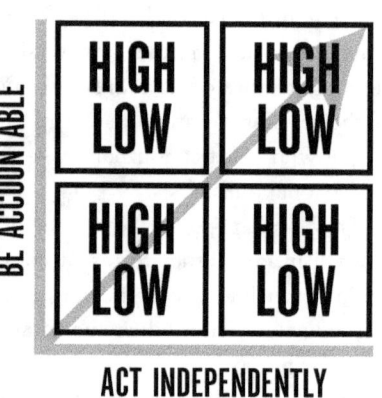

"Bad" journalism occurs when we do a lousy job of truth-telling and when sources or subjects are harmed for no good reason. ("Low/Low" on the horizontal and vertical axes.)

"Better" journalism might occur when we cause a lot of harm (disrupting people's comfort zones) during the process of telling highly significant truths ("High/Low") or when we cause only a small amount of harm while telling an insignificant story ("Low/High"). Ethical and excellent journalism, of course, maximizes the amount of truth and the minimization of harm.

The same goes for the principles of independence and accountability.

The bulk of this collection of real-life ethical dilemmas shows how communications professionals in some four dozen case studies attempted to deal with these four principles, consciously or not, when making decisions on deadline.

WHAT OTHER CODES SAY

Each of the chapters in the rest of this resource closes with excerpts from codes of ethics. These excerpts are primarily from employers' codes, which tend to be more detailed than aspirational codes, such as SPJ's or RTDNA's.

Not all media companies make their codes of ethics available to the public. We applaud those that do; it's an important way to live up to the principle of accountability and transparency. The excerpts that follow come from codes collected by the American Society of News Editors and by the Society of Professional Journalists from sources available online to anyone who wants to look them up. They include both employers' codes of ethics and associations' aspirational codes and provide further guidance to the subjects covered in that chapter.

There is also a collection of principles concerning the use of social media — both personally and as a source of information — that could be pertinent to several chapter subjects, such as accuracy, or conflicts of interest, or transparency. Somewhat arbitrarily, the social media principles follow the chapter on reporter-source relations.

WHAT THE CODES SAY: General Principles

In the 21st century ... news is transmitted in more ways than ever before — in print, on the air and on the Web, with words, images, graphics, sound and video. But always and in all media, we insist on the highest standards of integrity and ethical behavior when we gather and deliver the news.

—*The Associated Press*

The Washington Post is pledged to an aggressive, responsible and fair pursuit of the truth without fear of any special interest, and with favor to none.

Washington Post reporters and editors are pledged to approach every assignment with the fairness of open minds and without prior judgment. The search for opposing views must be routine. Comment from persons accused or challenged in stories must be included. The motives of those who press their views upon us must routinely be examined, and it must be recognized that those motives can be noble or ignoble, obvious or ulterior.

We fully recognize that the power we have inherited as the dominant morning newspaper in the capital of the free world carries with it special responsibilities:

to listen to the voiceless
to avoid any and all acts of arrogance
to face the public politely and candidly

The Washington Post

If all the philosophy of ethical behavior could be boiled down to a few words, they could be these: behave as though everything you did would be reported on the front page of tomorrow's paper.

That means, of course, that we as journalists and citizens should hold ourselves to the same high standards of truth, sensitivity and fairness, which we expect from public officials on whom we report.

Tacoma Morning News Tribune, Washington

We believe that the Internet is the most powerful communications medium to arise since the dawn of television. As digital delivery systems become the primary source of news for a growing segment of the world's population, it presents complex challenges and opportunities for journalists as well as the news audience.

Editorial Integrity. The unique permeability of digital publications allows for the linking and joining of information resources of all kinds as intimately as if they were published by a single organization. Responsible journalism through this medium means that the distinction between news and other information must always be clear, so that individuals can readily distinguish independent editorial information from paid promotional information and other non-news.

Online News Association

Mike Keefe, The Colorado Independent. Reprinted with permission.

We believe that it is the duty of journalists to serve the truth. As practitioners of the press freedom that is essential to democracy, we believe that journalists have a higher duty than others to avoid the appearance of conflicts of interest in their professional and private lives.

Asbury Park Press, New Jersey

These guidelines are intended to serve in a variety of situations. They apply to everyone working for the Free Press newsroom — full-time and part-time staff members, and freelancers on assignment. They obviously cannot envision all circumstances. These are not legal standards. Other news organizations may view some matters differently. Those affected by our coverage may differ with us over what is "fair" or "accurate." Occasions will arise where news decisions must be made that will be at variance with these guidelines; nevertheless, they represent what we ourselves strive for.

Whenever doubt exists on a question of ethics or taste or sensitivity, please discuss that doubt with a supervising editor.

Detroit Free Press

Like most institutions, the press is under attack. We are being harassed by government officials and judges. Our motives and methods are challenged. Our fairness is questioned. Our credibility with the public is undermined.

In this climate, it is more important than ever that we act fairly and responsibly in reporting the news, that we reject any conduct — any conflict of interest or special favor — which might lessen public confidence in our integrity.

Professional tradition and lively individual consciences are the best defenders of journalistic ethics. But many issues, equivocal or morally ambivalent, are difficult to decide in concrete terms. Because this is so, it seems advisable to have specific guidelines for The News.

The New York Daily News

The good news organization is fair, accurate, responsible, independent and decent. Truth is its guiding principle.

Associated Press Media Editors

The mission of ProPublica is to practice and promote investigative journalism in the public interest. All of the values stated here, and the rules set out here, are intended to contribute to that mission. Much of the language below draws on similar policies in place at distinguished American news organizations, including Dow Jones & Company, the Associated Press, the Washington Post and Time Inc. We do this because, while our entity is new, and our business model somewhat innovative, our ethics are neither. They reflect what we and others have learned over many years. At the same time, however, this Code is not immutable. Most of it consists of guidelines; exceptional circumstances may require exceptions to these rules. We expect to continue to learn, and as we do so, to revise this document in light of further insight and experience.

ProPublica

Inform objectively! Edit out subjective bias.
　Comment editorially to inform and guide.
　Campaign for the desirable — help eliminate the undesirable. Play the role of a good citizen.
　Serve as friendly counselor, information bureau and champion of the readers' rights. Try to respond to a reader's responsible doable requests.
　Be courteous to the public. It is good public relations.

The Phoenix Republic

Thou shalt not:
1. Make up sources or quotes. This includes "composite" sources.
2. Deliberately distort the truth.
3. Take bribes. This means accepting cash in any amount, trips or substantial gifts in exchange for doing our jobs. The IRS gift standard ($25 value) is the outside limit on what would be considered a "substantial gift."
4. Plagiarize from sources outside the newspaper. If you have any doubt, attribute or discuss it with your editor.
5. Alter the content of news photos through technological or other means. Photo-illustrations are acceptable, but should be clearly labeled.
6. Use our standing with the newspaper for personal financial gain or special treatment.

7. Pay sources for news stories.
8. Stage or re-create news events for photographers.
9. Physically or verbally abuse a source, reader or colleague.

Statesman Journal, Salem, Oregon

Beneath these guidelines rests the Golden Rule: Treat others as you would have them treat you.

Our news judgments should be influenced by intellectual honesty; by compassion for individuals; by the consequences of publication; and by readers' need to know. There are occasions when an exercise of self-restraint will be in the public interest, when significant harm can be reasonably anticipated as a result of publication, with no balancing public benefit.

That weighing of benefit against potential harm — particularly to an individual who is thrust into the light of publicity not by choice — should be a constant exercise in the application of news judgment. We should approach it as a green-light question — is there sufficient reason to publish this information? — rather than a red light — is there sufficient reason not to? And we should fall back on that Golden Rule.

The need to publish immediately is likely to come into conflict with our consideration of other ethical obligations. Surely information of public interest loses its value to our readers with the passage of time. Still, even under the pressure of deadline we must apply reasonable judgment, weighing the good that will be achieved with speed against the harm that could be inflicted by compromising other values.

Daily Press, Newport News, Virginia

Managers, by virtue of their positions of authority, must be ethical role models for all employees. An important part of a manager's leadership responsibility is to exhibit the highest standards of integrity in all dealings with employees, customers, and the world at large. Managers must avoid even implicit or unspoken approval of any actions that may be damaging to the reputation of Dow Jones, and must always exercise sound business judgment in the performance of their duties.

Dow Jones & Company (publishers of the *Wall Street Journal*)

An ethics policy should be a living document. The committee that crafted these guidelines anticipated that the Mercury News, on occasion, must revisit the important ethical issues of the day to ensure its ethics policy does not become obsolete or, worse, ignored. Therefore, these are broad outlines; the newspaper will establish a fair method of dealing with ethical questions.

San Jose Mercury News, California

We will seek solutions as well as expose problems and wrongdoing.

Gannett Newspaper Division

Our goal is to begin and end each day with a primary obligation to the public's right to know.

With every ethical scar, we threaten a delicate relationship with readers. Ethical breaches violate hard-earned trust and shatter our credibility.

To properly understand and reflect the community, we must live thoroughly and wholeheartedly in it. The constant tension of demanding a better society, while still living in it, is an obligation of a passionate and compassionate journalist. We should be independent, without being detached.

Ethics is the constant process of examining and drawing these lines. It is a continual effort, and we should hold each other accountable in the protection of our values. These values must come through a discussion with our conscience, our colleagues and our leaders, both for the public interest and our own professional education.

The Denver Post

The explosion of new technologies is changing the marketing and advertising landscape both domestically and globally. New media, new ideas, new challenges, new cultural opportunities are swirling around the industry and impacting the way it does business.

The one constant is transparency, and the need to conduct ourselves, our businesses, and our relationships with consumers in a fair, honest, and forthright manner.

This is especially true in today's often hostile environment, with revelations of wrongdoing in particular industries and government programs resulting in an erosion of public confidence and trust in all our institutions.

It is particularly fitting in such times that we remind ourselves of the ethical behavior that should always guide our personal and business conduct.

The eight Principles and Practices presented here are the foundation on which the Institute for Advertising Ethics (IAE) was created. They are based on the premise that all forms of communications, including advertising, should always do what is right for consumers, which in turn is right for business as well. For while we are in an age of unparalleled change, this overriding truth never changes.

American Advertising Federation

The Public Relations Society of America (PRSA) is committed to ethical practices. The level of public trust PRSA members seek, as we serve the public good, means we have taken on a special obligation to operate ethically.

The value of member representation depends upon the ethical conduct of everyone affiliated with the Public Relations Society of America. Each of us sets an example for each other — as well as other professionals — by our pursuit of excellence with powerful standards of performance, professionalism, and ethical conduct.

PRSA Code of Ethics

CHAPTER FOUR:

Guidelines and Rules: Ethics and the Law

By Paul Fletcher
Publisher & Editor-in-Chief, Virginia Lawyers Weekly
SPJ National President, 2015-16

The Society of Professional Journalists Code of Ethics provides precepts for reasoned, ethical decision-making in a newsroom.

But the Code contains only "guidelines," not "rules." The Code is not enforceable in a court of law. Its guidelines and tenets are aspirational, designed to help journalists decide the most ethical way to handle a dilemma.

There *are* enforceable rules that journalists must follow — the laws of the United States and of their respective home states. These rules will be found in two places — in the statute books and in case law as decided by state and federal courts.

The laws, coupled with the ethical guidelines, provide a framework for journalists as they do their work.

Words Matter

Lawyers are trained to parse statutes and laws carefully. The way a statute is worded matters: just what did the drafters in the legislature mean?

Journalists similarly should read the Code with care. The words used throughout the Code were selected intentionally. As an aspirational document, it often contains words such as "consider," or "weigh" or "balance." In a few places, it calls for journalists to "be cautious when" doing something or to "be wary of" certain fact patterns.

Journalists looking for hard-and-fast rules in the Code won't find many. There are only three direct imperatives in the Code:
- Never plagiarize.
- Always attribute.
- Do not pay for access to news.

Those few black-and-white statements qualify as rules. The rest of the Code deals in a lot of different levels of gray.

Legal v. Ethical

When the SPJ Code of Ethics was revised in 2014, there was a new section added that had not been part of the prior 1996 Code. Under the second guideline, "Minimize Harm," it states:

- Journalists should "[r]ecognize that legal access to information differs from an ethical justification to publish or broadcast."

The section provides a clear reminder: There is a difference between what is legal and what is ethical.

The law might allow you to do one thing, but ethical guidelines might not. Put another way, the fact that you *can* publish doesn't mean you *should*.

And under the same guideline is a cautionary observation, "Pursuit of the news is not a license for arrogance or undue obtrusiveness."

How would this play out in an actual newsroom? Here's an example:

The Journal News in Westchester County, New York, in December 2012 published the names and addresses of citizens who had obtained gun permits, in Newtown, Connecticut. The paper is based about 40 miles from Newtown.

The week before, Newtown had been the site of a horrific mass shooting at Sandy Hook Elementary School.

The Journal News obtained all of its information through appropriate, legal channels. The publisher of the newspaper justified printing the data by saying, "New York residents have the right to own guns with a permit and they also have a right to access public information."

But Al Tompkins, a senior faculty member at the Poynter Institute, the Florida-based journalism think tank, took the Journal Record to task.

He said, "Just because information is public does not make it newsworthy. People own guns for a wide range of law-abiding reasons. If you are not breaking the law, there is no compelling reason to publish the data.

"Publishing gun owners' names makes them targets for theft or public ridicule," he added. "It is journalistic arrogance to abuse public record privilege, just as it is to air 911 calls for no reason or to publish the home addresses of police or judges without cause."

Tompkins concluded, "Unwarranted publishing of the names of permitted owners just encourages gun owners to skip the permitting."

SOURCE: Julie Moos, https://www.poynter.org/reporting-editing/2012/where-the-journal-news-went-wrong-in-publishing-names-addresses-of-gun-owners/Dec. 26, 2012.

Here is another example, one anticipated by the drafters of the Code:

Under "Minimize Harm," there is a caution to "[c]onsider the implications of identifying criminal suspects before they face legal charges." Many newsrooms handle this situation by simply drawing a line: A suspect doesn't get named until he or she actually is charged.

But not all do. And police authorities make it harder when they identify a "person of interest," that is, someone they are investigating but who hasn't been charged.

> Accuracy is not the same as truth. Different people have different truths.

In a competitive news environment, the temptation to publish the name of a "person of interest" might overcome a journalist's best ethical impulses. Anyone who thinks of naming a person of interest before charges are filed should recall the examples of Richard Jewell and Stephen Hatfill.

At the Atlanta Olympics in 1996, someone set off a nail bomb that killed two people and injured 111 others. Jewell, a security guard, earlier had noticed a suspicious backpack and alerted the Georgia Bureau of Investigation. As authorities sought to clear the area, the backpack exploded.

Jewell was hailed as a hero at first, then the situation turned ugly. Authorities started to take an interest in Jewell as a possible suspect. The local media fueled the fire on the hero-turned-goat story.

As Ronald Ostrow wrote in a Columbia University case study on Jewell, "Papers like the [Atlanta] Journal-Constitution feel enormous internal pressure to 'own' the story—to be first with every important new development. To be beaten by an outside news organization in your own back yard is the ultimate competitive humiliation."

As Jewell's life became a living hell, the hoopla became one of the most egregious examples of "trial by media." Ultimately, the story didn't pan out and Jewell was exonerated.

SOURCE: Ronald Ostrow, http://www.columbia.edu/itc/journalism/j6075/edit/readings/jewell.html, June 13, 2000.

Stephen Hatfill was a government researcher who was wrongfully accused in the 2001 anthrax mailings that killed five people. He had been identified as a "person of interest" by Attorney General John Ashcroft in a letter to Sen. Charles Grassley, R-Iowa.

The anthrax incident came right after 9/11, when nerves were raw and hysteria easy to incite. But Hatfill was not the perpetrator. He went on the offensive, filing numerous lawsuits to clear his name.

For journalists, though, there was a dilemma identified by Donna Shaw, who wrote a piece on the problem with the term "person of interest" in American Journalism Review. "How do you not use his name?" she quoted one source as saying, when Hatfill's lawyer had gone public with denunciations of the government.

SOURCE: Donna Shaw, American Journalism Review, http://ajrarchive.org/Article.asp?id=4042. Feb/March 2006.

Libel, Slander and Defamation

This is a media ethics book, not a treatise on media law, but a few observations on defamation law are in order.

Every reporter must be aware of the laws on defamation in his or her state. That's not just ethical, that's smart. And required. Journalism schools teach courses on libel, slander and defamation; lawyers stay on retainer for media organizations to provide counsel when reporters and editors come close to the line. Know what you can publish or not, and if part of your story is questionable, you must, as a matter of ethics, take it up the chain so you don't publish something untruthful.

There is a strong argument that publishing inaccurate work is unethical. The preamble to the first guiding principle in the Code, "Seek Truth and Report It," states, "Ethical journalists are accurate and fair." A sloppily written story that has factual errors, then, is unethical work. And worse, a reporter who doesn't seek to write an accurate story exposes herself and the organization that publishes it to a lawsuit. Getting fired could be the least of her problems.

Protecting Sources (And Yourself)

Sometimes journalists need to promise confidentiality to sources in order to get the information they need for a story.

(**Note:** Some outlets still will allow information from "unnamed sources" to be published. Given the modern trend toward transparency in journalism — reflected in the 2014 Code, which urges journalists to be "accountable and transparent" — that practice has become somewhat suspect.)

But where a journalist makes a promise of confidentiality, the promise should stick. The Code states that ethical journalists should "[b]e cautious when making promises, but keep the promises they make."

When the story at issue involves a criminal matter, that's when a journalist might find trouble. Thanks to the 1972 U.S. Supreme Court decision in *Branzburg v. Hayes,* a reporter has no constitutional privilege from being compelled to testify before a grand jury about his sources if the information is relevant to a criminal investigation. There have been cases where reporters have stood their ground and they got thrown in jail for contempt of court:

- Judith Miller of *The New York Times* spent 85 days behind bars for refusing to reveal Central Intelligence Agency sources in a story about CIA operative Valerie Plame.

Or sometimes the sanction is monetary.

- A federal judge found Toni Locy, writing for USA Today, in contempt for not revealing a source in a story on the anthrax investigation; he fined her $5,000 a day. She prevailed on appeal, and the contempt finding and the fines were thrown out.

These are cautionary examples for any reporter caught in a similar scenario. The good news is that there are laws that provide some safe quarter. They are called "shield laws," and they provide to some degree the reporter's privilege lacking in the *Branzburg* case. Forty-nine of the 50 states and the District of Columbia have reporter protections either in an enacted statute or a decision from the state's highest court. Wyoming is the one state without a shield law.

Some shield laws are stronger than others — New York has one of the best. In the Empire State, the reporter's privilege is absolute: a journalist cannot be hauled into court and threatened with jail if she doesn't reveal who gave her sensitive, confidential or embarrassing information.

New Yorkers always have supported freedom of the press. Go back to colonial times. In 1735, one of the earliest press freedom cases was tried there. John Peter Zenger published an anonymous article criticizing the colonial governor. He refused to identify the author and was brought up on libel charges. But a jury refused to convict him, setting an important precedent for all the colonies, and later, the United States.

The first version of the state's press-shield law was passed in Albany in 1970, during an era when the Nixon administration was warring with the press. The investigative reporters at *The New York Times* were a particular target. Gov. Nelson A. Rockefeller hailed the law: "A representative democracy, such as ours, cannot exist unless there is a free press both willing and able to keep the public informed of all news."

> These aren't just laws to aid journalists — they are laws for everyone. The request mechanisms in FOI statutes can be used by any citizen.

The current absolute protections in the New York law were adopted in 1990. And an absolute approach makes sense. New York City is the media capital of the world.

The case of Jana Winter, an investigative reporter at Fox News, is illustrative. Winter, who lives in New York, published a story involving James Holmes. Holmes was convicted of shooting up a theater in Aurora, Colorado, the night that the Batman movie "The Dark Knight Rises" premiered. Twelve people died and 70 were injured. Winter's story focused on a notebook that Holmes had mailed to a University of Colorado psychiatrist. In her piece, Winter referred to two anonymous sources. In Colorado, 20 different law enforcement officials denied being the source. Holmes' lawyers filed a subpoena across state lines, seeking to force Winter to travel to Colorado to tell them with whom she talked.

Winter lost twice in intermediate court proceedings, but in December 2013, the New York Court of Appeals quashed the subpoena, freeing her from any obligation to testify.

The case of author James Risen in 2014 serves as a bitter reminder that there is no federal shield law. Risen wrote a book entitled, "State of War," about CIA efforts to damage Iran's nuclear program in the 1990s. Jeffrey Sterling, a former CIA officer, faced criminal charges after the publication of the book; his lawyers subpoenaed Risen, who resisted.

Risen was ordered to testify in federal court. He appealed that order to the 4th U.S. Circuit Court of Appeals, which affirmed the finding. The U.S. Supreme Court declined to take the case, leaving Risen in the unenviable position of testifying or going to jail. Attorney General Eric Holder announced the government's position with a statement that "no reporter is going to jail while I'm attorney general." Ultimately Risen was not called to testify.

But the Risen matter provided some impetus to the effort to pass a federal shield law, a measure called "The Free Flow of Information Act." Since the turn of the century, there have been numerous efforts to pass a federal shield law, and it always has been a bipartisan issue. In 2007, for example, one of the lead sponsors was an Indiana Republican congressman named Mike Pence, later to become vice president.

Proponents of the federal shield law came close in 2014, as the proposed act passed the House and gained approval from the Senate Judiciary Committee. But the bill never made it to the Senate floor. Sen. John Cornyn, R-Texas, had vowed to filibuster the bill, and groups working for passage, including SPJ, could not reach a head count of 60 needed to break the filibuster.

In November 2017, Attorney General Jeff Sessions was asked in a House Judiciary Committee hearing whether he would make a commitment not to prosecute journalists who were doing their jobs. Sessions would not provide those assurances. That night, two Congressmen, Democrat Jamie Raskin of Maryland and Republican Jim Jordan of Ohio, introduced "The Free Flow of Information Act of 2017," the latest incarnation of a federal shield law bill. At the time of this writing, it remained in the House Judiciary Committee.

SOURCE: Paul Fletcher, Forbes.com, https://www.forbes.com/sites/paulfletcher/2017/11/29/sessions-testimony-prompts-new-federal-shield-law-bill-protecting-journalists/#1ed665d04912, Nov. 29, 2017.

An Obligation to Be A Watchdog

Journalists long have been called upon to see that public business is indeed public. But this aspiration was turned into an obligation in the 2014 Code of Ethics. Under "Seek Truth and Report It," there is a revised tenet:

- Journalists should "[r]ecognize a special obligation to serve as watchdogs over public affairs and government. Seek to ensure that the public's business is conducted in the open, and public records are open to all."

The second sentence appeared, with slightly different wording, in the 1996 Code. The first sentence is new.

There is some important wordsmithing at play here. It is an *obligation* to be a watchdog, one that is *special*. This is not a mere duty, or just an aspiration, or a really nice idea. Journalists *must* be watchdogs. With the use of the word "obligation," consider the need to serve as a watchdog a fourth direct imperative, joining "Never plagiarize" and the others mentioned at the outset of the chapter.

Consider also the discussion above, in Chapter 2, about the rights and obligations of journalists. There is a long, proud history of journalists' service as watchdogs. Back in the 1960s, a group of open-government advocates started a push for greater transparency and openness in the federal government.

Among the journalists who pushed, lobbied and cajoled Congress were the leaders of Sigma Delta Chi, as SPJ was then known. These men (yes, women were not admitted as members to SDX, later SPJ, until 1969) sought a federal open-records law as early as 1960. It took several years but ultimately, the bill known as the Freedom of Information Act was passed in 1966.

President Lyndon Johnson, suspicious and private by nature and sinking into the mire of the Vietnam War, hated this act and opposed it year after year. Once it was on his desk, he signed it reluctantly. But he signed it. That led to passage of numerous state FOI laws, many of which were pushed by state SDX leaders. Those statutes remain on the books today.

SOURCE: Bert Bostrom, *Talent, Truth and Energy,* chapter 5.

Some of the early efforts for state-level laws started in Florida, with that state's chapter of the American Society of News Editors pushing the Florida legislature for open-government statutes. Because Florida is nicknamed "The Sunshine State," these laws were called "sunshine" laws, and aptly so, since they allow access to the documents and records from the inner workings of government.

With FOI laws allowing scrutiny of government actions, including contracts with outside parties, expenditures of public money, journalists throughout the country have filed FOIA requests for documents on which to base their stories. This ray of sunshine on government activity is one of the most useful for reporters who heed the ethical call to serve as a government watchdog.

And it's worth noting that journalists aren't mentioned in the FOI laws, and with good reason. These aren't just laws to aid journalists — they are laws for everyone. The request mechanisms in FOI statutes can be used by any citizen.

There are many resources for journalists that are available on the Freedom of Information Act and how to make a request. Almost every state has some open-government group for assistance. Most of them have "[state] Coalition for Open Government" as their name (e.g., Virginia Coalition for Open Government, or VCOG).

These groups maintain websites that provide state-specific advice and help on open records, including lists of what exemptions might have been passed by a state legislature or how the local courts have interpreted the state law. A simple Google search or similar internet query will provide access to this information when needed.

Not Legally Enforceable

And this chapter comes to a close by coming full circle. We considered at the outset the difference between what is legal and what is ethical. Here's a thought on what is ethical and what is legally binding. In 2009, SPJ added a disclaimer section at the end of its Code of Ethics. It currently states:

The SPJ Code of Ethics is a statement of abiding principles supported by additional explanations and position papers that address changing journalistic practices. It is not a set of rules, rather a guide that encourages all who engage in journalism to take responsibility for the information they provide, regardless of medium. The code should be read as a whole; individual principles should not be taken out of context. It is not, nor can it be under the First Amendment, legally enforceable.

Why would SPJ need to include such a disclaimer? Clever lawyers. There were numerous instances in which plaintiffs' lawyers in defamation claims sought to establish that a violation of the ethics code was tantamount to journalistic malpractice. Indeed, some of the debates within SPJ over enforceability of the Code against offending journalists echo those thoughts. But journalists are not regulated or licensed and there is no disciplinary authority watching over them.

Lawyers sought to shoehorn the SPJ Ethics Code into the legal system by making it the "standard of care" for the profession. In a legal or medical malpractice case, the plaintiff's team will seek to set the standard of care for the defendant, then show that the defendant breached that standard, causing injury to the plaintiff, resulting in damage. The standard of care in malpractice cases often is established by expert testimony by someone in the field of the defendant.

Despite the explicit disclaimer at the end, efforts to use the SPJ Code as a weapon in litigation continue. The most recent high-profile case was in 2016, in the $100 million defamation suit filed by pro wrestler Hulk Hogan (real name: Terry Bollea) against the now-defunct website Gawker, which had published an excerpt of a sex tape involving Hogan. Hogan's lawyers put a University of Florida journalism professor, Mike Foley, on the stand. Foley testified that there was "no question" Gawker had violated the SPJ Code of Ethics in publishing the sex tape. Foley acknowledged that the Code wasn't legally binding, but clearly Hogan's lawyers sought to establish that Gawker had done wrong.

Whether publishing a sex tape ever can be ethical (highly unlikely) is a question for another day. But give the last word to SPJ Ethics Committee Chair Andrew Seaman, who was quoted by Peter Sterne in Politico's reporting on the Hogan case:

"What's legal is not always ethical and what's ethical is not always legal," [Seaman] said, adding that the SPJ's ethics code "has no bearing on a legal case deciding what is legal and what is not."

SOURCE: Peter Sterne, Politico, https://www.politico.com/media/story/2016/03/journalism-group-responds-to-invocation-of-its-ethics-code-in-hogan-v-gawker-004421, March 10, 2016.

CHAPTER 5:

To Tell the Truth: Accuracy and Fairness

The principles of accuracy and fairness stand at the very heart of journalism's "prime directive" (to borrow from the philosophy followed by notable "Star Trek" explorer, Capt. James T. Kirk), and that is to tell the truth.

Indeed, accuracy and fairness speak to the obligation of providing meaningful information to citizens who depend on its quality, authenticity and lack of bias to understand issues and to make important decisions.

Accuracy means "getting it right." It is an essential responsibility of individual journalists and news organizations. To provide wrong information is a disservice to the public and a sure way to erode the credibility of journalism.

Audiences deserve, and in most cases still pay for, a reasonably accurate and unbiased picture of the world they live in. Every effort should be made to ensure that statements of fact are correct and that information is presented in context. It is not appropriate to use deadlines, or competition, or personal excuses, or equipment problems, or wardrobe malfunctions, or staffing shortages, or any other reason to justify inaccuracies or bias.

Fairness means pursuing the truth with both vigor and compassion and reporting information without favoritism, self-interest or prejudice.

Accuracy and fairness mean challenging traditional definitions of news, ensuring coverage of society issues and groups of people under-reported in the past.

Accuracy and fairness also mean portraying individuals and issues with a basic sense of open-mindedness, avoiding biased reporting, stereotypical portrayals and unsubstantiated allegations.

To be sure, journalism can never tell the full truth in every story, because facts compete against each other, and additional facts and more information emerge over time. Many stories must be reported piecemeal, as they develop. But the fuller picture will come only from journalists committed to the fundamental principles of accuracy and fairness.

Accuracy Checklist

- ☐ Do you have a high level of confidence about the facts in your story and the sources that are providing them? If not, can you tell your story in a more accurate manner? If you have any doubts about your sources, can you delete them or replace them and achieve a higher likelihood of reliability?
- ☐ Have you attributed or documented all facts?
- ☐ Have you double-checked all facts?
- ☐ Can you provide the properly spelled name and accurate telephone number of every source cited?
- ☐ Are you highly confident that all the factual statements in your story reflect the truth?
- ☐ Are you prepared to defend publicly your fact-checking and whatever other measures were taken to verify your story?
- ☐ Are the quotes in your story presented fairly, and in context?
- ☐ Are you quoting anonymous sources? Why are you using those sources? Are you prepared to defend publicly the use of those sources?
- ☐ Are you using any material, documents or pictures provided by anonymous sources? Why? What is your level of confidence about the validity of this material? Are you prepared to defend publicly the use of that material?
- ☐ Have you described persons, minority groups, races, cultures, nations or segments of society — e.g. businesspeople, combat veterans, cheerleaders — using stereotypical adjectives? Are such descriptions accurate and meaningful in the context presented?
- ☐ Have you used potentially objectionable language or pictures in your story? Is there a compelling reason for using such information? Would the story be less accurate if that language or picture were eliminated?
- ☐ Do your headlines (or broadcast promos or teases) accurately present the facts and context of the story to which they are referring?

Accuracy and social media

The internet offers many challenges and opportunities for journalists. The challenges include that the internet is luring away a chunk of mainstream media's readers and viewers, as well as the risk for reporters of using the web as a resource when much of its content may not be accurate. The opportunities of this electronic environment include almost unlimited research and interviewing possibilities.

Social media have been widely touted as the source of choice for a new generation of news consumers. But a closer examination of the figures suggests the new media aren't fully replacing the old media. The growth in new media doesn't match the loss of viewers and readers of old media. Perhaps some people simply have decided to live news-free lives.

Then there's the problem that much of this new-media content is not reliable information. One recent survey reported that only 25 percent of the people who read them think blogs can be trusted to give accurate information.

On the web, it's all supposed to be hammered into something approaching reality as other individuals weigh in with their own version of the truth. But what if you as an information seeker access the site before the hammering is finished? (And it very rarely is truly finished.)

Still, the internet is an important tool for a journalist. But it's important to think about what you can get from the world wide web with some sense of confidence and what you have to be careful about.

Email interviews are convenient, and email provides an easy tool for fact-checking. Blogs provide a good access to opinion, even if they're a questionable source for facts.

In this world of multiple choices for information — or affirmation — how can the mainstream media compete? By providing consistently trustworthy information, comprehensive and free of bias. By remembering the importance of accuracy, fairness and reliability in reporting.

Accuracy is not the same as truth. Different people have different truths. Evolution. The age of the Earth. Whether a fetus is the same as a baby, or global warming is caused by humans. Your job is to report those beliefs, those sometimes disparate truths, accurately.

Reliability means that people can trust your accuracy consistently. You don't make mistakes — or you make as few as is humanly possible, and what you report is an accurate reflection of what people think.

Fairness means you give everyone with a stake in the story a chance to explain his or her version. It's not often a 50-50 balance. You have to use your judgment. Some points of view don't carry as much weight as others.

Traditional media will survive only if they insist on providing accurate, reliable and fair information.

Let others give readers what they want to see. Your responsibility as an ethical journalist is to give them information that they need to make sound decisions. And a sense of responsibility is what divides an ethical journalist from a careless polemicist.

— *Fred Brown, SPJ Ethics Committee*

Using the Internet for Accuracy and Fairness

The internet is a mixed bag. It can't always be relied upon for accuracy and fairness. For some things, though, it's a great tool for traditional reporters. Such as:

1. Online interviews: A great way to let people think about what they're going to say; a lousy way to get a "gotcha" moment. And you can't be sure, if you're interviewing a famous person, celebrity or politician this way, that it isn't some spokesperson responding — or, worse, an impostor.
2. Fact-checking: When you're uncertain you've got a fact right, you can email your proposed sentence or paragraph or two to the source to see if it's phrased correctly. Make it clear you're not going to change it unless it's inaccurate. But accuracy is more important than independence.
3. Blogs are a great way to gauge sentiment. They can be a sort of informal poll. But remember that they're best as a source for opinion; be skeptical of accepting them as fact.

CASES: Truth and Accuracy

CASE STUDY: Cooperating with Government

WHAT: It was the longest prison standoff in recent U.S. history. On January 18, 2005, two inmates at the Arizona prison complex near Buckeye armed themselves with homemade weapons and took over a prison guard tower. They held two correctional officers hostage, releasing one of them, a male, a week into the standoff and the second, a female, before surrendering two weeks later, on February 1. But the public didn't know about any of this until after it was over.

The governor's office, explaining that it feared for the safety of the two prison guards, telephoned news executives around the state and urged them not to reveal certain basic information. As the standoff continued, authorities said they were worried that publicity would reach the inmates and foil negotiations.

Television viewers, radio listeners and newspaper readers were not told the names of the hostages or the names, criminal histories or disciplinary records of their captors until after the siege ended. State officials refused to confirm their identities or to release most details about how the standoff began or what happened afterward.

But also, Arizona news organizations agreed to wait until the standoff ended before publishing many details or any names they might learn from other sources. They held off on interviewing relatives of the inmates they suspected might be the captors. Media were not allowed within half a mile of the prison; the airspace was closed to helicopters.

The inmates eventually were charged with kidnapping, aggravated assault, escape and sexual assault, which gives you some idea of what went on during the standoff. The names of the guards weren't made known after they were released.

QUESTION: Should your news organization agree to the information blackout?

WHO: Put yourself in the position of a managing editor at a newspaper or a news director of a television station. You're the one who has to decide.

The stakeholders you must consider include, obviously, the hostages, who have more at stake than anyone else, including possibly the prisoners who took them captive, who also are major stakeholders.

WHY: As is so often the case, the major principles involved here are the reporter's duty to tell the truth and the competing principle of minimizing harm. Did the Arizona media do the right thing in this case? What would you have done? Would you have cooperated with the authorities? Would you have put conditions on your cooperation? How much would you worry about what the competition is doing? How long would you have waited to release information? Should the media have worked together to develop a unified position? Would you change your stance if media outlets outside the state began reporting details the Arizona media agreed not to report.

by the SPJ Ethics Committee

Other questions: This is one of several cases throughout this text that can also be analyzed from the perspective of a student majoring in strategic communications. Do you think the governor's press officer did the right thing? If you were advising the governor, what would you have done differently?

CASE STUDY: A Congressman's Past

WHAT: Three weeks before the 2004 election, *The* (Portland) *Oregonian* published a sensational story. David Wu, a Democratic congressman seeking a fourth term, had been accused by an ex-girlfriend of a sexual assault some 28 years previously. But criminal charges never were filed, and neither Wu nor the woman involved wanted to discuss the case so many years later.

The *Oregonian* spent months trying to discover the truth about this persistent rumor. Finally, on Oct. 12, 2004, it published an article more than 3,000 words long explaining what it found out.

On that same day, Congressman Wu held a news conference to say he did something regrettable in his youth, but he didn't think it was relevant now. Other media picked up the story, of course, and his Republican opponent used it in her campaign.

Here's a quick summary:

Wu and his ex-girlfriend were science majors at Stanford University. She broke up with him in the spring of 1976. That summer, Wu was questioned by Stanford campus police after his ex-girlfriend said he tried to force her to have sex with him.

Wu told police it was consensual. He was not arrested. The woman declined criminal prosecution and didn't file a formal disciplinary complaint.

Wu refused to be interviewed or to answer written questions about the incident when *The Oregonian* asked him about it 28 years later. Wu's ex-girlfriend also declined to comment, either in person or through a representative. Stanford officials wouldn't discuss it either, citing university policy and student confidentiality laws.

So how did *The Oregonian* get its story? Here are some quotes from the newspaper's initial article:

"Reporters contacted scores of former Stanford students, current and retired university officials and professors, law associates, and former campaign staffers and friends of Wu to determine what occurred. ...

"The account that follows is based on recollections of the Stanford patrol commander, the woman's counselor, two professors who supervised dormitories at the time and several classmates who were on campus that year."

QUESTION: If you are *The Oregonian*, do you publish this story three weeks before the election? If you're a competing news media outlet, do you follow it?

WHO: Wu, obviously, is the major "Who." Almost as equally affected is the unnamed woman who filed the complaint against him. Wu's opponent most likely would benefit from the story. The public is a stakeholder, in that it will go to the polls in less than a month to make a decision about who should represent the district in Congress. The newspaper itself also is putting its reputation on the line, as is often the case in controversial stories.

WHY: Certainly, there is a truth to be told here, and the truth potentially could change the outcome of the election. But is the congressman's youthful indiscretion all that important more than a quarter-century later? The woman who made the complaint doesn't want to rehash the events of the episode. Readers might think that the news side of *The Oregonian* is only furthering the editorial page's agenda, because it endorsed Wu's opponent.

HOW: Clearly, the newspaper decided to run the story. But it may have had second thoughts (see the sidebar by Michael Arrieta-Walden, *The Oregonian*'s public editor, published October 17, 2004). Wu, by the way, won re-election in a landslide.

THE PUBLIC EDITOR:
STORY ON LONG-AGO INCIDENT WORRIES READERS, EDITORS

More than 350 readers called or wrote last week to criticize *The Oregonian*'s publication of a story about an allegation that David Wu sexually attacked a college girlfriend 28 years ago. The newspaper explained its decision in an editor's note and invited comment from readers. They responded.

Reader after reader raised questions about fairness, relevancy and timing. Many of the questions were ones that editors struggled with for weeks leading up to the publication of the story, issues of journalistic judgment that editors, let alone readers, disagree about. Here are several of the major questions readers raised and an attempt to address them:

Timing of the article: Many readers asked why the newspaper published the story only three weeks before the election, especially given that the allegation was 28 years old and Wu already had served three terms in Congress. They argued the timing was unfair to Wu. "I'm insulted by it," said reader Nathan Whittlesey of Newberg. "I don't think you are honorable."

The timing troubled editors, as well. A reporter had heard a rumor about the allegation in 2000 but hit a dead end. When new information emerged earlier this year, editors devoted three reporters to the story and worked for months to confirm it as soon as possible. Critical information did not emerge until September, and then editors' questions and concerns generated the need for even more reporting and editing. The final drafts were edited over the weekend and prepared for publication on Tuesday. Although the story would be published just days before ballots were mailed, editors believed voters still would have enough time to weigh any response and to consider other information about Wu.

Relevancy of the allegation: Many readers questioned whether a 28-year-old allegation involving behavior as a 21-year-old college student is relevant to an election today. Several readers recalled their sexual and drug activities from college days that would be embarrassing or criticized today.

"We all made mistakes when we were in college," says Steve Dimeo of Hillsboro. "I can't believe that you published the article. It's beneath you."

Editors would agree that most of us have events in our pasts we'd prefer to forget. But Editor Sandy Rowe says that the seriousness of the allegation — an attempted sexual assault — demanded investigation by reporters, and that people who seek public office offer themselves for such scrutiny. She also concluded that an allegation that could have generated a criminal charge — even one as old as this one — is especially relevant in Oregon, where sexual scandals involving public officials have heightened Oregonians' awareness and concern.

Second-hand sources: Readers were troubled that the newspaper would print such a serious allegation based on sources, as the story acknowledged, who themselves could not know the whole story. "This article on David Wu is pure hearsay," said Carolyn Landsverk, in deciding to cancel her subscription to the newspaper after 32 years. "It's so uncharacteristic of the paper."

The lack of eyewitnesses was deeply troubling to editors; no one other than Wu and his former girlfriend can know what went on in that dorm room. That's why editors insisted that reporters talk to as many sources as possible and that only named sources be used. Their confidence in the accuracy of the story was bolstered by the fact that they were able to interview university officials involved at the time, including a campus police officer, counselor and professor. Rowe said editors had to accept that precisely what went on in that room was unknowable. And although Wu admitted after publication to "inexcusable behavior" for which he was disciplined by the university and didn't challenge the accuracy of the story, the details of the incident will likely never be known.

No cooperation from the victim: Readers said that if the victim did not want to revisit the issue because of her privacy, the newspaper should have honored that wish.

That also received strong consideration, but it's not unusual for the newspaper to report on criminal incidents in which the victim would prefer there was no publicity. Those incidents are considered newsworthy, often because of the public service the information provides. In this case, Rowe said the newspaper went to lengths to try to shield her identity, including making even more changes at the 11th hour to obscure her identity after talking again with her representative.

Editorial opinion and story: Many readers suspect that the newspaper published the story because it had recently endorsed Wu's opponent, Goli Ameri.

The appearance of the article four days after the endorsement makes that conclusion understandable. But those who made the decision and wrote the editorial endorsing Ameri had no role in the story about Wu, and the reporters on the Wu story had begun pursuing it even before his opponent emerged from the primary in May. The editorial board did not know the full details of the story when it made its decision, or whether a story would be published.

Goldschmidt influence: Many readers charged that the Wu story was an attempt by the newspaper to repair its reputation, which was damaged by its lack of aggressiveness in the original pursuit of the allegations of sex abuse by former Gov. Neil Goldschmidt.

In *The Oregonian* newsroom, the influence of the Goldschmidt story is undeniable. Rowe says the Goldschmidt case made the reporters more persistent in pursuing the allegation over several months, but that it wasn't what pushed her to publish the story. The Wu story had to stand on its own, although the reader reaction to the stories of Goldschmidt and former Sen. Bob Packwood did make it abundantly clear to her that allegations of serious sexual misconduct matter to readers of the newspaper.

On the Wu story, I admire the reporters and their editors for their persistence, diligence and thoroughness. They were not intimidated by the attempts by Wu's camp to undermine the reporting and to keep the newspaper from pursuing the story. All of that serves readers well.

I also admire how the newspaper's editors struggled and deliberated over the decision to publish. Despite the contrary view of many readers last week, reporters and editors dislike these types of stories and knew they would face significant criticism for publishing the story.

As with any difficult ethical decision in journalism, there is no clear right or wrong answer. It's a judgment call, a subjective choice that no editor relishes. You must weigh your responsibility to the public against potential harm and make the best decision you can. In this case, while I find the stories reflect exhaustive reporting and editing and are ethically justified, many of the concerns voiced by readers resound with me, causing me to disagree with the judgment of those editors.

With only three days left before the mailing of ballots, the bar for publication of any allegation against a candidate should be exceedingly high to reach. Too many hurdles loom for me and many readers: You must accept that the 28-year-old incident is relevant. If you do so, you still must overcome concerns about not knowing with absolute certainty what happened in that room, no public records or criminal charges, no firsthand accounts from the two people most closely involved and no established pattern of behavior.

I understand and respect how the journalistic duty of never wanting to withhold important information from voters — especially about such a serious allegation — trumped those and other concerns, but I'm not comfortable with it.

My discomfort is aggravated by how I think the newspaper has failed to serve those voters in other ways.

In its pursuit of the story, the newspaper essentially has neglected to cover the race for the 1st Congressional District. Until last week, only one local story of any substance has been written about the tight race between Wu and Ameri.

And until a profile on Friday, the newspaper also failed to deliver a fuller portrait of Wu, with the story on the allegation or in coverage in past months. Wu provided no help by refusing to grant the newspaper an interview on any subject, but the newspaper should have shared more with readers about his public service and character.

That neglect allows the story about Wu's college incident to have a potentially disproportionate effect on voters and readers and leaves them understandably questioning its fairness.

Another question: This case can also be analyzed from the perspective of the congressman's office staff. If you were Congressman Wu's public affairs officer, what would you have done?

CASE STUDY: Satire as Journalism

Journalism so far has managed to adapt to the age and to new media, but there's another element in the mix, one that combines journalism and satire. It's a question worth considering by journalists and other professional communicators.

News-based shows like HBO's "Last Week Tonight with John Oliver" have redefined "journalism" and raise an ethical **question**: what is journalism in this day and age, and do these satirical comedians qualify?

The American Press Institute defines journalism this way: "Journalism is the activity of gathering, assessing, creating, and presenting news and information. It is also the product of these activities …"

Some of the identifiable characteristics of journalism are the effort to be neutral in reporting while following a code of professional ethics. One of the primary goals of journalism is to encourage fair reporting, exemplified by neutral language and limited opinion, as well as investigating all sides of a story (which can have its shortcomings, as seen with most climate change discussions).

Satire, on the other hand, is defined by Merriam-Webster as "trenchant wit, irony or sarcasm used to expose and discredit vice or folly." The purpose of satire is to use opinion and exaggeration to add humor to a topic, and is therefore fundamentally separate from journalism's striving for neutrality and fair reporting.

"Last Week Tonight with John Oliver" is a prime example of a satirical investigative news show that many consider to qualify as news — excluding the show's creators and host. Oliver has denied any affiliation with journalism. "I'm doing the job of a comedian," he says. "I make jokes about the news, so I'm pretty clear about the lane that I'm in."

But from net neutrality to the Trump presidency, "Last Week Tonight with John Oliver" takes a single topic and investigates its components in detail. That's what journalists do. The show's team of researchers pores through all aspects of a topic; their thoroughness and consistency won them one of broadcasting's most prestigious awards, the Peabody.

The Peabody's website explained that Oliver's "resolve not simply to explore headline news, but to pull back the proverbial curtain and show us the subtle mechanics at work in our nation's democracy and culture is to be commended. For bringing satire and journalism even closer together, 'Last Week Tonight with John Oliver' receives a Peabody Award."

CNN Senior Media Correspondent Brian Stelter, in an interview with HBO's CEO, Richard Plepler, highlighted Oliver's interview with Edward Snowden, who leaked highly classified U.S. government documents, saying, "I heard from a source close to Snowden who said, 'The reason we chose John Oliver... was because of his journalism.' "

Oliver, though, steadfastly denies any relationship to journalism. In an episode of the show that focused on the field, he said, "... Stupid shows like ours lean heavily on local papers. In fact, whenever this show is mistakenly called journalism, it is a slap in the face to the actual journalists whose work we rely on." (Season 3, Episode 20).

The United Nations Educational, Scientific and Cultural Organization (UNESCO), describes investigative journalism as "the unveiling of matters that are concealed either deliberately by someone in a position of power, or accidentally, behind a chaotic mass of facts and circumstances—and the analysis and exposure of all relevant facts to the public."

By that definition, "Last Week Tonight" *is* an example of investigative journalism, with or without the comedic spin. That contrasts with monologues from shows like "The Late Show with Stephen Colbert," which do not qualify as original journalism because they often rely heavily on stories already reported.

When John Oliver and TV journalist Jorge Ramos discussed the nature of today's journalism, they concluded that the very definition of the field has begun to shift, even to accommodate comedians like Oliver:

Ramos: "Why do you think [Snowden] chose you? And not a, should I say, respected journalist?"

Oliver: "... You're right! I'm not a respected journalist, because I'm not a journalist!"

Ramos: "... But let me just say that, you have more credibility than most journalists here in the United States, and I would say many other countries."

Oliver: "But that is more of an insult to the current state of journalism than it is a compliment to the state of comedy."

A crucial component of journalism is the very reason journalism was created — as a regulating force for government, corporations and society. The goal of journalism is to investigate issues, and by revealing them to the public, help spur movement to a solution. The idea is that journalism can make the American people more aware of how their democracy is serving them, and mold how it could serve them better.

Few comedians can claim to "change the world," but Oliver's show has had a significant impact. In an interview with CBS Morning News, Gayle King highlighted what has been labeled "The John Oliver Effect": "A month after your story on bail, New York City Mayor Bill De Blasio announced he will ease policies for low-level offenders, that's one. After your rant on U.S. territory rights, a judge cited the episode in a court decision on a class action case brought by Guam citizens over a tax refund, and... Your famous net neutrality segment got the public to react so strongly, John, it crashed the FCC [website]."

Ramos summarizes the "John Oliver Effect" best: "That is what Oliver does: spark a national dialogue."

If, based on these standards, Oliver is in fact a journalist, the next important question to ask is by what code of ethics should he operate. The satirical commentary he presents already opposes the concept of neutral journalism, but the impact is the same, and arguably even more effective. "Last Week Tonight" has been accepted as journalism, and Oliver has been (mis?)labeled as a journalist; but this ready acceptance of satire could be a sign that journalism's fundamental values are more pliable than initially thought, and that biased commentary, or at least reporting with a point of view, could become a more ingrained aspect of the field.

"Last Week Tonight" takes relevant or obscure news pieces and investigates them, much like investigative journalism, but presents the information in a satirical package. So Oliver is indeed presenting the news, but without the neutrality typically expected of journalists and reporters.

Is John Oliver a journalist? Despite the objections from Oliver himself, his work at "Last Week Tonight" seems to fulfill the requirements expected of journalists, and with the significant impact it has made on society in inspiring Americans to get involved in their own government, it's possible that satirical news shows may become yet another permanent branch of journalism.

—*Selene McConachy, University of Denver*

References

Bilton, Nick, et al. "The New Establishment 2015." The Hive, Vanity Fair, 9 Sept. 2015, www.vanityfair.com/news/photos/2015/09/new-establishment-list-2015.

CBSThisMorning. "John Oliver: I'm Not a Journalist." YouTube, YouTube, 30 Oct. 2015, www.youtube.com/watch?v=1lFoyDOi-Ww.

CNNMoney. "Why Snowden Chose John Oliver." YouTube, YouTube, 8 Apr. 2015, www.youtube.com/watch?v=zpYW1fpuyNA.

Fusion. "John Oliver to Jorge Ramos: 'I'm Not a Journalist.'" YouTube, YouTube, 12 May 2015, www.youtube.com/watch?v=l17TPkXGVCo&t=192s.

LastWeekTonight. "Journalism: Last Week Tonight with John Oliver (HBO)." YouTube, YouTube, 7 Aug.2016, www.youtube.com/watch?v=bq2_wSsDwkQ.

"Satire." Merriam-Webster, Merriam-Webster, www.merriam-webster.com/dictionary/satire.

"What Is Journalism? Definition and Meaning of the Craft." American Press Institute, American Press Institute, 9 Oct. 2013, www.americanpressinstitute.org/journalism-essentials/what-is-journalism/.

CASE STUDY: The BTK Killer and the Eagle

It started three decades earlier. "It has always been part of the paper's lore," Rick Thames, former editor of *The Wichita Eagle* told *Editor & Publisher*'s Joe Strupp.

Beginning with his first murder in 1974, the "BTK" killer — his own acronym, for "bind, torture, kill" — sent the newspaper four letters and one poem. The *Eagle*'s Web site was subpoenaed last year when investigators thought BTK might be posting items on a discussion board. And in 2004, the killer sent the paper a letter after 16 years of silence, apparently sparked by a story about the 30th anniversary of the first killing.

New elements continued to crop up from time to time, almost up until the arrest of the suspected killer. *Eagle* Reporter Hurst Laviana, who followed the case for more than 20 years, was one of three reporters who were asked to give DNA samples. "It seemed like a logical thing for them to do," Laviana told *E&P*, adding that police told him they'd received five tips from people urging that he be tested. He never heard back from investigators after that June swabbing.

BTK had killed eight people since January 15, 1974, the last 20 years previously, in 1986. The killer's first communication with the newspaper was 10 months after the first killing. A reader found a letter inside a book at a local library and called the newspaper.

The last letter arrived in March 2004 and included photos from the 1986 crime scene, as well as a copy of that victim's driver's license.

The killer also has sent letters and made phone calls to a local television station, but his main media connection has been the Eagle.

The newspaper also has involved itself in the case. In 1974, when it was still the *Eagle-Beacon*, it offered a $5,000 award for information leading to an arrest. And a 1978 poem from BTK was mistakenly included in romantic messages the paper runs on Valentine's Day.

In 2004, the Sedgwick County District Attorney subpoenaed the identities of six people who had posted items to a BTK bulletin board on the Eagle's Web site. The *Eagle* cooperated without a fight but was criticized by the DA for running a story about the subpoenas.

All of this put the newspaper in an awkward position. The killer seemed almost to be using it as an agent of communication. It was both a provider of evidence and chronicler of the news. Some employees worried that BTK might target them as attention increased.

Questions: What do you think? How should the *Eagle* have handled communications from the serial killer? Did it do the right thing? Did it cooperate too closely with law enforcement? With the killer?

(Epilogue: Dennis Rader, who admitted to being the BTK Killer, was arrested February 25, 2005, by Wichita Police. On June 28, 2005, he pleaded guilty to 10 counts of murder.)

CASE STUDY: A Suspect "Confession"

WHAT: John Mark Karr, 41, was arrested in mid-August 2006 in Bangkok, Thailand, at the request of Colorado and U.S. officials. During questioning, he confessed to the murder of JonBenet Ramsey, who had been beaten and strangled to death in the basement of her Boulder, Colorado, home sometime during Christmas night 1996. The murder was a media obsession for much of 1997, and video clips of the young beauty contestant competing in various costumes ran, it seems, every few hours.

Karr was arrested after Michael Tracey, a journalism professor at the University of Colorado, in Boulder, alerted authorities to information he had drawn from e-mails Karr had sent him over the past four years. Karr had initiated the correspondence, apparently intrigued by Tracey's argument, in documentaries and elsewhere, that John and Patsy Ramsey had been unfairly implicated in their daughter's death. Karr was returned to Boulder for DNA testing and ultimately cleared. But he wasn't freed; he also faced misdemeanor child pornography charges in California.

> Do you break a confidence with your source if you think it can solve a murder — or protect children half a world away?

WHO: Put yourself in the shoes of a news director or managing editor. Could you resist this story, especially if you were in Colorado? In the first three weeks after Karr's "confession," the now-defunct *Rocky Mountain News* ran 150 stories about him, including this first-day lead: "The decade-long search for JonBenet Ramsey's killer came to a startling end in Thailand on Wednesday." *The Denver Post* probably ran a similar number, but its web site list cuts off after 10 hits. In JonBenet's home town of Boulder, the *Daily Camera* ran 120 stories during the same period.

Or imagine you're Professor Tracey. Do you break a confidence with your source if you think it can solve a murder — or protect children half a world away?

There are many stakeholders in this case, including the media, Tracey and, of course, Karr himself. Add Boulder law enforcement authorities, who had been criticized for bungling the original case 10 years previously, and now for spending $23,656, including two business-class airfares, to bring a delusional man back to face dubious charges. Ramsey family members are major stakeholders. Even the University of Colorado j-school is among many parties with a peripheral interest.

WHY: The principles involved in deciding what to do include the media's obligations to their readers and viewers to present the news in full while maintaining a sense of responsibility and balance. For Professor Tracey, there's a struggle between confidentiality and collaboration. And should the media be critical of authorities who, after all, pulled Karr away from the temptation of children in Thailand, where he was about to begin a teaching job?

HOW: We've seen how the media reacted to this story — at full throttle. Was it overkill? A bit more skepticism and proportionality would have been more professional. Was Professor Tracey's role appropriate? He considers himself an academic, not a journalist. But even if he were a journalist, wrote *Rocky Mountain News* media columnist David Kopel, he should act like an ethical human being. Kopel's argument is worth repeating:

"Some critics claim that if journalists cooperate with the police, they will lose the trust of their audience. But just imagine how much less most readers would trust the newspapers if readers learned that a reporter refused to reveal non-confidential information which could have led to the capture of a notorious murderer."

ANALYSIS: Some principles (from the SPJ Code of Ethics), and comment
- Journalists should be honest, fair and courageous in gathering, reporting and interpreting information. (Quantity, more than quality, is the question.)
- Test the accuracy of information from all sources and exercise care to avoid inadvertent error. (In a highly competitive rush, it's difficult — but still necessary.)
- Show good taste. Avoid pandering to lurid curiosity. (Lurid curiosity is sometimes unavoidable.)
- Be judicious about naming criminal suspects before the formal filing of charges.
- Be vigilant and courageous about holding those with power accountable.
- Clarify and explain news coverage and invite dialogue with the public over journalistic conduct. (There was plenty of explaining where the information came from, and a flood of letters to the editor.)

— *SPJ Ethics Committee*

CASE STUDY: Pre-publication review

Once upon a time, a reporter would never let a source see what the reporter intended to write. But there has been growing acceptance of the idea that it's more important to be accurate than to be independent.

Actually, both are great ideals, but accuracy takes precedence. That's why attitudes have changed. It's a credibility thing. Some argue that pre-publication review gives a journalist's sources more confidence that the reporter is going to get it right. And, let's face it, there are some very complicated topics where it is probably a good idea to go back to one's source and say something like: "Here's what I understood you to say about cold fusion's potential as a power source. Please tell me if I've got it right."

College texts for reporting students have made note of this change in the acceptance of prepublication review (or PPR for short). Steve Weinberg, former head of Investigative Reporters and Editors, is quoted in one as saying, "I have practiced PPR as a newspaper staff writer, a magazine free-lancer and a book author. Never have I regretted my practice. What I do regret is failing to do it during the first decade of my mindless adherence to tradition."

Weinberg says the offer of review makes sources more willing to talk on the record. And it doesn't compromise the writers' control over their stories. If a source wants to change a story, remind the source that the review is only for accuracy, not for interpretation or tone.

This is not about turning over your story to your source. There are rules, after all. And the No. 1 rule is "no editing." You're not going to let a source edit your copy — or change its tone, context or organization, either. You're just checking the facts.

Make that clear to your source. Accuracy is your motivation; not accommodation.

There are other rules, too:

Don't change direct quotes, especially if you have them on tape. Sometimes a source will say that isn't really what he intended to say and will want to rephrase it. You can either play "gotcha" or negotiate — especially if the rephrasing is more accurate or pertinent. After all, the source did say both the old and the new versions.

The best time to double-check is during the initial interview. "I think I understood what you said about bird flu and down pillows, but let me read it back to you from my notes to be sure I have it right."

You might occasionally want a source to review an entire story, but it's better practice simply to go over specific passages. You can do it by phone or by e-mail — or, better yet, e-mail the snippets to the source and then discuss it over the telephone.

A few journalists routinely ask their sources to review entire stories to see if there are any errors. Jay Mathews, a veteran education reporter for The Washington Post, made a practice of showing entire stories to sources, even though it made his editors uneasy. He wrote about that in The Post's May 31, 2003, edition:

"I have shown every story I have written to all the sources I could find," he said. "… They are welcome to argue about the tone, the analysis or anything else that bothers them, but I change only the things that I am convinced are inaccurate."

Pre-publication review gives sources confidence that the reporter cares about getting it right. Offering to let them check what you've written gets them to open up. It enhances your credibility and reputation.

You won't lose control of your story. You're still the one who has the final say on what goes into your story before it's submitted to an editor — who is, other than you, the only one who can change what you've written.

It's best to have a written newsroom policy on this, something written down that a reporter can refer to when a source asks to check a story before it's published.

And when does fact-checking become excessive? Texas Republicans in 2005 accused an Austin American-Statesman writer of collaborating with a Democratic district attorney to criticize the Republican Party. E-mails showed the political reporter/columnist gave the prosecutor advance versions of an article he was writing. The writer says he was only trying to avoid errors. The Republicans claimed the journalist and DA were in cahoots, trying to make their party look bad.

Journalists have mixed reactions, although most of them feel it's not a good idea to be quite so accommodating. But they do want to get it right.

— *Fred Brown, SPJ Ethics Committee*

One possible policy on PPR:

1. Make it clear that your source is not your editor. He or she can't change what you've written.
2. The review is for accuracy only. Just the facts, not context, tone or organization.
3. Don't change direct quotes. You should have them on tape. But it's OK to negotiate.
4. The best time to double-check is during the interview.
5. It's better to review specific passages with the source than to hand over the entire story for review.
6. Remember: YOU DON'T HAVE TO CHANGE ANYTHING! But if it's incorrect, you certainly should.

CASE STUDY: The Media's Foul Ball

WHAT: The Chicago Cubs in 2003 were five outs from advancing to the World Series for the first time since 1945 when a 26-year-old fan tried to grab a foul ball, preventing outfielder Moises Alou from catching it. The Florida Marlins rallied for an 8-3 victory to tie the National League championship series in game 6, then went on to defeat the Cubs. The man in the left field seats who deflected the ball was escorted by security guards from Wrigley Field after he was threatened and cursed by angry fans and pelted with beer and debris.

The hapless fan's identity was unknown. But he became recognizable through televised replays as the young baby-faced man in glasses, a Cubs baseball cap and earphones who bobbled the ball and was blamed for costing the Cubs a trip to the World Series.

QUESTION: Given the potential danger to the man, should he be identified by the media?

WHO: After working through the night and the next morning, the *Chicago Sun-Times* identified the infamous Cubs fan as Steve Bartman, the Lincolnshire, Ill., consulting firm where he worked and the suburb where he lived. *Sun-Times* reporter Frank Main, who covered the story, explained why the *Sun-Times* editor at the time decided to reveal Bartman's identity. "He was the center of a national news story and there was no legal or moral problem in naming him. We did not think there was a serious possibility of his being assassinated by fans. We decided to go with the story and tell readers what we knew." *Chicago Tribune* editors said they printed Bartman's name after he released a statement saying, "I am truly sorry from the bottom of this Cubs fan's broken heart." James Burke, a member of the Ethics AdviceLine for Journalists team, said identifying Bartman was "an act of irresponsible journalism" and a violation of the SPJ ethics code that urges journalists to minimize harm. Chicago's Mayor Richard Daley chastised the media for identifying Bartman, and was quoted by the *Sun-Times* saying "do you put your CEO's name and address out?... You wouldn't do that. You'd be fired tomorrow... And that is not fair to that young man..."

WHY: One of the highest principles in the SPJ Code of Ethics is to seek truth and report it. But journalists also should balance that principle with others, such as whether revealing Bartman's identity could result in harm. Other than the statement expressing regret for deflecting the ball from Alou's glove, Bartman made no further comment or allowed interviews. For years, he remained a private figure who insisted on his privacy and made every attempt to avoid the publicity he was getting. The *Chicago Tribune* justified identifying Bartman by saying other media were doing it.

HOW: Journalists have an obligation to consider the honorable course of action, such as whether Bartman should have been identified and whether his identity was something the public needed to know. This was, after all, a baseball game in which Bartman was a mere spectator. Bartman did not lose the game; the Chicago Cubs lost the game and the series. Each news organization should consider acting independently.

At least one journalist at the time thought the *Chicago Tribune* might have distinguished itself by continuing to refuse to identify Bartman even though he issued a statement and others were identifying him. The SPJ Code of Ethics urges journalists to show compassion and special sensitivity when dealing with inexperienced sources or subjects. That could have applied to Bartman. Journalists could have asked him if he wanted to be identified before doing so. This was not a case where the public needed to know his identity. And in retrospect, Bartman has never surfaced again from his momentary, unwanted celebrity. It was thrust upon him against his will. He was a victim of fate and happened to be where a foul ball fell from the sky.

In his statement, Bartman said in part: "I had my eyes glued on the approaching ball the entire time and was so caught up in the moment that I did not even see Moises Alou, much less that he may have had a play." The media could have taken pity on the guy.

— *by Casey Bukro, Chicago Headline Club*

CASE STUDY: A Confrontational Confirmation

WHAT: In 2018, President Donald Trump nominated Brett Kavanaugh, a judge on the U.S. Court of Appeals in Washington, D.C., to fill a U.S. Supreme Court vacancy. There was a deep divide nationwide over Kavanaugh's nomination, partly because a Republican-controlled Senate had blocked a Supreme Court nomination by Trump's Democratic predecessor, Barack Obama, from even having a hearing.

But the controversy over Kavanaugh's nomination mushroomed when an allegation that he committed sexual assault in his youth — in the 1980s — became public shortly after his Senate Judiciary Committee confirmation hearing.

In a story published on September 14, 2018, *The New Yorker* reported on allegations Christine Blasey Ford sent confidentially to U.S. Sen. Dianne Feinstein about Kavanaugh. In a letter, Blasey Ford alleged that when she and Kavanaugh were teenagers, he attacked her at a party while a second boy was in the room. She alleged that Kavanaugh pinned her to a bed, tried to remove her clothes and put his hand over her mouth to keep her from screaming.

The New Yorker published its story, without naming Blasey Ford, a week after Kavanaugh finished three days of questions and answers with the Judiciary Committee related to his nomination. On September 16, *The Washington Post* published a story based on an interview with Blasey Ford in which she shared details of her allegation. She agreed to be named.

In both the letter and the interview, Blasey Ford recalled some details, such as where in the house the attack occurred and how it was carried out, but was unsure of others, such as the approximate date.

The accusation shook up the confirmation process and forced a delay on a final Senate vote. The Judiciary Committee invited Blasey Ford to testify. In highly charged proceedings on September 27, Blasey Ford shared with the committee what she remembered about her encounter with Kavanaugh. Separately, Kavanaugh came back before the Judiciary Committee the same day and insisted he was falsely accused and was the target of political opposition.

After *The New Yorker* and *The Washington Post* published stories about Blasey Ford — but before the Judiciary Committee reconvened for further testimony — two more women came forward with other accusations of sexual misconduct by Kavanaugh, also from decades earlier.

One, Deborah Ramirez, alleged that Kavanaugh exposed himself to her, close to her face, while they attended Yale University. She recalled the circumstances of the encounter and others who were in the room.

Another, Julie Swetnick, alleged that Kavanaugh pressed himself and grinded against girls while in high school and attempted to remove their clothes. She also alleged that Kavanaugh, a friend and others caused girls to get inebriated and disoriented before other boys "gang-raped" them. She did not accuse Kavanaugh of committing rape and provided no other specific details about circumstances or witnesses.

The FBI was called on to investigate. But its review was limited in time and scope and didn't include Swetnick's accusation. At the end of its work, the FBI reached no conclusions about the accuracy of Blasey Ford's or Ramirez's allegations.

A week after the Judiciary Committee heard from Blasey Ford and Kavanaugh about the sexual assault allegation, the Senate moved ahead with a procedural vote on Kavanaugh's nomination. The following day, the Senate voted — almost entirely along party lines — to confirm him.

As unusual and chaotic as the confirmation process was, it was affected by journalists' attempts to ferret out the story. Blasey Ford had almost remained silent. It was only in July, when she heard that Kavanaugh was a serious contender for the Supreme Court seat, that she decided she needed to contact Feinstein, a California Democrat on the Judiciary Committee. Blasey Ford also sent a message to *The Washington Post's* tip line at around the same time. Blasey Ford, a California resident and professor at Palo Alto University, got in touch with her congresswoman, Anna G. Eshoo, to help connect her to Feinstein.

On July 30, Blasey Ford sent Feinstein a letter detailing her memories of Kavanaugh sexually and physically assaulting her in the 1980s. She asked Feinstein to keep the letter confidential. Feinstein forwarded the letter to the FBI on September 12, according to a message she later wrote to Sen. Chuck Grassley, the Judiciary Committee chairman.

When asked why she didn't raise Blasey Ford's allegation during Kavanaugh's initial confirmation hearing before the Judiciary Committee, Feinstein said, "She had asked to remain confidential."

Blasey Ford retained a lawyer who advised her to take a polygraph test, which she did in early August. But in late August, Blasey Ford decided not to come forward, reasoning that it would upend her life but probably not affect Kavanaugh's confirmation, the *Post* reported.

However, the existence of the letter to Feinstein leaked. Feinstein publicly acknowledged receiving a message about Kavanaugh, but didn't describe anything in it and said she referred it to the proper authorities.

Additional details filtered out in news reports. Then, reporters figured out Blasey Ford's connection. According to the *Post*, one reporter visited her at home and tried to talk to her as she was leaving a classroom where she teaches; another reporter called her colleagues to ask about her. The new developments caused Blasey Ford to change her mind and speak out publicly.

Questions: Was unmasking the woman behind a confidential message sent to Feinstein (a) fair game or (b) necessary for a full account? Were there other ethical obligations? Were the media correct to air these allegations in the late stages of the confirmation process? Should they have ignored or given lesser coverage to any of the three allegations?

WHO: Journalists helped drive a critical national story by the decisions they made on what to cover and how thoroughly to cover it. Even though Feinstein knew Blasey Ford's allegation, she and the Senate Judiciary Committee did not bring it up during Kavanaugh's confirmation hearing. When word of the allegation leaked and journalists reported on it, the confirmation process took a very different path.

Stakeholders: Blasey Ford might have been resigned to be a silent observer. But journalists tracked her down, making her feel pressure to speak out, overcoming her reservations.

Coming, as it did, in the weeks leading up to a midterm election, the episode affected the public's perception of the political parties involved.

Kavanaugh and Blasey Ford said they and their families were harassed after her allegation emerged. About a week after she testified before the Judiciary Committee, Blasey Ford told supporters raising money for her that her family had to move four times and invest in additional security measures.

WHY: The fact that Blasey Ford's letter and identity were not made public did not stop reporters from investigating. Blasey Ford weighed her choices and tried to keep her identity private while sharing her allegation. But journalists were not obligated to balance concerns in the same way.

The SPJ Code of Ethics urges journalists to "Seek Truth and Report It" and "Minimize Harm."

For Blasey Ford, harm could come from being injected into a charged political debate. That meant public pushback from those who support Kavanaugh's nomination, either for the political ramifications or because of concern about a decades-old allegation being raised at a critical time, or both. Harm, for Kavanaugh, was being accused of criminal acts when he was a teenager, and, despite his denials, possibly losing his chance to serve on the nation's highest court.

But the significance of the allegation pushes the balance toward the pursuit of truth. Many people considered what Kavanaugh was accused of doing, as well as his temperament in responding to the allegation, to be relevant in whether he should sit on the Supreme Court.

Whether to cover every allegation, relying on one person's word and a hazy recollection, is a tougher call. None of the three women had a pristine account of what she remembered, largely because of how many years had passed.

Blasey Ford provided names of people she said were involved or present in the house the day of the attack, but none corroborated her account. Ramirez said she was intoxicated and had gaps in her memory. She named people who she said were in the room, but they and others disputed her story. Swetnick offered no possible corroborating witnesses.

DECISION/DISCUSSION: As media have become more experienced in covering allegations of sexual misconduct, especially outside the criminal justice system, they have become more thorough in seeking verification and corroboration.

Reporters look for people who, if they didn't witness an attack, recall being told about it at the time, especially firsthand from the victim. Records, documents or even journal entries also are used to check if someone shared details of misconduct at the time. Sometimes the choice is tough but necessary, to report on damaging allegations that arise shortly before a deadline and could affect an outcome simply by mentioning them.

A notable example is a report *The Los Angeles Times* published in 2003 about allegations against California gubernatorial candidate Arnold Schwarzenegger. Six women accused Schwarzenegger of touching them in a sexual way without their consent over a period of three decades. Four of the six would not allow their names to be used in the story.

The *Times* published its piece less than a week before the election. But Schwarzenegger still won.

–by Andy Schotz, SPJ Ethics Committee

WHAT THE CODES SAY: Truth and Accuracy

Accuracy always comes first. It's better to be late than wrong. Before pushing the button, think how you would withstand a challenge or a denial.

Reuters Handbook of Journalism

We strive to be fair, accurate, responsible, independent and sensitive to the feelings of our readers. We respect individual rights to privacy. We strive for balance. If we represent a point of view, we want it to be the public interest.

Asbury Park Press, New Jersey

Question continually the premise of the stories and adjust accordingly.

Gannett Newspaper Division

Facts should be presented honestly, fully and fairly. This applies to news stories, columns, editorials, headlines, graphics, illustrations, captions, photographs, layouts and any other editorial component. Writers, editors, photographers and artists should always strive to inform readers accurately and represent situations fairly. We will not knowingly place any person in a false light, such as racial or ethnic stereotyping.

The Arizona Republic, Phoenix

A fair-minded reader of Times news coverage should not be able to discern the private opinions of those who contributed to that coverage, or to infer that the organization is promoting any agenda. A crucial goal of our news and feature reporting — apart from editorials, columns, criticism, blog posts and other content that is expressly opinionated — is to be nonideological. This is a tall order. It requires us to recognize our own biases and stand apart from them, including in social settings and in our own statements made on social media. It also requires us to examine the ideological environment in which we work, given that the biases of our sources, our colleagues and our communities can distort our sense of objectivity.

The Los Angeles Times

Our preference, when time and distance permit, is to do our own reporting and verify another organization's story; in that case, we need not attribute the facts. But even then, as a matter of courtesy and candor, we credit an exclusive to the organization that first broke the news. Attribution to another publication, though, cannot serve as license to print rumors that would not meet the test of The Times's own reporting standards. Rumors must satisfy The Times's standard of newsworthiness, taste and plausibility before publication, even when attributed. And when the need arises to attribute, that is a good cue to consult with the department head about whether publication is warranted at all.

The New York Times

"Fair" means that we present all important views on a subject. This range of views may be encompassed in a single story on a controversial topic, or it may play out over a body of coverage or series of commentaries. But at all times the commitment to presenting all important views must be conscious and affirmative, and it must be timely if it is being accomplished over the course of more than one story. We also assure that every possible effort is made to reach an individual (or a spokesperson for an entity) that is the subject of criticism, unfavorable allegations or other negative assertions in a story in order to allow them to respond to those assertions.

KUOW/Puget Sound Public Radio

Look for good things to write of as well as bad. Life is not a dirge.

The Phoenix Republic

We do not write or edit stories primarily for the purpose of winning awards. We avoid blatantly commercial journalism contests and others that reflect unfavorably on the newspaper or the profession.

We recognize that it is not unusual for corporate officers of a newspaper to be involved in civic activities. However, that involvement should never color the news coverage of those activities, and staff members should be no less vigilant in their coverage.

Asbury Park Press, New Jersey

As we seek out the other voices that will give our coverage balance and fairness, we should also take care that our quest for "the other side" does not create imbalance. Too frequently a marginal dissenter or heckler finds prominent play in a story where the vast majority of the activity was focused elsewhere. The result is neither fair nor accurate. Of course, history has heard many lonely "crackpots" who turned out to be right, but we have an obligation to ask for some demonstration of factual basis or expertise before we necessarily buy their arguments or even given them the weight that appearance in print can impart.

Daily Press, Newport News, Virginia

[W]e always strive to identify all the sources of our information, shielding them with anonymity only when they insist upon it and when they provide vital information — not opinion or speculation; when there is no other way to obtain that information; and when we know the source is knowledgeable and reliable....

We must explain in the story why the source requested anonymity. And, when it's relevant, we must describe the source's motive for disclosing the information....

These are the AP's definitions:

On the record. The information can be used with no caveats, quoting the source by name.

Off the record. The information cannot be used for publication.

Background. The information can be published but only under conditions negotiated with the source. Generally, the sources do not want their names published but will agree to a description of their position. AP reporters should object vigorously when a source wants to brief a group of reporters on background and try to persuade the source to put the briefing on the record. These background briefings have become routine in many venues, especially with government officials.

Deep background. The information can be used but without retribution. The source does not want to be identified in any way, even on condition of anonymity.

In general, information obtained under any of these circumstances can be pursued with other sources to be placed on the record.

The Associated Press

We strive to identify all the sources of our information, shielding them with anonymity only when they insist upon it and when they provide vital information — not opinion or speculation; when there is no other way to obtain that information; and when we know the source is knowledgeable and reliable. To the extent that we can, we identify in our stories any important bias such a source may have. If the story hinges on documents, as opposed to interviews, we describe how the documents were obtained, or at least to the extent possible. We do not say that a person declined comment when he or she is already quoted anonymously.

ProPublica

The Washington Post is pledged to disclose the source of all information when at all possible. When we agree to protect a source's identity, that identity will not be made known to anyone outside The Post.

Before any information is accepted without full attribution, reporters must make every reasonable effort to get it on the record. If that in turn is not possible, reporters should request an on-the-record reason for concealing the source's identity and should include the reason in the story.

In any case, some kind of identification is almost always possible — by department or by position, for example — and should be reported.

No pseudonyms are to be used.

However, The Washington Post will not knowingly disclose the identities of U.S. intelligence agents, except under highly unusual standards which must be weighed by the senior editors.

The Washington Post

Be wary of going "off the record." News makers who go "off the record" can maneuver you into the position of not being able to report or pursue what they have told you. What good is information if we cannot publish it? In the vast majority of cases, a hard-nosed attitude against going off the record prods the news maker to go ahead and say what he wanted to say anyway, or it at least leaves you free to seek the information without restriction elsewhere.

The Journal News, White Plains, New York

"He said" means the journalist got the quote from the source — in person, at a press conference, or on the phone. "He said in a statement" or "in a report" means the quote came from a written statement or press release, or from a document such as an analyst's report. "He said in an e-mail interview" means exactly that. If the quote comes from another news outlet, the journalist must credit it: "President Smith told the Associated Press."

BusinessWeek

Reporters and editors should discuss general conditions under which promises of confidentiality can be made. Reporters should not make a pledge or promise of confidentiality they are not empowered to honor and enforce, and editors should honor promises properly made by reporters. Reporters and editors should respect the confidentiality of our newsgathering and internal editing processes in conversations with sources and readers.

Sources are not paid for news, either in cash for tips or interviews, or in promises of future coverage or other favors.

The Arizona Republic, Phoenix

Candidates/Elections — Do NOT run stories in which candidates say they are going to file a complaint or charges. Wait until the complaint or charge is actually filed. Do not print charges against a candidate in stories that appear in the Sunday or Monday papers before the Tuesday Election. No political stories are carried in an Election Day paper.

St. Paul Pioneer Press and Dispatch, Minnesota

- Describe an unnamed source's identity as fully as possible (without revealing that identity) to help readers evaluate the credibility of what the source has said or provided.
- Do not make promises you do not intend to fulfill or may not be able to fulfill.
- Do not threaten sources.

. . . All sources should be informed that the newspaper will not honor confidentiality if the sources have lied or misled the newspaper.

Gannett Newspaper Division

On some stories, editors might ask reporters to discuss with confidential sources what the source's reaction would be if a court orders the newspaper and/or the reporter to divulge its source of information. The source's willingness to be publicly identified and attest to the information he or she provided might determine whether certain sensitive information is published.

An agreement to protect a source's identity creates an agreement with both the reporter and The Post. The agreement should be based on the understanding that the source is honest. We should tell the source that if he/she is dishonest with us, the promise of identity protection will be negated. In other words, "The Post will protect you. But if you lie to me, that promise of confidentiality is void."

The Denver Post

Since the U.S. Supreme Court has ruled that the First Amendment does not extend to journalists the absolute right to protect the confidentiality of news sources, reporters on their own cannot guarantee sources confidentiality in a published story. If a demand is made after publication for the source's identification, a court may compel us to reveal the source. In circumstances where the demand for absolute confidentiality is made a condition for obtaining the story, that situation needs to be discussed with a supervising editor before a commitment is made. Trust works both ways — the editor must be able to trust the reporter fully, and vice versa.

Detroit Free Press

The grant of anonymity should be a last resort.

KUOW/Puget Sound Public Radio

We report in environments — Hollywood and Washington, to name two — where anonymity is routinely sought and casually granted. We stand against that practice and seek to minimize it. We are committed to informing readers as completely as possible; the use of anonymous sources compromises this important value.

These standards are not intended to discourage reporters from cultivating sources who are wary of publicity. Such informants can be invaluable. But the information they provide can often be verified with sources willing to be named, from documents or both. We should make every effort to obtain such verification. Relying on unnamed sources should be a last resort....

The Los Angeles Times

The news organization should guard against inaccuracies, carelessness, bias or distortion through emphasis, omission or technological manipulation.

It should acknowledge substantive errors and correct them promptly and prominently.

Associated Press Media Editors

Much of popular journalism today comes with a political or ideological slant: it aims to win people to a point of view, not necessarily to an understanding of the facts. CNN does not try to appeal to a specific point of view or political constituency. To the contrary, the reporters, producers, editors and writers at CNN aim for comprehensive journalism. In their news coverage, they strive to present the whole story, fairly and completely, so that readers and viewers may come to their own conclusions. And in their presentation of opinion and analysis, they strive to represent a range of viewpoints.

Time Warner Inc. (CNN)

On this newspaper, the separation of news columns from the editorial and opposite-editorial pages is solemn and complete. This separation is intended to serve the reader, who is entitled to the facts in the news columns and to opinions on the editorial and "op-ed" pages. But nothing in this separation of functions is intended to eliminate from the news columns honest in-depth reporting, or analysis or commentary when plainly labeled.

The Washington Post

Plagiarism is one of journalism's unforgivable sins — and, at this newspaper, a dismissible offense. Material taken from other newspapers and other media must be attributed.

Grand Forks Herald, North Dakota

It is unacceptable to hedge an unverified or unverifiable assertion with words such as "arguably" or "perhaps." Our job is to report what is true, not what might be.

The Los Angeles Times

- Preserve the integrity of the process of communication.
- Be honest and accurate in all communications.
- Act promptly to correct erroneous communications for which the practitioner is responsible.
- Preserve the free flow of unprejudiced information when giving or receiving gifts by ensuring that gifts are nominal, legal, and infrequent.

PRSA Code of Ethics

Advertising, public relations, marketing communications, news, and editorial all share a common objective of truth and high ethical standards in serving the public.

American Advertising Federation

CHAPTER 6:

Deception

The issue of deception is a significant ethical matter; it deals with truth, and seeking truth is what journalism is all about. Only recently has the debate over deception reached the stage where media organizations have begun to address the issue head-on in their codes of ethics. The discussion has intensified of late because of the conversion to digital photography and the ease with which reality can be manipulated, along with the disturbing tendency of so many news operations to turn to surreptitious reporting and hidden cameras as a first rather than a last resort when conducting investigations.

Deception in journalism can take many forms, from outright lying, to misleading, or misrepresenting or merely being less than forthright. All of these actions are intended to cause someone to believe what is not true.

Our society depends on a level of trust, a belief that people will exchange and share information that is true. Without such trust, interaction among people will be stifled, and the functioning of society will be thwarted.

Given the premium value on truth, when, if ever, is it appropriate for a journalist to deceive someone in gathering information or reporting a story?

Journalists disagree. Some subscribe to a rigid rule, saying that any form of deception to obtain information is unacceptable in a profession whose mission is truth-telling. Others would argue that while deception is to be avoided, it may be acceptable in those rare instances in which the value of the information sought is of overwhelming importance, and the information can be obtained in no other way. Others would suggest there is a distinction among forms of deception, between outright lying and merely not revealing everything, between using hidden cameras in a public place and hiding cameras on the person who is at the same time pretending to be someone else.

The issue of deception places a premium on the ability of individual journalists and news organizations to do solid, ethical decision-making. In some cases, deception might allow journalists to come closer to exploring the truth, but those who deceive can cause great harm to the credibility of journalism and may harm individuals who are deceived.

Deception: Checklist

What does it mean to lie? Ethicist Sissela Bok wrote an outstanding book on this subject, called *Lying: Moral Choice in Public and Private Life*. In that book, she says lying is one form of deception. "I shall define as a lie any intentionally deceptive message which is stated." The act of deception, Bok says, can be much broader. "When we undertake to deceive others intentionally, we communicate messages meant to mislead them, meant to make them believe what we ourselves do not believe. We can do so through gesture, through disguise, by means of action or inaction, even through silence."

In an effort to determine when the use of deception at whatever level might be justified by journalists, the participants in an ethical decision-making seminar at The Poynter Institute for Media Studies created the following criteria:

- ☐ When is deception by a journalist justified? What are the criteria for a "Just Lie"? To justify a lie or deception one must fulfill all of the criteria.
- ☐ When the information sought is of profound importance. It must be of vital public interest, such as revealing great "system failure" at the top levels, or it must prevent profound harm to individuals.
- ☐ When all other alternatives to obtaining the same information have been exhausted.
- ☐ When the journalists involved are willing to fully and openly disclose the nature of the deception and the reason for it to those involved and to the public.
- ☐ When the individuals involved and their news organization apply excellence, through outstanding craftsmanship as well as the commitment of time and funding needed to fully pursue the story.
- ☐ When the harm prevented by the information revealed through deception outweighs any harm caused by the act of deception.
- ☐ When the journalists involved have conducted a meaningful, collaborative and deliberative decision-making process in which they weigh
    - the consequences (short- and long-term) of the deception on those being deceived
    - the impact on journalist credibility
    - the motivations for their actions
    - the deceptive act in relation to their editorial mission
    - the legal implications of the action
    - the consistency of their reasoning and their action

CASES: Deception

CASE STUDY: Who's the "Predator"?

SITUATION: "To Catch a Predator," a ratings-grabbing series on NBC's *Dateline*, appeared to catch on with the public. But it also raised serious ethical questions for journalists.

The television newsmagazine, working "as a wall" with law enforcement, trolled for men to engage in sexually charged on-line chats with minors, then invited them to a face-to-face meeting, supposedly at the child's home. Armed with liquor, condoms and little common sense, the men arrived at the front door. The kids weren't home, but the suspects don't know that when they walked into a kitchen and came face to face with reporter Chris Hansen.

The conversations were recorded by a bevy of hidden cameras, and the men were met by law enforcement officers once they left the house. The "suspects" were portrayed as sexual predators without any apparent constitutional protections.

Critics questioned this blending of reporters, "watchdog" groups and police, arguing that the men caught in the sting were entrapped at worst and faced public ridicule and humiliation at best. One target of the sting, a Texas district attorney who made contact on-line, but never ventured out for a personal meeting, committed suicide before facing the cameras. When police, armed with a search warrant — and a *Dateline* camera crew — showed up at prosecutor Louis Conradt Jr.'s home in Terrell, Texas, no one answered the door, according to the police who took part in the attempted arrest. After forcing their way into his home, police found the 56-year-old prosecutor in a hallway holding a semiautomatic handgun. "I'm not going to hurt anybody," he told police before firing a bullet into his own head.

Dateline isn't the only media organization that has been involved in these stings. They date back to at least 2003, and what they have in common is a website called Perverted-Justice.com. It's a highly motivated advocacy group, committed to finding perverts and removing them from circulation.

Perverted-Justice.com scanned chat rooms looking for men who could be lured into sexually explicit conversations with correspondents pretending to be underage boys and girls. It worked with police and news media to entice the unsuspecting marks to set-up trysting places where the cops — and the cameras — were waiting.

Judging from the ratings, the public loved this. Perverts who would harm children are exposed and made to account for their perversion.

But the media should be more questioning. Is it ethically defensible to take part in the deceit that is a sting? Should a journalist buy into the agenda of an advocacy group, even if it's a worthy agenda? Is it ethical to work with law enforcement authorities in this manner?

QUESTION: If your newspaper or television station were approached by Perverted Justice to participate in a "sting" designed to identify real and potential perverts, should you go along, or say, "No thanks"? Was NBC reporting the news or creating it?

ANALYSIS: Once Perverted-Justice.com had an alliance with a national network, the smaller local stations that first cooperated with the group probably no longer faced the decision of whether to join forces in similar "stings." NBC aired the last new episode of "To Catch a Predator" in December 2007, but episodes are still available on MSNBC.com.

The biggest stakeholders in this ethical decision clearly were the men lured before the cameras. Their wives and families also faced major consequences from what NBC did. Law enforcement officers provided plenty of "perp walks," arrests and bookings in clear view of cameras for additional video footage of the suspects, in return for coverage of their cleaning up the community of predators. Perverted Justice got airtime for its cause and financial reward for its efforts. NBC had a primetime audience of more than 8 million viewers.

The public had a stake, too. There is no question that law-abiding citizens want to bring sexual predators to justice. Even one communication ethics student, a young mother, said she could find no reasonable arguments against using a sting to trap potential perverts.

"I do not see in any way that a news station would be looked down upon for giving society what I would consider this service," she wrote. "… If one child can be saved from this horrific event, then by all means do it. I think if you were to take a poll the majority of society would agree."

That's most likely true. But responsible media shouldn't base their ethical standards on what's popular.

Enticing (the term Hansen preferred to use, as posted on his blog) or entrapping subjects holds many legal and ethical issues. Should reporters seek out criminals? Is this indeed a public service as NBC contends? There is also an evidentiary problem when law enforcement and media join forces to prosecute criminals. Are outtakes, notes and other reporting tools now part of a criminal investigation?

In one case a district attorney's office announced it would not prosecute cases during one of NBC's stings, citing a lack of evidence. The office claimed Perverted Justice members refused to testify and turn over records (they deny these accusations) and NBC needed to provide additional footage to help build a case. Running the on-line trolling and sting house in two different counties caused a jurisdictional dispute, creating another legal issue.

Media critics and ethicists question the reporting methods and standards of running this type of "undercover" operation. Al Tompkins of the Poynter Institute said, "The project, from the very beginning, had lawsuit written all over it," a competing network reported.

Critics cite the Society of Professional Journalists Code of Ethics as a guideline for fair and accurate reporting, including:
- Avoid undercover or other surreptitious methods of gathering information unless traditional open methods will not yield information vital to the public.
- Avoid …activities that may compromise integrity or damage credibility.

- Be wary of sources offering information for favors or money, do not pay for access to news.
- Avoid misleading re-enactments or staged news events. If re-enactment is necessary to tell a story, label it.
- Diligently seek subjects of news stories to allow them to respond to criticism or allegations of wrongdoing.
- Avoid conflicts of interest, real or perceived.
- Avoid pandering to lurid curiosity, even if others do.
- Balance a suspect's right to a fair trial with the public's right to know. Consider the implications of identifying criminal suspects before they face legal charges.
- NBC engaged the services of Perverted Justice, inviting scrutiny of creating a news story. By paying actors to pose as minors and engage in sexual chat, did the newsmagazine become the story? NBC surrounded the criminals with law enforcement waiting patiently outside to record the outcome. This was the reverse of most crime scenes. Justice and the media were both perverted throughout this predatory process.
- The important thing is to have a discussion, and to ask the right questions. Among them: Is this a justifiable, ethically defensible use of deception? Should you buy into the agenda of an advocacy group? How ethical is the group itself? Do you compromise your "watchdog" role by cooperating with law enforcement authorities?

DECISION: Let law enforcement conduct sting operations and the media report on the arrests.

— *By Robbie Rogers and Sara Stone, Baylor University*

CASE STUDY: The Masquerading Mortician

SUMMARY

Free-lance reporter Jonathan Franklin posed as a mortician and entered the mortuary at Dover Air Force Base, the sole Desert Storm casualty processing center, during the Persian Gulf War. He wanted to find out if the military had been underestimating the number of casualties. He found that it had.

On the basis of previous reporting he had done on the war dead after the invasion of Panama, Franklin was convinced the Pentagon was "screwing with the numbers." The Pentagon had forbidden journalists to photograph or witness the unloading of the dead at Dover Air Force Base, and Franklin was stymied in all his above-board efforts to penetrate the cloak of security around the returning dead.

He tried contacting the undertaker who won the government contract to prepare the bodies returning from the Gulf for burial, attempted to get the number of dead from airlines shipping the bodies home, and sought unsuccessfully to locate the officers who were informing the families of the dead. After exhausting those avenues of inquiry, Franklin decided to go undercover.

Craig McLaughlin, then managing editor of the *Bay Guardian*, a weekly newspaper in San Francisco, said he chose to run Franklin's freelanced piece, although he usually turns down story ideas involving undercover work. He said he felt it was his responsibility as an editor to show the public what the war really resulted in: not just flashy graphics on the television, but mangled American sons and daughters.

McLaughlin said the deception perpetuated on the military's mortuary "was not a lie directed at an individual. It wasn't an invasion of privacy. It was directed at a government body failing to uphold the Constitution."

McLaughlin gave Franklin's story the green light because it passed his two requirements for undercover work:

There are no other means by which the story can be reported.

The information in the story is politically vital to the readers, with important public policy ramifications.

Inside the morgue, Franklin apparently was the only journalist to actually see the Gulf casualties. He found that many of the combat deaths due to friendly fire were being reported inside the morgue as "training accidents," a practice that also occurred after the Panamanian invasion. And Franklin discovered a source who estimated there were "about 200" combat deaths, compared to the official Pentagon figure at the time: 55.

Franklin's one-page story in the Bay Guardian prompted at least one letter to the editor, in which the writer complained only about the gruesome descriptions of the bodies Franklin had seen inside the morgue. The story also won second place in the annual Project Censored awards for the most important stories bypassed by the mass media each year.

ANALYSIS

The use of deception to gain access to information is always an ethical concern. The primary principle of journalism, truth-telling, requires reporters **to be honest themselves in their gathering, reporting and interpreting of information.**

At the same time, there can be rare cases in which the only way to inform the public fully about significant events necessitates misrepresentation or deception. Craig McLaughlin's two criteria outlined in the case above provide the base of a meaningful process for determining when it might be appropriate to be deceptive. There is another important criterion to add: If a journalist uses deception in the news-gathering process, that deception must be disclosed to the public when the story is published. McLaughlin said the *Bay Guardian* demanded that Franklin include that full disclosure in his article. That level of accountability forces journalists to be judicious in their choice of exceptions to the truth-telling principle and requires them to be ultimately accountable to the public.

Journalists must accept that when they are less than honest about who they are in gathering information, whether it be through actively misrepresenting their identity, using hidden cameras or microphones, or passively deceiving someone, they are lying, pure and simple.

In the case of Jonathan Franklin's decision to pose as a mortician at the Dover Air Force Base, that lie must be balanced against the significant public policy interests inherent in this case and the responsibility of the media to hold the government accountable. Furthermore, Franklin's decision to misrepresent himself must truly be the last and only alternative available in gathering and reporting that information.

News organizations and individual reporters who consider using deception should also weigh both the short-term and the long-term consequences of their actions. It is possible that lying may provide access to significant information for a particular story; it also could keep government agencies honest. It is also possible that lying may erode the credibility of journalism and undermine its overall and long-term ability to function effectively as the primary information-provider in society.

— *from the Third and Fourth Editions of "Doing Ethics,"*
Black, Steele and Barney

CASE STUDY: ABC and Food Lion

WHAT: This case has been a classic study in the use of deception since the report first aired in the early 1990s. It's been discussed hundreds of times in media law and media ethics classes, and it continues to be a hot topic.

ABC News journalists have used hidden cameras on a number of occasions over the years, the reports often airing on the network's *PrimeTime Live* program. Stories revealed dangerous or illegal situations in board and care homes, child care facilities and veterans' hospitals. In other cases journalists used hidden cameras to help expose insurance scams and racial discrimination by landlords and real estate agents.

Yet, no *PrimeTime Live* story up to that time generated as much public attention and journalistic soul-searching as the reporting on the Food Lion supermarket chain. To investigate allegations of unsanitary food-handling practices at Food Lion, two ABC producers worked briefly in the spring of 1992 at several of the company's supermarkets in the Carolinas. The producers misrepresented themselves on their job applications, and once employed they concealed cameras in wigs and clothing to tape video and sound for their report.

The *PrimeTime Live* exposé aired in November 1992. The hidden camera video revealed rat-gnawed cheese, and spoiled meat and chicken being washed with bleach, repackaged and given a new sell-by date. In interviews, Food Lion employees and former employees attested to being told to take part in such practices, and many former store workers signed affidavits swearing to the same effect.

Food Lion claimed its reputation was severely damaged by the revelations and that it lost $1.7 billion to $2.5 billion in sales and stock value.

Still, Food Lion did not sue for libel, where the truth of the report would be the standard. Instead, Food Lion sued on grounds of fraud and trespass, seeking to show that the ABC employees spent their time on the job at the stores performing their journalistic role instead of performing the work they were hired to do. Food Lion lawyers also said the journalists had made some mistakes in reporting, even helping to create some of the bad conditions they exposed. The plaintiff's lawyers also sought to discredit statements by some people it characterized as union supporters dissatisfied with management at the non-union chain.

So when the case of *Food Lion vs. Capital Cities/ABC* went to trial in December 1996, the judge did not allow jurors to view the news report but rather directed them to assume that the facts of the report were true.

The network did not deny that it had used deceptive news-gathering methods, but it did deny committing fraud and trespass. Fraud requires intent to injure, and by performing their supermarket jobs well, the undercover journalists could do no harm as food workers.

The jury found in favor of Food Lion. Although the grocery chain sought as much as $1.9 billion from ABC, the jury awarded it $5.5 million. In August 1997, an appellate judge reduced the award to $315,000. In 1999, a federal appeals court overturned the jury verdict, ruling that ABC News did not commit fraud. The court did find the two producers liable for submitting fake employment applications and trespassing in Food Lion stores and ordered each to pay $1 to Food Lion.

There is a pivotal question. Is it ever appropriate for journalists to lie to get to the truth? Put another way, is it ever justifiable for a journalist to violate the principle of honesty in order to honor the principle upon which journalism is founded, a duty to provide the public with meaningful, accurate and comprehensive information about significant issues?

WHO: *PrimeTime Live* must make a convincing argument that the use of deception to get journalists inside Food Lion supermarkets was justifiable. ABC had considerable anecdotal evidence, including dozens of interviews with current and former Food Lion employees, that Food Lion supermarkets were selling tainted meat and fish products and violating other health, safety and employment standards. But ABC News needed firsthand evidence to be sure of the accuracy of those allegations and to document the extent of wrongdoing. While undercover reporting is clearly intrusive and invasive, the journalist's direct observation can heighten fairness to the accused by minimizing reliance on other sources who might have tainted motives.

ABC must also make a convincing argument that in this case no other reporting methods would provide the same level of verification as undercover reporting. Granted, ABC could have purchased meat and fish products at the counter and tested them, but that approach is not foolproof, nor could it have revealed the behind-the-meat-counter story that would indicate the extent of wrongdoing and the reasons for it.

In a forum on ethics, ABC News must justify the level of expertise it brought to this story. Did the quality of reporting measure up to the highest standards required for a case where it lied to get to the truth? Were the journalists comprehensive and exhaustive in their investigation? Did they offer a contextual as well as factually accurate picture of what was happening at Food Lion? Finally, there is this critical question: If ABC News used the threat to public health as a reason for the extensive undercover investigation and the use of deception, why did it take so long to ring the warning bell? Why did the network wait six months after going undercover before *PrimeTime Live* aired the report?

WHY: Absolutists will argue that a journalist should never lie, no matter what is at stake. That position avoids the essence of ethical decision-making and ignores the unique and essential role journalists play in a democratic society. Ethics involves making difficult choices when faced with competing values, conflicting principles and multiple stakeholders. Ethical decision-making often involves choosing a course of action among several options, each of which carries negative consequences.

Journalists can and do face these agonizing dilemmas when reporting on issues of national security, government corruption or public safety. The consequences can be profound, sometimes involving risk to human life, the ruin of a person's reputation or the downfall of an institution or business enterprise. Even on routine stories about health care, crime, education and government, journalists face hard choices about what to report and what to hold back, about when and how to approach vulnerable people and when to step back.

ABC News encountered such ethical dilemmas in the past in deciding to use deception and hidden cameras to get to the truth. *PrimeTime Live* journalists went undercover to produce reports on abhorrent treatment of patients in VA hospitals and in board and care homes, spotlighting government regulatory failures that jeopardized the welfare of patients. *PrimeTime Live* used deception and hidden cameras to document the insidious racial discrimination that threatens the fabric of our society.

To be sure, hidden cameras are overused and misused by both network and local television, and journalists too often use forms of deception and misrepresentation as a shortcut in their reporting. These tools have extremely sharp edges, and when improperly used, they harm innocent people and erode journalistic integrity. When the tools are overused, they become dull, losing their impact.

Hidden cameras and any form of deception should be used judiciously and rarely. They should be reserved for those exceptional stories of great public interest involving significant harm to individuals or system failure at the highest levels. Furthermore, deception and hidden cameras should be used only as a reporting tool of last resort, after all other approaches to obtaining the same vital information have been exhausted or appropriately ruled out. And news organizations that choose to use deception and hidden cameras have an obligation to assure their work meets the highest professional standards.

There is no judge or jury to offer a verdict on whether ABC measured up to such high ethical standards in the Food Lion case. The public and other professionals render that verdict. Perhaps more importantly, ABC must scrutinize its own journalism to see if it met the highest standards.

HOW: This case clearly demonstrates how courtroom verdicts are cast in the extremes of black and white while ethical decisions most often emerge from situations painted in multiple shades of gray.

With the law, juries vote on right or wrong after listening to polarizing arguments from two sides of a case. With ethics, there is no defined forum with a witness stand and jury box, and there is no volume of case law. It is the public, and to some degree professional colleagues, who will judge the moral positions of both this major network news organization and this huge supermarket corporation.

In the court of law, a federal jury said ABC News and *PrimeTime Live* journalists trespassed and committed fraud when researching accusations that Food Lion supermarkets sold spoiled meat.

The debate over ethics in this case continues in the court of public opinion, focusing on issues of honesty, accuracy and fairness.

ABC had good reasons to appeal the legal ruling in the Food Lion case. It is equally important that ABC hold its own news reporting to the highest standards journalists need considerable freedom to do their work on behalf of the public. They have a responsibility to honor that freedom by being ethical and excellent at what they do.

— *from the Third and Fourth Editions of "Doing Ethics," Black, Steele and Barney*

Another question: Did the grocery chain do the right things for damage control before it went to court? If you were advising Food Lion as a strategic communicator, what would you have suggested?

What the Codes Say: Using Deception

[W]e don't misidentify or misrepresent ourselves to get a story. When we seek an interview, we identify ourselves as AP journalists.

The Associated Press

No staffer will represent himself or herself as anything other than a Dallas Morning News reporter, editor, photographer, artist, columnist or other occupation. If for security or other reasons you must avoid identification, you must inform your editor as soon as possible. The managing editor and editor must also be informed.

The Dallas Morning News

Fictional Devices. No reader should find cause to suspect that the paper would knowingly alter facts. For that reason, The Times refrains outright from assigned fictional names, ages, places or dates, and it strictly limits the use of other concealment devices.

Masquerading. Times reporters do not actively misrepresent their identity to get a story. We may sometimes remain silent on our identity and allow assumptions to be made — to observe an institution's dealings with the public, for example, or the behavior of people at a rally or police officers in a bar near the station house. But a sustained, systematic deception, even a passive one — taking a job, for example, to observe a business from the inside — may be employed only after consultation between a department head and masthead editors. (Obviously, specific exceptions exist for restaurant reviewing and similar assignments.)

The New York Times

KUOW journalists do not record phone calls without permission. KUOW journalists do not use hidden microphones, recorders or cameras.

KUOW/Puget Sound Public Radio

Except in rare and justifiable instances, we do not tape anyone without that person's knowledge. To do otherwise violates a general policy of treating people as we would want to be treated. An exception may be made only if we are convinced the recording is necessary to protect us in a legal action or for some other compelling reason, and if other approaches won't work. Such circumstances require a managing editor's approval in advance.

Detroit Free Press

In an era when the press' role in society is under intense public scrutiny, it is essential that each staffer goes the extra step to assure that his or her identity, affiliation and purpose are explained to those from whom information is sought. This is especially true in dealing with members of the public who might not have had prior exposure to the news-gathering process.

This goes beyond the ethical question of whether reporters ought to pose as something else. That should not be an ethical question: in fact, we should be honest in describing our role at all times.

This has to do with stressing what to us is basic: identifying ourselves as reporters and naming the newspapers we work for.

We want to avoid the allegation that we somehow cloak the fact we seek information which we intend to provide for public consumption.

Spokane Spokesman-Review and Chronicle, Washington

Nothing in our news report — words, photos, graphics, sound or video — may be fabricated. We don't use pseudonyms, composite characters or fictional names, ages, places or dates. We don't stage or re-enact events for the camera or microphone, and we don't use sound effects or substitute video or audio from one event to another. We do not "cheat" sound by adding audio to embellish or fabricate an event. A senior editor must be consulted prior to the introduction of any neutral sound (ambient sound that does not affect the editorial meaning but corrects a technical fault).

The Associated Press

CHAPTER 7:

Minimize Harm

Minimize Harm. It's one of the four major sections of the SPJ Code of Ethics. It's also a major factor in moral reasoning and ethical decision-making.

Many ethical decisions, in journalism and elsewhere, are a struggle between doing one's duty and being responsible about the consequences of that action.

The important thing is to have that debate — either with yourself or preferably with colleagues — and to ask the right questions. A key pair of those questions is this: Who gets hurt if we tell this story? And does the benefit to the public of knowing that truth outweigh that harm?

The heavyweight in this balancing act is the truth. Telling the truth is a journalist's overriding duty. Considering the consequences is a tempering element — a smaller element, but nonetheless an important one.

In the simplest terms, minimizing harm requires being sensitive to the consequences of what you do as a journalist. "Balance the public's need for information against potential harm or discomfort," the code of ethics says, and remember that "[p]ursuit of the news is not a license for arrogance or undue intrusiveness."

Before the code of ethics was revised extensively in 1996, it didn't say much about minimizing harm. Years ago, we journalists were more confident in our righteousness. But while the older SPJ codes of ethics don't actually use the words "minimize harm," they did include some evidence of sensitivity.

> Considering the consequences is a tempering element.

The 1984 version is an interesting document. This code of ethics has one section, out of six, labeled "ethics." It's all about conflicts of interest — the principles that are now part of the code's "Act Independently" section, in both the 1996 and 2014 revisions. Of course, there's much, much more to ethics than merely avoiding conflicts of interest.

There's another section in that 1984 code called "fair play." Parts of it correspond to the "Minimize Harm" and "Be Accountable" sections of today's code. It says, "Journalists at all times will show respect for the dignity, privacy, rights and well-being of people encountered in the course of gathering and presenting the news." Journalists shouldn't "pander to morbid curiosity," it says, and should "make prompt and complete correction of their errors."

The "Fair Play" section represents about one-sixth of that 1984 code. By contrast, "Minimize Harm" is nearly a quarter of the 2014 code. Add the "Be Accountable and Transparent" provisions and you've got close to a third of the whole thing.

There is some sentiment in the profession that journalists shouldn't fret about consequences. It makes them timid. Throw it all out there and let come what may. Tell the story and run.

That attitude gives ammunition to journalism's critics, and it helps to explain dwindling trust. Civic journalism's response was to try to show the public that journalists do care, and to pay more attention to readers' and viewers' wants. The recent code revisions, beginning in 1996 with the inclusion of "Minimize Harm," and "Be Accountable," were in part an effort to recognize that new sensitivity.

"Minimizing harm" means letting your humanity show through. Show a little compassion for the people who are affected by what you write. Remember that, for many people, being part of a story is a rare, even once-in-a-lifetime experience. They live with the consequences of what you've written long after you've moved on to other stories.

Minimize Harm (from the SPJ code of ethics, 2014 version)

Ethical journalists treat sources, subjects, colleagues and members of the public as human beings deserving of respect.

Journalists should:
- Balance the public's need for information against potential harm or discomfort. Pursuit of the news is not a license for arrogance or undue intrusiveness.
- Show compassion for those who may be affected by news coverage. Use heightened sensitivity when dealing with juveniles, victims of sex crimes, and sources or subjects who are inexperienced or unable to give consent. Consider cultural differences in approach and treatment.
- Recognize that legal access to information differs from an ethical justification to publish or broadcast.
- Recognize that private people have a greater right to control information about themselves than public figures and others who seek power, influence or attention. Weigh the consequences of publishing or broadcasting private information.
- Avoid pandering to lurid curiosity, even if others do.
- Balance a suspect's right to a fair trial with the public's right to know. Consider the implications of identifying criminal suspects before they face legal charges.
- Consider the long-term implications of the extended reach and permanence of publication. Provide updated and more complete information as appropriate.

Fairness Checklist

- [ ] Is the meaning distorted by over- or under-emphasis?
- [ ] Are facts and quotations in proper context?
- [ ] Have you given this story the length and display appropriate to its importance, and have you presented it with dignity and professionalism?
- [ ] Are the headlines and teases warranted by the text of the stories?
- [ ] Have you done your best to report all sides of the story, not just one side — or, just as problematic, two artificially polarized points of view?
- [ ] Have you been compassionate in your reporting?
- [ ] Have all relevant people, particularly those who may be affected or harmed by the story, been given an opportunity to reply? If they have not been reached or have no comment, have you explained why in the story?
- [ ] If sources are not fully identified, is there a justifiable reason?
- [ ] When substantive errors or distortions appear in your paper or on the air, do you admit and correct them voluntarily, promptly and with a prominence comparable to that given the inaccurate statement or statements?
- [ ] Are you fostering an open dialogue with your readers, viewers and listeners? Do others, both in the newsroom and outside it, feel the story is fair to those involved?

CASES: Minimize Harm

CASE STUDY: Moral Decisions in a Massacre

SITUATION: In October 2017, a lone gunman opened fire on a music-loving crowd gathered in Las Vegas for the Route 91 Harvest Festival in what has since been labeled the "deadliest mass shooting in modern U.S. history." More than 500 people were injured and 59 were killed; Justifiably, the massacre remained the dominant news story at nearly every news outlet for weeks. Perhaps less justifiable, however, was the consistency with which these news outlets—both large and small—included the many very graphic and upsetting pictures and videos of the tragedy.

Time magazine, for example, published an online article entitled "Las Vegas Was the Deadliest Shooting in Modern U.S. History" that was accompanied with a deeply upsetting video taken by festival-goers during the shooting. The video was placed above the text of the article, and it begins playing as soon as the viewer enters the webpage. In it, gunshots can be clearly heard and distressed festival attendees are seen fleeing, screaming and attempting to shield themselves from the raining bullets. It's particularly disturbing to watch the video knowing the gravity of the situation and the immense loss of lives.

Perhaps *Time's* only saving grace is a five-second trigger warning displayed before the violence begins: "Warning: Graphic Content...Viewers may find the following footage disturbing." However, since the video is on auto-play, readers who focused on something else—such as the written article itself—might not pay attention to this warning and be exposed nonetheless. This example is just one of a seemingly endless number of news outlets that themselves posted or broadcast images and/or videos from the Las Vegas massacre.

Questions: Does a high degree of public interest in a matter justify journalists in funneling offensive, disturbing or violent images directly to viewers—especially when they could access it elsewhere? And furthermore, do such images serve a legitimate news use, or do journalists propagate them simply because of fear that they would be the only ones who wouldn't?

ANALYSIS: The moral agents in this scenario are journalists, who have a myriad of ethical considerations to weigh when reporting stories about violent or disturbing events. But there are a number of constraints posed by the industry that make this difficult. The Society of Professional Journalists Code of Ethics does not expressly address the issue of graphic images, but in its "minimize harm" section, it asserts that journalists should "show compassion for those who may be affected by news coverage." The language, intentionally non-specific, allows journalists to decide for themselves what is and isn't acceptable. And in the struggling and highly competitive industry of modern media, this vagueness can mean that ethics not expressly prioritized can be lost in the shuffle. In other words, when a breaking story—such as the Las Vegas massacre—rocks a newsroom, then reporters, editors, etc. might get more caught up in all the potential views an image might garner, rather than all the potential harm it might cause. Ultimately, the rapid pace of news today almost necessitates that journalists, already hampered by dwindling resources and increasingly meager salaries, throw out ethical concerns.

Many individual media employers, however, have instituted more specific policies that more directly address photojournalism ethics. Journalists still need to take the time to properly judge the harshness of an image precisely because of the powerful reach of news stories.

The stakeholders for this ethical dilemma (and really any dilemma faced by journalists) are vast and diverse: viewers and readers of the story/video, concert-goers and the families of concert-goers. The extent to which each of these stakeholders was or could be affected in viewing or hearing this video also differs greatly. Viewers without any personal connection to the Vegas massacre might be impacted in smaller ways for a shorter length of time—e.g., having trouble sleeping that night. Whereas someone with a personal connection could be impacted much more seriously, such as suffering from PTSD.

DECISION: With stakes this high, in cases of tragic digital news stories with this much gravity, *at most*, journalists may decide to post hyperlinks to the graphic image(s)/videos. This permits readers more agency and control in their exposure to the story, rather than having it virtually shoved down their throats. But there may be one exception to this rule: if the images have strong potential to incite real societal, political or legal change. For example, the viral 2015 photo of a drowned Syrian toddler on a Mediterranean beach played a significant role in awakening the world to the Syrian refugee crisis. Even in the case of this exception, journalists still need to weigh the potential benefits against the potential harm.

> The grisly footage had the potential to perhaps effect gun reform.

One could argue that the Vegas massacre falls into this category, that the grisly footage had the potential to, perhaps, effect gun reform. But if the mass murder was really going to do that, it would be the 59 lives lost that would be the deciding factor, not *Time's* decision to post a video. If *Time* had given more consideration to ethics, and less to attracting attention, its editors might have come to another conclusion.

— *Chloe Barrett, University of Denver*

References

Waxman, Olivia B. "Las Vegas Was the Deadliest Shooting in Modern U.S. History. Here's Why 'Modern' Is So Important." *Time Magazine*, 4 Oct. 2017. http://time.com/4968108/las-vegas-deadliest-shooting-modern-us-history/ Accessed 19 Jan. 2018.

Another question: This case also can be analyzed as a daunting public-relations challenge — to both the organizers of the music festival and the management of the hotel where the shooter had set up his sniper's nest. Pick one, or both, and say what you might have done as a strategic communications adviser.

CASE STUDY: TV Doctors in Haiti

WHAT: It didn't take long after the Haiti earthquake in January 2010 before news organizations, especially television, started sending in their medical experts. In almost every case these experts are in fact accredited medical doctors — fully capable of tending professionally to the injured and the sick. And not just capable of ministering to the needs of the victims, but professionally and ethically obligated to do it, as well.

But these M.D.s are also journalists. And journalists have an obligation to a certain degree of detachment. They're expected to be impartial observers, not to be involved in the stories they cover.

Dr. Sanjay Gupta, CNN's medical expert, was the first to arrive, a couple of days after the January 12 disaster. He was soon followed by Dr. Richard Besser of ABC News, Dr. Nancy Snyderman of NBC News and Dr. Jennifer Ashton of CBS News. All four answered the basic ethical conflict by dividing their time between caring for patients and reporting on what they observed.

Dr. Snyderman said this in an e-mail to *Fortune* editor-at-large Patricia Sellers on January 19: "I have worked whenever possible triaging patients and sewing patients up, operating to clean dirty wounds. But there aren't enough hands on the ground. The bodies keep coming — in wheelbarrows, on mattresses and on shoulders."

Dr. Besser helped a pregnant woman in labor; Dr. Gupta performed surgery on a girl with a suspected skull fracture. Dr. Ashton helped surgeons operate on a girl in shock from a botched amputation. "When I see a situation where there's something I could do to help somebody, I'm going to do that," Dr. Besser told the *Los Angeles Times*. "It would be cruel and heartless to do anything but."

All of the physician-journalists soon faced criticism, though, that in reporting on their own efforts to fulfill their medical responsibilities, they were exploiting their good deeds and thus tainting their journalistic responsibilities. Journalism ethicist Bob Steele told the L.A. *Times*, "I think it's very hard for an individual who is professionally and emotionally engaged in saving lives to be able to simultaneously step back from the medical work and practice independent journalistic truth-telling." News organizations that focus on work being done by their own staff "at some point appear to be capitalizing for promotional reasons on the intervention by journalists," Steele added.

QUESTION: What are the professional obligations of a medical doctor who is also a journalist? Which obligation takes top priority, telling the story or tending to the victims?

WHO: The doctor-journalists themselves are the moral agents in these circumstances, the ones who have to decide which approach to take. Their employers also must decide what demands to put on them, including what stories to assign, what video to use and how much time to allow them to attend to ministering to victims of the quake. Those two — the doctors and their media employers — also are the key stakeholders in whatever decisions are made. Their professional reputations are under scrutiny. The people of Haiti, especially the quake victims, also have a major stake in the outcome of the decision; they can use help from even just a few extra skilled physicians, and the images that the media carry worldwide will increase awareness of their plight.

WHY: This is a clear example of the often-encountered dilemma between impartial truth-telling and minimizing harm. Both the SPJ Code of Ethics and the Statement of Principles of the Association of Health Care Journalists have similar language. The AHCJ principles recognize "that gathering and reporting information may cause harm or discomfort" and urges "special sensitivity … when dealing with children, mentally handicapped people, and inexperienced sources or subjects." Neither deals specifically with the choice faced by doctor-reporters, but both are similar in intent to the Hippocratic Oath: "Whatever I see or hear in the lives of my patients . . . I will keep secret, as considering all such things to be private."

Journalists are taught not to make themselves part of the story. And yet they often do. Travel writers, food critics and theater reviewers have been known to write in the first person. Columnists do it from time to time. And then there are those pieces where reporters tell what it's like to live on the street as a homeless person, or to try to get by on food stamps for a month. Reporters are human beings, too. Is it realistic to expect them not to act when they might save a life — or in this case, many, many lives?

> Journalists are taught not to make themselves part of the story. And yet they often do.

There's another question here: Is it really helpful to inundate a disaster scene with journalists? Every news outlet, it seems, wants its own take on what happened, and how recovery efforts are going. But that coverage can get to be redundant, and reporters run the risk of getting in the way of people whose sole function is to try to provide assistance.

In an article published in *Electronic News*, Dr. Tom Linden, an M.D. and journalism professor at the University of North Carolina, Chapel Hill, proposed three rules for physician-journalists covering disasters:

"(1) When physician journalists face medical emergencies, their duty to treat might take precedence over their responsibility to report. When that's the case, the medical professional should perform health care duties as he or she sees fit. However, it's usually inappropriate for medical professionals to report about their own health care efforts. In most cases, this type of first-person journalism is self-centered and simply bad journalism. When physician journalists become the story, medical reporting loses its way.

"(2) Standard practice for reporters in the United States is to seek a parent's or guardian's approval before interviewing and featuring a child in a radio or television news report. Those same standards should apply when physician reporters travel to trauma zones, whether they're in the United States or abroad.

"(3) A physician reporter who treats a patient shouldn't feature that patient (or ask that patient for permission to be featured) on a radio or television report. Such a request puts the patient in an unacceptable bind. If the patient refuses consent, then the patient might fear that the physician will withdraw treatment. This fear might be especially acute in a disaster zone or in impoverished areas where limited or no other medical help is available. Moreover, physician journalists should bear in mind the Hippocratic Oath's admonition about keeping private what they 'see or hear in the lives' of their patients.

"News executives might well chafe at these restrictions, but physician journalists should stand their ground and not allow themselves or their patients to be used to boost ratings for commercial gain. The public has a right to know, but physician reporters have a duty to protect their patients from exploitation and to keep the boundaries between their dual professions intact."

HOW: The doctors covering this story decided they could be both physicians and journalists, although it wasn't an easy choice, and they continued to have their doubts. "I don't think our intention is ever to make the story about myself," Dr. Gupta told the L.A. Times. "I think people innately understand that there is a tremendous medical need down here, and if you can help, you should help." "Morally," Dr. Snyderman said, "I have a responsibility to help people. From a journalistic standpoint, I have a responsibility to tell stories. And in between is a very delicate balance that I wrestle with."

CASE STUDY: Admiral Boorda Suicide

SUMMARY

This is a case that is both a journalistic and a public relations challenge. When he committed suicide May 16, 1996, Admiral Jeremy Boorda was the Navy's top officer, a highly decorated veteran of the Vietnam era who had risen from the enlisted ranks to command NATO as it engaged in its first offensive action.

Boorda killed himself roughly an hour before he was to be interviewed by *Newsweek* correspondents about whether he had worn a medal for valor that he hadn't earned. In the aftermath of the tragedy, *Newsweek* and other news organizations were accused of hounding Boorda to his death, which provoked the magazine and other media members to do a little soul-searching over the question: Is any story worth a life?

Although the Pentagon did not blame *Newsweek,* it was clear that Boorda changed his lunch plans and went home to kill himself upon learning that reporters were on their way to ask him unsettling questions. Boorda's suicide note, the *Washington Post* reported, "indicated he was not taking his life in the belief he had been caught in a lie, but out of fears that the media would accuse him of one and blow it out of proportion." Navy spokesman Admiral Kendall Pease said, however, "*Newsweek* did nothing wrong."

Some media critics, however, did blame *Newsweek* and other news organizations that had begun to investigate Boorda for what syndicated columnist Nat Hentoff called a story that "had no legs." *Newsweek* acknowledged that letter writers complained vociferously about the magazine's role, and some canceled subscriptions.

In a "full accounting" by its media critic, Jonathan Alter, the magazine looked inward to examine whether it had violated some unwritten but understood ethical tenet. Alter chronicled how the story idea had been generated: a Washington-based outfit called National Security News Service provided documents and photos showing Boorda began wearing the valor pin in the 1980s, then stopped. He described the reporting: part-time contributing editor David Hackworth had been working on the story with Washington bureau chief Evan Thomas and national security correspondent John Barry. His conclusion was that *Newsweek's* position was "defensible."

Acknowledging the sometimes grave consequences that journalism can produce, Alter also raised the issue of "whether the story was worthy or not. Was it too trivial to pursue?" Although Hentoff and others believed so, some current and former military officers disagreed. Among them was Hackworth, a retired Army colonel often referred to as the nation's most highly decorated officer. Accompanying Alter's article was an essay by Hackworth titled "Why Medals Matter." Referring to an officer's wearing of decorations he is not entitled to, Hackworth wrote: "There is no greater disgrace."

Hackworth's involvement in the story included this ironic footnote: Almost a year to the date after Boorda's suicide, CNN and CBS reported that Hackworth also had military decorations he hadn't earned. Hackworth told CNN he had learned he was not entitled to a Ranger tag and a second Distinguished Flying Cross. Hackworth said he had listed the medals on the résumé posted on his personal page on the Internet but removed them. CNN reported that Hackworth might have made an honest mistake — just as Boorda claimed he had.

> Was it too trivial to pursue?

ANALYSIS

This is a troubling case study about journalistic fairness. Whenever the public jumps to the conclusion that the media have caused egregious harm, it is time to take stock — regardless of the merits of the public's opinion.

It may have been a mark of lingering Vietnam-born media paranoia among the military over what most civilians would consider a trivial story: A man at the top of the military ladder takes his own life rather than face a reporter's questions.

Reporters often must weigh the effect of reporting a story when determining whether audiences need any particular information. Each time a reporter inquires into an individual's personal behavior there is risk that the source will react in an extreme way. However, it's unlikely *Newsweek* reporters could have anticipated Admiral Boorda's suicide.

Still, reporters must have been aware that their story would be more than an embarrassment to Boorda. It was bound to damage an otherwise honorable officer's professional reputation.

A former officer, who himself was later found to have worn undeserved medals, took a strict stance in calling such behavior "no greater disgrace" — a difficult statement for most civilians to comprehend.

Truth is important, and comprehensive media reports relating to public figures are doubly important.

But the suicide aside, harm to Boorda's reputation may have been difficult to justify when considering the usefulness of the information to *Newsweek* readers. On the other hand, scrutiny of public figures and such mundane behavior as wearing unearned medals is critically important if citizens are to make informed judgments about their leaders.

If Boorda had told the reporter he would commit suicide if the story ran, would the reporter have been justified in killing the story? Such threats do occur. In this case, the *Newsweek* reporters would probably have been puzzled at the extremity of the response. Their puzzlement, however, might have led to more thorough understanding of and better reporting on the military, a complex institution whose value system is not well understood by all journalists.

In the aftermath of Boorda's suicide, public discussion of the matter was effective in holding *Newsweek* accountable, whatever the magazine's justification. The soul-searching conducted by *Newsweek's* Alter was commendable — not just as a PR effort on behalf of the magazine but as an ethical post mortem. It's likely reporters familiar with the Boorda case will make greater efforts to determine the impact of their stories on their sources as they decide whether the story is worth the potential harm.

— *From earlier editions, Black, Steele and Barney*

CASE STUDY: Publishing Drunk Drivers' Photos

WHAT: As the publisher/editor of a 5,700-circulation, chain-owned weekly newspaper in Anderson County, Kentucky, Don White often received phone calls from local residents begging him to keep their names off the court records page of the paper. After learning from an anti-drunken driving coalition that the battle against drunk driving had "hit a brick wall," White decided to heed the group's call for more innovative sanctions against drunk drivers.

When readers of *The Anderson News* picked up the December 31, 1997, issue of the newspaper, stripped across the top of the front page was a New Year's greeting and a warning. "HAVE A HAPPY NEW YEAR," the banner read. "But please don't drink and drive and risk having your picture published." Readers were referred to the editorial page where White explained that starting in January 1998 the newspaper would publish photographs of all persons convicted of drunken driving in Anderson County.

"Most violators of the law dislike having their name in the local paper. We hope the certainty that their picture will also be published will keep more drunks off our highways," White wrote. He also published state and national drunk driving statistics and stories about seven people killed by drunk drivers.

In February 1998, White published 1-column by 3-inch-deep photos of two persons convicted of DUI during January. Both had been arrested before White announced his policy. In March, 12 mug shots appeared, followed by 20 in April and 11 in May. In May, White also revised his policy. Instead of publishing all DUI (driving under the influence) convictions in the county, he limited the photos to residents of Anderson County or surrounding counties where the *News* circulates. He also began publishing the photos weekly rather than monthly.

After a person charged with DUI was convicted or pleaded guilty, the county jailer (who is elected in Kentucky) supplied the information and the photo taken at the time of the arrest to the newspaper. Under each photo the newspaper printed the person's name, age, place of residence, date and time arrested, charge, blood alcohol level and date convicted. The paper published the photos regardless of the age of the offender and made no distinction between first offenders and those who had been arrested before for DUI. The only cases in which photos were not published were those where the DUI suspect was injured, taken to the hospital for treatment and, although charged, never processed at the jail and never photographed. Only once did White give any person special treatment. When the chairman of the county Democratic Party was convicted of drunk driving for the second time in five years, White published his mug shot and a story on Page 1 rather than on the district court page where the photos usually ran. Before someone's photo was published, the person's name usually had already appeared in the paper twice—after the arrest and after the arraignment.

> "I really don't think that the role of a community newspaper is to punish or embarrass anybody."

QUESTION: Is this an appropriate policy for a newspaper?

WHO: Circulation of *The Anderson News* apparently was unaffected by the policy. It's unclear whether publishing the photos directly affected DUI arrests or accident rates in the county. In 2003, Anderson was the only one of Kentucky's 120 counties to record no traffic deaths. However, for the years 1999 through 2003 the percentage of collisions involving alcohol is Anderson County was 4.7 percent, slightly higher than the state average of 4.4 percent for that time period. No one knows how many prominent local citizens did not drink and drive because of the policy. Some evidence is anecdotal. White knew of one group of teens who chose not to drive after drinking for fear their pictures would be in the paper.

Police told White one teenager tried to commit suicide after his DUI arrest because he feared his picture would be published. Some whose pictures appeared said the publication hurt their families, particularly their children. The management of the chain that owns *The Anderson News* did not interfere in White's decision to publish the photos.

The policy applied only to drunken driving convictions and not to any other misdemeanor or felony offenses. Apparently, no other newspaper followed White's lead and adopted a similar policy.

WHY: Newspapers have an obligation to seek the truth and report it. But in what form should that truth be reported? Is a listing of DUI arrests and convictions sufficient to inform the community or does publishing photographs of those who are convicted or plead guilty further the goal of truth-telling?

This case raises important questions about fairness and the role of a newspaper in a small community. Does fairness mean treating every individual convicted of drunken driving the same regardless of whether the person is an adult or a juvenile, or whether the person is a first or repeat offender? Is it fair to single out only those convicted of drunk driving while not routinely publishing photos of persons convicted of felony offenses such as rape or robbery? Is the newspaper imposing an additional punishment on drunk drivers that other convicted criminals in the community do not face? Is it the newspaper's job to determine the community will benefit more from publication of the photo of someone arrested for a misdemeanor DUI offense than the photo of a convicted child abuser or sex offender?

Undoubtedly, reducing drunken driving is a noble goal for the newspaper, but should the newspaper purposely embarrass individuals in an attempt to achieve that goal? No one disagrees with the need to keep drunk drivers off the road. The disagreement is over whether publishing the photos will, in fact, achieve the newspaper's goal. Will the policy keep alcoholics off of the road? Will prominent people who would lose face in their community if their photos were published be more likely to refrain from drinking and driving? What about the impact on the families of those whose pictures appear in the paper?

HOW: One can argue that *The Anderson News*' DUI photo policy was designed to minimize harm to the community by reducing the number of drunk drivers on the county's highways. On the other hand, the policy did not minimize harm to those convicted. Particularly harmed by the policy were the families of those arrested and convicted of DUI who usually had nothing to do with the offense but were embarrassed and humiliated by their family member's public exposure. One father, who managed a local restaurant frequented by teens, said his children's friends didn't say anything after his name appeared in the paper reporting his arrest on a DUI charge. However, after he pleaded guilty and his picture was published, his teenaged sons "got rode over pretty hard" by their friends who recognized their father's picture. The man, who had a blood alcohol reading of .16 (twice the legal limit in Kentucky) when he was arrested, said, "I deserved everything I got (from the legal system). Thank goodness no one got hurt." But he didn't think the photos were fair or reduced the number of drunk drivers on county roads.

This case also raised questions about the relationship between a newspaper and public officials. Without the cooperation of an elected county jailer, *The Anderson News* would not have been able to publish the photos. The SPJ Code of Ethics admonishes journalists to act independently, but the policy and practice of *The Anderson News* would have been impossible without the cooperation of an elected official. The *News* was also dependent on the jailer for the accuracy of the photo identifications.

Author's note: In May 2006, White retired as publisher and editor of *The Anderson News*. His replacement was General Manager Ben Carlson. In a column in August 2006, Carlson announced he would no longer publish the photos. He wrote that publishing mug shots of those convicted "adds a level of punishment, or at least embarrassment, beyond what is imposed by a judge." In an interview, Carlson told the *Lexington Herald-Leader*, "I really don't think that the role of a community newspaper is to punish or embarrass anybody. It's to report the news and provide information." Carlson told the *Herald-Leader* he had no negative response from county residents when he announced the change. The state director for Mothers Against Drunk Driving said she was disappointed by the decision to change the policy. In 2008, only 15 alcohol-related accidents — none of them resulting in fatalities — occurred in Anderson County. That was the lowest number in the 11 years since White first published the photos, but it came two years after the policy was dropped. In eight of the 11 years, Anderson County had no fatal accidents involving alcohol and only three alcohol-related highway deaths occurred during that time. In 2007, as in 2003 and 2001, no one died on the county's highways.

— *by Elizabeth K. Hansen, Eastern Kentucky University*

CASE STUDY: Naming Victims of Sex Crimes

WHAT: On June 5, 2002, 14-year-old Elizabeth Smart was abducted from her bedroom in Salt Lake City, Utah. Elizabeth's parents worked with local and national media to increase visibility of the case; public interest in the kidnapping of the attractive, accomplished blonde teenager was immense. Nine months after the abduction, Elizabeth's younger sister, who had witnessed the kidnapping, remembered that the abductor's voice sounded like that of a vagrant who had done some work for the family some months before the kidnapping. That detail ultimately led to Elizabeth's rescue, which was a major media story nationwide.

Elizabeth's suspected kidnappers, a man and a woman, were charged with several crimes, including sexual assault. Their trial was indefinitely postponed, as both suspects have been deemed mentally unfit to stand trial. Then in November 2009, the woman pleaded guilty, apologized to Elizabeth, agreed to testify against the man and was sentenced to 15 years in prison. A new competency hearing for the man was held in late 2009.

> Which is more important, the obligation of the journalist to tell the story well, or the obligation of the journalist to minimize harm to the abused child?

After Elizabeth was returned to them, her parents, Ed and Lois Smart, wrote a book about their family's ordeal. They and Elizabeth gave a number of interviews. Some reporters were sensitive in questioning Elizabeth about painful subjects. Others grilled her about the details of the time she spent with her captors, leaving her visibly upset. The Smarts authorized a made-for-television movie about Elizabeth's kidnapping and eventual rescue.

* * *

On May 16, 2005, a man, a woman and a teenage boy were found brutally murdered inside their rural Idaho home. Two children, eight-year-old Shasta Groene and her nine-year-old brother Dylan, were missing. For six weeks, police and volunteers searched for the children; their names and descriptions were widely distributed in hopes someone would recognize them and alert authorities. Eventually, that is just what happened. A waitress in a Coeur d'Alene, Idaho, Denny's restaurant recognized Shasta with a man who would later be identified as Joseph Duncan, a 42-year-old registered sex offender. Dylan's body was eventually found in a Montana campsite.

As the story unfolded, it became evident that the brother and sister had been sexually abused by their kidnapper. Although the identities of sexual abuse victims are usually shielded in the media, many media outlets continued to identify Shasta Groene in this case, since the children's identities had been widely circulated while the search efforts were ongoing.

* * *

On January 8, 2007, 13-year-old Ben Ownby disappeared while walking home from school in Beaufort, Missouri. A tip from a school friend led police on a frantic four-day search that ended unusually happily: the police discovered not only Ben, but another boy as well—15-year-old Shawn Hornbeck, who, four years earlier, had disappeared while riding his bike at the age of 11.

After the boys' discovery, the families of both victims held press conferences at which the young victims were present and answered a few questions. Shawn and his parents appeared on *The Oprah Winfrey Show*, as did Ben's parents. Shawn's parents spoke to Winfrey about the mental changes their son had undergone and speculated that he had been sexually abused.

Media scrutiny on Shawn's years of captivity became intense. Shawn had apparently had a certain amount of "freedom" while he was being held. (He played games and spent time with friends.) So why, analysts asked, didn't he try to escape? Psychologists pondered the matter on air; one pundit even posited that Shawn preferred life with his kidnapper and had chosen to remain with him. Others cited the Stockholm syndrome in defending the young man for not attempting to escape years earlier.

Questions: Should children who are thought to be the victims of sexual abuse ever be named in the media? What should be done about the continued use of names of kidnap victims who are later found to be sexual assault victims? Should use of their names be discontinued at that point?

WHO: Decision-makers in this case are reporters, editors/producers and management who have to weigh the potential to cause further harm to already-victimized minors against the desire to tell the whole story, pressure to improve ratings/circulation and pressure to beat other news organizations to the story. They are also under pressure from the public, which, accustomed to 24-hour, speed-of-light news availability, has come to expect immediate, detailed coverage of the big stories.

The stakeholders are obviously the children in question. These children have already been through more than most of us can even imagine. Is it a healing experience for them to share their stories with the world? Or will the scrutiny add further turmoil to their already-fractured lives, perhaps causing irreparable damage?

Other stakeholders include the children's families, who have been through the wrenching ordeal of losing a child and are sometimes eager to share their joy at being reunited with their children and to thank those officials and volunteers who helped bring their children home. In the Smart and Hornbeck cases, the parents gave their consent for their minor children to be interviewed and were present during the interviews.

WHY: Does the charge to "seek the truth and report it" in the face of enormous public interest outweigh the potential for causing further harm to children who have already been victimized? It is a journalist's job—and obligation—to tell compelling stories in detail. But is there ever a point when it is better for a journalist to step back, give the story's subject her privacy, and, if necessary, tell the clamoring public to mind its own business? Even if the child declares that he wishes to speak in an interview or press conference, given the child's age and what he has been through, is he really in a position to make that choice?

On the other hand, in the Smart and Hornbeck cases, the journalists had permission from the children's parents to interview them. The children were apparently willing to be interviewed. The children or parents could have ended the interviews at any time.

In the Groene case, the child's identity was already very well known, particularly in Idaho. It would have been impossible to remove her name from the news stories that had already been published, so referring to her by oblique descriptors would have seemed pointless at best, and disingenuous at worst. After all, you can't un-name a name any more easily than you can un-ring a bell. Further, some journalists reasoned that it would be irresponsible to refrain from informing the public that the search for these children was, in fact, at an end.

The first guideline in the code of ethics of the Society of Professional Journalists is "seek truth and report it." But the second guideline is "minimize harm." Items under that dictum include "avoid pandering to lurid curiosity" and "be cautious about identifying juvenile suspects or victims of sex crimes." However, with words like "seek," "minimize," "avoid," and "be cautious," there is always room for interpretation. One can take caution, and then go ahead, if he or she truly believes it is the right thing to do, without having breached the code of ethics.

So the question remains: Which is more important, the obligation of the journalist to tell the story well, or the obligation of the journalist to minimize harm to the abused child?

HOW: Do you release the name of a child who is thought to have been abused? Do you interview the child? Increasingly, we are seeing instances of this scenario playing out in the media. A precedent has been set, so we may continue to see cases like this unless news organizations change their policies.

This issue is not black and white; it is a wide range of grays. Every case is different, and a journalist could certainly choose either course while remaining true to the SPJ code of ethics. In some cases, the best course of action might be to name the child, but refrain from publishing graphic details about the abuse the child endured. Perhaps in other cases, there is no pressing public interest for the child's identity to be released, and his or her privacy is the utmost consideration.

Most importantly, journalists must closely examine their own motives. Whatever path they choose, they should be guided by professional ethics and never simply by a desire to be first with a detail that will increase ratings or circulation.

—*By Amber Orand and Sara Stone, Baylor University*

CASE STUDY: When the Crime is Incest

THE SITUATION: Sexual abuse is one of the most sensitive topics to report. The victims often want to avoid publicity, but reporting sex crimes may help prevent future sex crimes and direct victims to sources of help. Reporters must strive to show respect for the subjects of their stories.

A story published in July 1995 in *The Wabasha* (Minn.) *County Herald*, a weekly newspaper in a town of about 2,500 people, offers a case study of the steps that should be followed from start to finish. The newspaper reported the sentencing of a father who was convicted of incest. The victim was his only daughter.

The daughter complained that the newspaper's report was insensitive, and the Minnesota News Council ruled in her favor. The complaint would likely have never reached the Minnesota News Council had the principles underscored at the hearing been practiced by the newspaper in pursuing the story.

The News Council's near unanimous decision to uphold the complaint should not be interpreted as a blanket condemnation of the newspaper or that the staff was callous in its decision to identify the victim as the daughter. The publisher and editor said it was a gut-wrenching decision.

ISSUES AND ANALYSIS: A case like this presents numerous questions for evaluating whether any story is fit for publication.

Is it news?

Values frequently collide when editors seek to balance victims' rights with a responsibility to inform. There was no doubt that reporting the father's sentencing stirred painful childhood memories for the victim. But from the editor's standpoint, the story held the individual accountable for his crime. The seriousness of the crime warranted front-page coverage, he said.

Part of the article was about the judge's apparent leniency in the punishment. Further examination, however — principally, talking to the victim — would have revealed the daughter's role in advocating a shorter sentence. The father was sentenced to one year in jail even though state guidelines recommended 13 years in prison. The father also was placed on 30 years' probation.

The story could have prompted a review of sentencing patterns in sex-abuse cases. It also could have raised the overall awareness of sexual abuse, especially if it included follow-up stories on the signs of sexual abuse and where to turn for help.

Even if it's true, should we publish it?

Must all facts be reported? The sex-abuse case offered instruction.

The editor pointed out that he printed exactly what was in court documents. His intent was to prevent sensationalism and to circumvent gossip about what had happened in the family. It's fair to ask, however, whether all details were necessary for public examination.

The family brought the complaint to the News Council on the basis of two issues: identifying the child and giving excessive detail.

The descriptive narrative of charges often is the more sensitive and bigger problem when reporting from court summaries. In this case, simply reporting the charges — repeated instances of abuse during several years — would have allowed readers to deduce the victim was a family member. (But that is not always true in such circumstances. Extensive cases of abuse also have been reported between an adult and a baby sitter or neighborhood youth.)

> Most newspapers have policies that protect the identity of victims, but that can become difficult in small towns where word spreads quickly.

In any case, the community still would have had a clear picture of the abhorrent circumstances had the newspaper not identified the victim as the daughter.

What if you were the subject?

Had the publisher and editor pictured themselves as the subjects of the story, they may have changed the final version. There's no better test than editors putting their own names in the headline. If editors have opportunity, they also should discuss approaches to stories with their families or other people they hold in high regard.

Did you talk with the subject of the story?

Editors should try to interview the involved parties, or at least alert them to the story. Most individuals expect to be contacted as part of the news gathering, but that does not always occur, as illustrated in this case. The newspaper's failure to talk to the victim directly almost certainly altered the story's presentation.

The editor and publisher said they spoke to each other and to the prosecutor, who had urged full disclosure. They did not talk to the family or a mental health therapist, and they did not seek a woman's perspective. The editor said he had all the information and only a weekend to write the story.

In hindsight, as revealed at the News Council hearing, the decision to rely only on the county prosecutor resulted in a significant omission in the story. The victim herself had asked that her father be given a lenient sentence so, in her words, her family could be reunited and try to get back to living a normal life.

The newspaper may have had only a few days to sort through the court appearance and sentencing, but the staff had months to sort through questions and prepare the coverage. The father had been charged with the crime a year earlier.

Editors may even consider sharing a story in advance with key participants. Many journalists reject the idea of letting someone preview a story, and for good reason. The practice can result in problems, not the least of which is setting a precedent. But sometimes pre-publication review — with explicit ground rules established in advance — can head off serious problems.

Reviewing a story with the individuals involved does not assure that everyone will leave the room on the same page. However, it's likely that all parties in the sex-abuse case — the victim, the community and the newspaper — would have been served better had a discussion occurred.

Is the report fair?

Reporting the facts does not necessarily guarantee balance. Omission of certain information, or failure to get a response from a party, can put a completely different slant on a story, especially in crime and court news.

It's easy to produce a story from a police report or criminal complaint. Getting a comment from the accused is not as easy. If a response is tracked down, comments often are tacked on the end of a story and appear almost as an afterthought.

The sex-abuse report may have fulfilled expectations of the prosecutor, but few others. In fact, the victim — who was represented by the prosecutor — was most upset by the coverage. In a story as important as this one, including the comments of others would have produced a stronger and more accurate story.

Lastly, don't be afraid to admit an error in judgment or a mistake. It's the right thing to do, and it goes a long way toward restoring credibility.

Is it a public or strictly private issue?

The Wabasha County Herald and the victim agreed that the story was important.

The editor said he believed that by fully reporting the incest, the newspaper would discourage others from committing the crime for fear of publicity. He also said the newspaper had been sensitive to the well-being of the girl by choosing not to run a story when her father was first charged with the crime a year before sentencing.

The girl, who said she first wanted to keep the case secret, said she decided she wanted to help others.

The differences, of course, surfaced in how the story was reported.

The impact of such stories on victims cannot be overstated, as pointed out by Dr. Frank Ochberg, a psychiatrist and adjunct professor who helped launch and sustain the Victims and the Media Program at Michigan State University's School of Journalism. "Victims in our society already feel that they have been labeled as losers, weak and pathetic, so when you add the stigma of sexual assault, it is easy to see how vulnerable this makes them," says Ochberg, an expert on posttraumatic stress disorder who has treated many victims.

Most newspapers have policies that protect the identity of victims, but that can become difficult in small towns where word spreads quickly. Community newspapers still should make the effort.

Will the story make a difference?

The Wabasha County Herald and the victim agreed — or at least had hoped to agree — on this point, too. The editor said the publicity given the perpetrator would deter others from carrying out a similar crime. And the victim said she hoped the publicity would help others who might be in similar situations.

Newspapers must give equal attention to how a story will affect those directly involved as well as the good provided to the broader community. An equally large part of the sex-abuse story was the reason the judge handed down a punishment far less than that recommended by sentencing guidelines. It can be argued that residents needed to know it was an incest case to put the county attorney's comments in context and to hold everyone in the criminal justice system accountable. Even to that point, the story identified the case as first-degree criminal sexual conduct, which in itself underscores the severity.

Will the truth quash rumors?

The opportunity to quash rumors is one of the strongest arguments editors can present to an otherwise unwilling or uncooperative news source. If a rumor has reached the newspaper, rest assured it has circulated throughout the community. One word of caution, though. Rumors are never-ending, especially in small towns. Editors must establish that a particular rumor is significant enough to warrant a story.

Sex-abuse reports are especially problematic. *The Wabasha County Herald* believed the story would put rumors to rest. Even the victim's therapist in this case encouraged newspapers to bring the problem to public attention.

Does a story meet journalistic and community standards?

All newspapers strive to protect victims, but it is not always possible. Consider these three cases, which all occurred during the span of a few months at the *Red Wing* (Minn.) *Republican Eagle*:

- A defendant, in what the judge characterized as a highly unusual request, asked for a three-hour furlough from jail once a week to visit with his daughter, the victim. It was difficult to report the court proceedings without identifying

The Minnesota News Council

Journalists, as a rule, don't like people looking over their shoulders. While other countries, notably Great Britain, have created official panels to review public complaints about press performance, the idea never has been popular in the United States.

The Minnesota News Council was one exception, and it may have been the longest-lived. It had a 40-year run from 1971 to 2011, when it folded due to a shortage of funding and complaints. It was a hybrid of press and public; half its members were from the public and half were from the news media.

Its funding came mostly (40 percent) from companies not engaged in the news business. It also said 20 percent of its money came from media organizations, 30 percent from nonprofit foundations and 10 percent from individual contributions.

It was strictly voluntarily; it made findings — about half the complaints it considered were upheld — but they were not enforceable in any way (except for apologies or expressions of embarrassment). The Washington News Council was similar, and was based on Minnesota's effort, but it lasted only from 1999 to 2014.

— but not actually naming — the daughter. A father was on trial for alleged sex abuse, but his attorney claimed what really was at issue was a custody battle between parents. The mother and daughter, the alleged victims, lived an hour away from Red Wing. A father was sentenced for sexual abuse that occurred during the course of 15 years. The newspaper identified the victim as a son, since he no longer lived in Minnesota. At an attorney's suggestion, the story also made it clear the abuse did not involve children who still lived in the area.

The Minnesota News Council [which shut down in 2011, citing a lack of funding and a shortage of complaints] took two actions on the complaint against *The Wabasha County Herald*. One was to uphold the victim's complaint. The council also urged the newspaper to consult others, including sex-abuse therapists, to develop a policy for covering such sensitive stories.

That's sound advice for any newsroom. The policy may not be black and white, but it will give the newspaper a basis for making sensitive decisions that still serve the need of informing readers.

— *Jim Pumarlo, SPJ Ethics Committee Former Editor, Red Wing (Minn.) Republican Eagle, 1982-2003*

[RULING BY THE MINNESOTA NEWS COUNCIL]

Minnesota News Council
Determination 106
August 24, 1995

In the matter of a complaint of anonymous juvenile incest victim against *The Wabasha* (Minn.) *County Herald*.

A 17-year-old incest victim attended the hearing to press her complaint. Accompanying her were her mother and her therapist. Representing *The Wabasha County Herald* were Michael Smith, editor, and Gary Stumpf, publisher.

Complaint: The complainant contended that the July 12, 1995, story about her father's sentencing:
- Invaded her privacy when it identified the victim of the sexual assaults as the convicted man's minor daughter (she was his only daughter)
- Was sensational and revictimized the daughter by publishing graphic details of the abuse she endured.

Determination: The Minnesota News Council chose not to vote on invasion of privacy or sensationalism, but after discussion decided that the newspaper had been insensitive to the girl. Members suggested that the newspaper should have consulted others in developing the story and could have talked with the family to prepare them for the story. A council member urged the newspaper to think not only of journalistic standards, but also community standards.

The council also voted unanimously to recommend that the newspaper create guidelines for covering sexual-abuse cases, consulting with outsiders including counselors and victims.

The Minnesota News Council addressed and promoted fairness in media through public discussion. The organization offered an alternative to legal action. Complainants stated their case at a hearing before a council comprised of media and public members. Media members participating in *The Wabasha County Herald* case included Jim Pumarlo, editor of the *Red Wing Republican Eagle*.

CASE STUDY: Turning Down a Political Ad

WHAT: CNN, NBC, Facebook and even Fox News banned a last-minute ad sponsored by the Trump presidential campaign that aired on the Sunday before the Tuesday, November 6, 2018, midterm elections. The 30-second spot, intended to support Republican Party candidates, centered on a large group of refugees from South and Central America who were making their way toward the U.S. Border.

The ad, by all appearances, was intended to raise fears about an "invasion" of immigrants from South and Central America, mostly Colombia, in a caravan making its way to the southern U.S. border. The video showed large groups of unkempt people, clinging to overcrowded truck trailers and other forms of transportation.

It highlighted a man, Luis Bracamontes, who had entered the United States illegally, been deported several times over the years, and yet kept returning to the United States. He eventually was found guilty of killing two law enforcement officers in Sacramento, California. But the homicides were in 2014, four years before the caravan, and some of Bracamontes's other crimes and illegal border crossings dated back to the Clinton and Bush administrations.

The ad closed with a prominent slogan, "Stop the Caravan. Vote Republican," and with a shot of President Trump at a desk, signing something and saying, in a voice-over,

"I'm Donald Trump, and I approved this message." Clearly, it was sponsored by the Trump re-election campaign, which had filed papers with the Federal Election Commission on the very day the president was inaugurated for his first term.

Questions: Should these news media outlets have written standards about what advertising is and isn't acceptable? If you pay for the message, should you be allowed to say whatever you want?

WHO: Network programmers were responsible for accepting the ads; network executives were responsible for the decision finally to remove them. Stakeholders include the Trump campaign, the two major political parties, the immigrant community (legal entry as well as illegal), the television networks and their reputations, and, finally, a public bombarded by campaign advertising that is overwhelmingly negative.

WHY: The principles involved in these decisions — truth, honesty and integrity — are all part of the codes of ethics adopted by associations of advertisers and public relations professionals as well as the Society of Professional Journalists, Radio Television Digital News Association and other journalists' organizations. Another principle, loyalty, is high on the list of ideals of the Public Relations Society of America.

Advertising is sometimes pulled if it can be shown to be inaccurate or offensive. But an argument also can be made that the principles of free speech should always come first, and that doesn't change when the "speech" is actually bought and paid for. In fact, the purchase of air time adds weight to the advertiser's claim that its viewpoint should be presented unaltered and uncensored.

> The purchase of air time adds weight to the advertiser's claim that its viewpoint should be presented unaltered and uncensored.

The media organizations that were airing the ad pulled it quickly after complaints started flying. CNN called the ad racist and refused to air it from the beginning. "CNN has made it abundantly clear in its editorial coverage that this ad is racist," the cable news network said in a statement. "When presented with an opportunity to be paid to take a version of this ad, we declined. Those are the facts."

NBC and its affiliates, after airing the ad initially, removed it from their programming. So did Fox News, whose opinion analysts have been very pro-Trump. The National Football League, in a statement, said it was unaware that the Trump ad had been scheduled to run during its highly rated "Sunday Night Football" broadcast. A spokesman for the league, Brian McCarthy, said the NFL "played no role in the airing of the spot" and added that the league "has no approval rights regarding campaign ads. That falls to the network that is selling the advertising and airing the game."

Fox's statement came from the network's president of ad sales, who said, "Upon further review, Fox News pulled the ad yesterday [Sunday] and it will not appear on either Fox News Channel or Fox Business Network." It had run on those channels about a dozen times.

Facebook pulled the 30-second spot, it said, because "this ad violates Facebook's advertising policy against sensational content. … While the video is allowed to be posted on Facebook [by individual users], it cannot receive paid distribution."

On the Monday after the ad aired, NBCUniversal said the ad had been pulled because of its "insensitive nature."

DECISION: The media outlets that had been offered the ad all decided that they would not allow a paid announcement that they considered to be unethical — and inaccurate — on their air.

DISCUSSION: Could this controversy have been prevented? Trump supporters said the way the situation unfolded was more evidence of the anti-Trump bias they ascribe to the mainstream media. If the ad never had been shown, would that strengthen their argument? Or did showing the ad, perhaps unwittingly, provide justification for the media's decision to pull it? Should policies on advertising be more specific about what's acceptable and what isn't? Or is it better to handle those air-it-or-not decisions on a case-by-case basis? For strategic communicators, in particular, even though loyalty is high on the list of PRSA principles, can you be loyal to a client who may be pushing the envelope too far?

What the Codes Say: Minimizing Harm

Reporters should use special care when interviewing people who don't regularly deal with the press. The rules that govern conversations with politicians and public relations people don't necessarily apply when you're interviewing a victim's neighbor or a parent angry about school boundaries. A reporter might not — should not — hesitate to embarrass a politician for uttering something truly brainless on the record. A plain, ordinary citizen in those circumstances can be granted some leeway and extra courtesy.

Daily Press, Newport News, Virginia

Be certain that any contacts related to a death are handled with care and sensitivity. We seek the cause of death for news obituaries, but that information can be withheld if the family requests it and our editors approve. Discuss with your editor whether we should report suicides, which we would do normally only if it involves a public figure or public suicide.

The Dallas Morning News

Those who are unaccustomed to dealing with the press deserve special consideration. You may need to tell them if they are being interviewed on the record, or when a conversation is being taped on the telephone.

The Journal News, White Plains, New York

Dealing with minors (generally defined as anyone under the age of 18) always invokes legal issues. An interview of a minor about a sensitive subject requires a KUOW journalist to secure permission from the minor's parent or legal guardian.... Examples of sensitive subjects include cheating, sexual activity, involvement in gangs or crime, difficult family relationships, probation violation, out-of-wedlock pregnancy or parenthood, victims' sexual abuse and similar topics that could have legal ramifications or lead to embarrassment. An interview of a minor in a special custodial situation, such as foster care, juvenile detention, or holding facilities for illegal immigrants, requires the consent of the person who has custody of the minor. Utah also requires the consent of both the custodian of the juvenile facility and the minor's parent.

An interview on a non-sensitive topic (normal childhood activities, sports, books, movies, trips to the zoo, baseball and the like) does not require consent. Generally, however, any interview on school premises will require the consent of the school authorities. If a minor is a witness to a crime, the KUOW journalist must weigh carefully whether we are exposing the minor to physical risk by identifying him or her by name as a potential witness, and whether there is potential for the minor to be accused as a participant.

Situations like school shootings require special care when interviewing visibly distressed minors who may have witnessed horrific scenes. Witnesses such as teachers or students over 18 are preferable interviewees. If continued interviewing substantially increases the distress of a minor who is a witness, the KUOW journalist should carefully balance the importance and quality of the information being obtained with the interviewee's emotional state and decide whether respect for the witness requires the interview to be ended. The KUOW journalist must also discuss with the editor whether that interview should be aired.

KUOW/Puget Sound Public Radio

Quoting in dialect or using a non-standard spelling will be done only rarely, must be in good taste and must serve an important journalistic purpose. Grammatical errors, when they are not important to the news or when they would make the speaker look foolish or take on undue importance, are to be avoided.

Detroit Free Press

It is not our job to make people look good by cleaning up inelegant turns of phrase, nor is it our job to expose them to ridicule by running such quotes. In most cases, this dilemma can be resolved by paraphrase and reported speech. Where it cannot, reporters should consult a more senior journalist to discuss whether the quote can be run verbatim. Correcting a grammatical error in a quote may be valid, but rewording an entire phrase is not. When translating quotes from one language into another, we should do so in an idiomatic way rather than with pedantic literalness. Care must be taken to ensure that the tone of the translation is equivalent to the tone of the original. Beware of translating quotes in newspaper pickups back into the original language of the source. If a French politician gives an interview to an American newspaper, it is almost certain that the translation back into French will be wrong and in some cases the quote could be very different. In such cases, the fewer quotes and the more reported speech, the better.

Reuters Handbook of Journalism

If our role as watchdog sometimes requires us to be firm, aggressive and insistent, we should never behave with arrogance or narrow self-righteousness. Our legitimate striving for detachment should never make us callous or indifferent to fear, anxiety, grief or suffering. Just as good journalists strive for balance in their stories, they should complement a healthy skepticism with courtesy and compassion.

Grand Forks Herald, North Dakota

Don't constantly dwell on the "bad" in a community or organization when there is also a "good" side to be told. Only finding fault is as bad as boosterism. Be aware of the trend of coverage and seek balance when appropriate.

The Journal News, White Plains, New York

PRINCIPLE 5: Advertisers should treat consumers fairly based on the nature of the audience to whom the ads are directed and the nature of the product or service advertised.

PRINCIPLE 6: Advertisers should never compromise consumers' personal privacy in marketing communications, and their choices as to whether to participate in providing their information should be transparent and easily made.

American Advertising Federation

CHAPTER 8:

Diversity

Only recently have news media codes of ethics and books on journalism ethics begun to mention issues related to diversity. It is clear, however, that diversity has an important place in any discussion of journalistic ethics.

Diversity is a critical component of accuracy and fairness, whether it relates to avoiding stereotypes or redefining news to better reflect a multicultural society.

Diversity is about the makeup of news organizations and who is making decisions. Diversity is about the way story ideas are developed and who does the reporting. Diversity is about inclusiveness in choosing sources and about giving voice to the voiceless.

> Diversity means talking to people who are different from you

Diversity means talking to people who are different from you, using people of different races, ages, religions and political beliefs in your reporting. Their viewpoints will enrich your story-telling and deepen your understanding of your audience and market.

There is no shortage of horror stories about news media thoughtlessly running roughshod over the sensitivities of various groups in society — ethnic, racial, religious, gender, physical ability, etc. While lessons can be learned from mistakes, the authors of this book believe we learn best from success.

Therefore you will find a relatively positive tone in much of this chapter's case studies, and in a number of suggestions for news organizations and for individual journalists relating to both staffing and story content.

Diversity Checklist

The following questions, protocols and recommendations for handling issues of diversity were written by the former diversity director and dean at the Poynter Institute for Media Studies in St. Petersburg, Florida.

Putting Diversity to Work in Your News Organization

By Kenneth Irby
Senior Pastor at Historic Bethel AMEC

1. Inclusion

    Who is on your staff? Who's on the freelance list? Who is reading your paper, watching your broadcast, listening to your station or navigating your site? What examples are you holding up as evidence of good work? What sources are being used by the journalists in your organization (books, articles, agencies, Web sites)?
    ... and

2. Combating Prejudice

    How are you helping your readers/viewers/listeners learn about the world around them and to recognize and work against prejudice, ignorance and stereotypes that get in the way of good journalism and good management? How can you help them to communicate better across difference? How do we help our readers, viewers, listeners and staffers challenge existing news values and newsroom practices that exclude, stereotype and marginalize and mislead?
    ... and

3. Improving Craft

    How do we help journalists increase truth-telling by bringing in seldom-seen faces, seldom-heard voices and seldom-shown places in your daily reports? Capturing diversity in the presentation of content is key. How do we help journalists and readers/viewers/listeners recognize when people and perspectives are missing in our daily reports? How do we help them strengthen their craft and understanding so that images and language are sharper, more precise, and fairer to the people we serve?
    ... and

4. Leading Change

    How are you helping your staffers and readers/viewers/listeners increase the diversity of people that they report on, hear and see? How are you doing as employers at hiring, recruiting and promoting people with diverse backgrounds? How are you managing diversity in your shop? How can you help people see the connection between a diverse team and high performance (excellence) in the newsroom.

Guidelines for Racial Identification

By Keith Woods
Vice President, Newsroom Training & Diversity at National Public Radio
Former Dean at the Poynter Institute

The use of racial identifiers in the media was for decades a means of singling out those who were not white. The practice helped form and fuel stereotypes and continues today to push a wedge between people. We can handle this delicate material better if we flag every racial reference and ask these questions:

1. Is it relevant?

    Race is relevant when the story is about race. Just because people in conflict are of different races does not mean that race is the source of their dispute. A story about interracial dating, however, is a story about race.

2. Have I explained the relevance?

    Journalists too frequently assume that readers will know the significance of race in stories. The result is often radically different interpretations. That is imprecise journalism, and its harm may be magnified by the lens of race.

3. Is it free of codes?

    Be careful not to use *welfare, inner-city, underprivileged, blue collar, conservative, suburban, exotic, middle-class, Uptown, South Side, or wealthy* as euphemisms for racial groups. By definition, the White House is in the inner-city. Say what you mean.

4. Are racial identifiers used evenly?

    If the race of a person charging discrimination is important, then so is the race of the person being charged.

5. Should I consult someone of another race/ethnicity?

    Consider another question: Do I have expertise on other races/cultures? If not, broaden your perspective by asking someone who knows something more about your subject. Why should we treat reporting on racial issues any differently from reporting on an area of science or religion that we do not know well?

CASES: Diversity

CASE STUDY: When Sources Won't Talk

WHAT: It began as a letter to the editor from a former editor. It ended with a record number of online postings and apologies from a fraternity and sorority.

Jamilia Gates, former news editor for *The Parthenon*, the student newspaper at Marshall University, learned that a campus sorority and fraternity had sponsored a thug- and gangsta-themed party. Gates, who is black, wrote in her letter that the party was an insult to black students and not an appropriate campus activity.

"Pictures from this party were posted all over Facebook. Pictures of representatives from these organizations showed members grabbing their lower limbs, with gum wrappers in their mouth representing gold teeth, baggy clothing, backwards hats and permanent-marker tattoos saying 'Thug Life,'" she wrote. "The people in those photos were basically displaying light-hearted racism."

Questions: The SPJ Code of Ethics offers guidance on at least three aspects of this dilemma. "Test the accuracy of information from all sources and exercise care to avoid inadvertent error." One source was not sufficient in revealing this information.

"Diligently seek out subjects of news stories to give them the opportunity to respond to allegations of wrongdoing." The newspaper editors knew the Greek community had often complained about The Parthenon's so-called negative coverage of Greek life.

"Tell the story of the diversity and magnitude of the human experience boldly, even when it is unpopular to do so."

How could the editors maintain credibility and remain fair to both sides yet find solid sources for a news tip with inflammatory allegations? Such a story could stir racial divisions on campus and risk the charters of both Greek organizations.

Reprinted with permission.

WHO: The newspaper's editors sat on the letter for a couple of days hoping the Greek affairs reporter could get details. Meanwhile, the editors found proof of the party in photos published on Facebook.

Managing editor Brian Dalek said: "As the person usually overseeing the opinion page and letters, the staff and I did want to verify that the party did, in fact, take place before publication. There was a little bit of concern that having a former editor submit the letter would lead to some in the Greek community on campus to see the paper as singling them out, as they had perceived in the past."

Members of the fraternity and sorority did not respond to the Greek affairs reporter's repeated requests for interviews.

"The photos were only taken down when we tried to get the Greek chapters' perspective on the party before we ran the letter," Dalek said. "After the initial inquiries, the reporter was basically shunned."

WHY: Knowing that further delays would detract from the event's news value, the editors made the unusual decision to break a news story in the letters column and published Gates' letter October 6, 2008.

Dalek said: "We did wait until we actually found several pictures on Facebook that appeared to have the theme of the gangsta/thug party. Sure, it could have been any party at Marshall, but we saw several pictures that actually had the name of the Greek chapters in the background. My only regret is that we did not print these photos or save them for proof that we did see photos before they were taken down."

HOW: Their strategy worked. Publication of the letter forced members of the fraternity and sorority to respond to *The Parthenon* reporter — but only off the record. They still didn't want to acknowledge the party. Over the next two days, the phone messages, online posts and letters from the Greek community flew. Online posts supported both sides — this type of behavior is unacceptable on a college campus versus no harm was intended as it was just a party.

Finally, the student government president urged both organizations to issue written apologies. Still, they refused to go on the record with the reporter who was finally able to pull together a story with reaction to the incident.

"After the publication of [Gates's] letter, Sigma Alpha Epsilon members submitted a letter that gave an apology on the taste of the party. Just hours before the page was sent to print, however, the chapter's president informed us that he had never seen the written apology and his signature was actually forged. They pulled the letter, thankfully, but it also gave us some clarification that there were individuals in the fraternity who were likely to be insensitive to different cultures based on the fact that they forged signatures as well. We no longer had second thoughts about the original letter by Jamilia Gates' take on the story," Dalek said.

Alpha Chi Omega's letter stated: "The sisters of Alpha Chi Omega would not and did not set out to hurt anyone's feelings or be insensitive to anyone's culture. We greatly regret choosing a theme with even the potential to be offensive … Please know that we have learned from this experience. We will share this valuable lesson with others in our organization. And we'll make every effort to ensure that it never happens again."

Sigma Alpha Epsilon submitted its letter: "Our fraternity prides itself on our creed, 'The True Gentlemen,' and our decisions regarding the social event did not live up to the beliefs to which we strive ... We are committed to reaffirming our actions to reflect those of a gentleman in order to better ourselves and our community."

The editorial board opted to follow up with an editorial October 10: "Hopefully this is the end of this controversy, but something can be taken from the situation. As individuals and as student groups at Marshall, we all need to take into account the impact of our decisions ... With the Internet, mobile videos and photos posted on MySpace and Facebook, anything you do can be a thorn in your side, and not just on a college campus."

The editors took a gamble in using the opinion page to break a story. However, their savvy use of social networking sites allowed them to independently confirm the party occurred. By the time Gates' letter was published, the photos had been removed.

The unusual strategy allowed the newspaper to cover an event with important ramifications to the campus. Had editors waited on a news story to cover it, the story would have been lost.

— by Nerissa Young, SPJ Ethics Committee and Parthenon adviser, Marshall University

CASE STUDY: Prejudiced and Persistent

WHAT: A reader of *The Durango* (Colorado) *Herald* complained to the Society of Professional Journalists in the spring of 2010 that the family-owned newspaper was regularly printing "hateful" letters to the editor attacking homosexuality. The particular sequence of events that appeared to spur the complaint was set off by a letter praising a parochial school in another Colorado community, the liberal university town of Boulder, for refusing admission to a child with lesbian parents. The letter, published March 24, 2010, included statements like this: "Satan is alive and well. This is why it is so important for Christ-based churches to offer special counseling to help the gay and lesbian community, including children trapped in their immoral existence."

Numerous letters were printed in response. Most of them challenged the initial letter, but one supporter wrote: "I am sick and tired of having sexual perversion crammed down my throat. Enough is enough. Sodomites are the ones filled with hate and evil — not God-fearing Christians."

This is the sort of language that drove the complainant to the SPJ Ethics Hotline. She said the *Herald* had even "created an editorial policy to justify" the practice. "The letters are so hateful that the community began to bombard them [the *Herald*] with requests not to print them, and that," she surmised, "is what inspired the policy." She asked if ethical journalists should ever publish such letters and complained that the newspaper's editorial defending its publication of such letters was "so weak." She did give the *Herald* some credit, though, for at least listening to the complaints. "I have written a response to the

> *There are three things that no one can do to the entire satisfaction of anyone else: make love, poke the fire, and run a newspaper.* **William Allen White, 1917**

Opinion — 4A — THE DURANGO HERALD

Bill Roberts, Opinion Page Editor · 375-4500 · letters@durangoherald.com — Wednesday, March 31, 2010

On publishing 'hateful' letters

A number of readers – see Page 5A – have responded to a letter published March 24 in the *Herald*. Most describe it as "hateful," and several have urged the *Herald* not to print further letters from that author or from authors they deem homophobic.

They are reasonable complaints from people honestly concerned about hurtful speech and intolerance. But they miss the point.

The *Herald* tries to keep the discussions on its Opinion page civil, if not always cordial, but there are some topics that are in themselves inherently ugly. The perceived need on the part of some Americans to limit the rights of their gay and lesbian neighbors is one example.

For starters, the *Herald* limits letter writers to 350 words and one letter per month. That some choose to address the same topic repeatedly may make it seem as if they are accorded more space. They are not.

But they are edited. The assertion that homosexuality is both forbidden by the Bible and a threat to society is theologically shaky and offensive to many. It is not an epithet.

As for whether anti-gay sentiments are a suitable topic, there are two reasons for printing such letters. The first is simply to educate readers about the diversity of thought in the community – good and bad. But admittedly, that goes only so far. The *Herald* would not print a letter proclaiming the inferiority of a given racial group.

But the equality of people of different races is settled law and a firmly established cultural ideal. The status of gay and lesbian Americans is another matter entirely. Issues such as "don't ask, don't tell," lesbian parentage and gay marriage are hotly contested public issues of a kind racial minorities have not faced in decades.

The discussion surrounding those questions cannot be limited to those who support full equality and opponents who express their homophobia only in euphemisms. It must also include those who would deny other's rights because they believe homosexuality is morally wrong and offensive to God.

They may be on the wrong side of history, but it is their country, too.

Reprinted by permission of the Durango Herald

policy that was published in the paper, a group of us went and met with the editorial page, and I wrote a letter to him after our meeting because I did not think that we had made an impact," she said in her e-mail to the Hotline.

QUESTION: What guidelines should a newspaper have for printing letters to the editor that attack a particular group?

WHO: The decision-makers here, the moral agents, are the *Herald's* publisher, Richard Ballantine, and its editorial page editor, Bill Roberts. They are responsible for setting the newspaper's policy on letters to the editor. The people most affected by their policy include members of Durango's homosexual community as well as the people writing the letters. Gays, lesbians, bisexual and transsexual individuals are offended and hurt. Their critics want to continue to be able to express their beliefs publicly.

The community itself, and its image, have a stake here, too. Durango is not large; about 16,000 people live within the city limits, and the *Herald's* countywide circulation area is about 50,000. But Durango is one of a number of scenic and sophisticated small towns that dot the American Southwest, attracting tourists, artists, galleries, students and good restaurants. It's the cultural hub of southwest Colorado. Its daily newspaper, owned by the same family since 1952, has a reputation to be concerned about — in particular, a reputation for an expansive world-view that contributes to Durango's level of sophistication.

WHY: This is a classic ethical struggle between freedom of expression and the ideal of minimizing harm. In a March 31, 2010, editorial defending the *Herald's* letters policy, editorial page editor Roberts, after what he called "considerable discussion" with the publisher and editorial board, wrote: "The Herald tries to keep the discussions on its Opinion page civil, if not always cordial, but there are some topics that are in themselves inherently ugly. The perceived need on the part of some Americans to limit the rights of their gay and lesbian neighbors is one example." The reasons for printing such letters, he said, are "to educate readers about the diversity of thought in the community — good and bad," and to permit debate about a controversial subject that covers hot-button issues like military service, gay marriage and adoption. The *Herald*, he conceded, would not be as permissive on issues of race, but racial equality "is settled law and a firmly established cultural ideal"; the issues still facing the homosexual community are still "hotly contested … of a kind racial minorities have not faced in decades."

This did not satisfy the woman who complained about the policy. "I cannot imagine *The New York Times* ever printing the types of letters that the *Herald* prints on a regular basis," she wrote to SPJ. "… My point is that I do not understand why gays and lesbians should be treated different." Another letter, published in the *Herald* on April 27, asserted that "religious belief is no justification for slander and hate-mongering. Homophobic hate speech, which these letters represent, is not 'discussion'; it is intimidation, pure and simple, and should not be tolerated."

> Should journalists' decisions be guided by racial or other sensitivities of their audiences?

SPJ's Ethics Hotline, staffed by volunteers, doesn't formally investigate complaints, but it does offer opinions and advice. In this case, the woman who complained was told that the editorial defending the *Herald's* policy appeared to be "a very thoughtful explanation of why journalists feel compelled to give voice to ideas and sometimes actions they don't agree with." She was invited to give more potentially damaging details about the letters' contents, but she did not reply. The facts in this case study were researched afterward.

Personally, Roberts said, he believes that sexuality is innate, not a lifestyle choice, "and as such should be treated much like race." But the half-dozen or so conservative Christians writing the anti-gay letters "really are offended," he said, by the growing acceptance of something they see as "profoundly immoral."

HOW: The *Herald's* policy on letters to the editor is similar to that of many publications that try to keep polemicists from dominating their op-ed pages. It limits letters to 350 words and writers to one letter a month. "That some choose to address the same topic repeatedly may make it seem as if they are accorded more space," the *Herald's* editorial said. "They are not." The discussion surrounding issues affecting gays and lesbians "cannot be limited to those who support full equality and opponents who express their homophobia only in euphemisms," the editorial continued. "It must also include those who would deny others' rights because they believe homosexuality is morally wrong and offensive to God. They may be on the wrong side of history, but it is their country, too."

Further discussion: Is there such a thing as fair criticism in this delicate subject area? Should there be more restrictions on letter writers who get to be predictable and repetitious? Is it fair to treat attacks based on sexual orientation different from criticisms based on racial or ethnic identity? Would you have a different, more specific, policy for letters to the editor?

CASE STUDY: The 'Art' of Darkness

WHAT: On June 27, 1994, both *Time* and *Newsweek* ran cover photos of O.J. Simpson, the former football and movie star who had been arrested 10 days earlier as a suspect in the stabbing deaths of his wife and a male acquaintance of hers. Both magazines used essentially the same photo — a police mug shot taken at the time of Simpson's arrest, after a bizarre, long-distance, slow-motion car chase followed worldwide on television.

Newsweek used the mug shot without altering it. *Time* used a darker, coarser image, symbolizing Simpson's fall from grace. Given three choices for a cover, *Time's* managing editor, James R. Gaines, said he chose one by Matt Mahurin, whom Gaines described as "a master of photo illustration."

Gaines wrote in a "To Our Readers" note the following week that he had found Mahurin's work "quite impressive. The harshness of the mug shot — the merciless bright light, the stubble on Simpson's face, the cold specificity of the picture — had been subtly smoothed and shaped into an icon of tragedy. The expression on his face was not merely blank now; it was bottomless. This cover, with the simple, nonjudgmental headline 'An American Tragedy,' seemed the obvious, right choice."

But the reaction was swift, and angry.

"I have looked at thousands of covers over the years and chosen hundreds," Gaines wrote. "I have never been so wrong about how one would be received. In the storm of controversy over this cover, several of the country's major news organizations and leading black journalists charged that we had darkened Simpson's face in a racist and legally prejudicial attempt to make him look more sinister and guilty, to portray him as 'some kind of animal,' as the NAACP's Benjamin Chavis put it. A white press critic said the cover had the effect of sending him 'back to the ghetto.' Others objected to the fact that the mug shot had been altered at all, arguing that photographs, particularly news photos, should never be altered."

There certainly was no racist intent, Gaines wrote, nor did the magazine or artist intend any suggestion of guilt. A week after the uproar, he still defended the cover:

"Our critics felt that Matt Mahurin's work changed the picture fundamentally; I felt it lifted a common police mug shot to the level of art, with no sacrifice to truth. Reasonable people may disagree about that. If there was anything wrong with the cover, in my view, it was that it was not immediately apparent that this was a photo-illustration rather than an unaltered photograph; to know that, a reader had to turn to our contents page or see the original mug shot on the opening page of the story. But making that distinction clearer will not end the debate over the manipulation of photographs. Nor should it. No single set of rules will ever cover all possible cases. It will remain, as it has always been, a matter of subjective judgment."

QUESTION: Was the decision to use this cover a defensible one? Did *Time* respond appropriately?

WHO: Gaines, the managing editor, made the decision to use the photograph, after Mahurin, the artist, made the decisions on how to make the image more compelling. They are the moral agents, the decision-makers in this case. They are also stakeholders, because their reputations — and their magazine's — are affected by their decisions. Others affected clearly include Simpson and the families of the victim, as well as the African-American community, potential jurists and even the entire judicial system. You may be able to think of others.

WHY: The principles involved here include a journalist's overriding responsibility to the truth — to be accurate and, as the SPJ code of ethics puts it, "honest, fair and courageous in gathering, reporting and interpreting information."

Certainly, there was a controversial amount of "interpretation" in developing this image. But should any news photo, in particular a police mug shot, be manipulated? Should journalists' decisions be guided by racial or other sensitivities of their audiences? Does the fact that the image was manipulated diminish the argument some journalists make that one should "tell the story and run" and not be cowed by the possible consequences?

HOW: *Time* clearly did not go casually into the decision to alter this cover the way it did. The managing editor's explanation in the July 4, 1994, issue explains the reasoning. But not many people agreed with what was done. Most photojournalists, in particular, argue that news photographs must be totally authentic. Manipulation alters the truth of what happened.

And yet, news images continue to be changed. In March 2005, the National Press Photographers Association took *Time*'s competitor *Newsweek* to task for publishing a cover picture of a smiling Martha Stewart, her head perched on a model's body. "NPPA finds it a total breach of ethics and completely misleading to the public," said Bob Gould, then-president of the organization. Rich Beckman, head of the School of Journalism and Mass Communication's visual communication program at the University of North Carolina in Chapel Hill, went on to list several other bad examples of photo manipulation, all of them in the decade since the flare-up over the Simpson cover:

"We've had the head of former Texas Governor Ann Richards placed on the body of a model sitting astride a motorcycle on the cover of *Texas Monthly* in July 1992, Oprah Winfrey's head placed on Ann Margaret's body on the cover of the August 26, 1989 issue of *TV Guide*, and in July 2003, *Redbook* published a cover photo of actress Julia Roberts that *USA Today* revealed to be a composite created by sticking the head of a year-old photograph of Roberts atop the body from a four-year-old photograph of her."

Said Beckman, "I wonder how many heads have to be attached [to other people's bodies] before the industry learns its lesson?"

CASE STUDY: Using the "Holocaust" Metaphor

WHAT: People for the Ethical Treatment of Animals, or PETA, is a nonprofit animal rights organization known for its controversial approach to communications and public relations. In 2003, PETA launched a new campaign, named "Holocaust on Your Plate," that compares the slaughter of animals for human use to the murder of 6 million Jews in WWII. The campaign centers around the power of emotion, and Lisa Lange, the vice president of PETA communications, stated that "The idea for the effort came from the late Nobel Prize-winning author Isaac Bashevis Singer, who wrote: 'In relation to them [animals], all people are Nazis; for them it is an eternal Treblinka' — a death camp in Poland" (CNN, 2003). A Jewish PETA member funded the campaign, but this has not lessened the backlash from the Jewish community toward the set of images.

"Holocaust on Your Plate" juxtaposes 60-square-foot visual displays of animals in slaughterhouses with scenes of Nazi concentration camps. Lange, quoted above, explains that the campaign "Is shocking, startling, and very hard to look at. We're attacking the mind-set that condones the slaughter of animals" (CNN, 2003). In 2003, the controversial set of images was released at an exhibit in San Diego, California, and a few months later, a more graphic version was released in Berlin, Germany. The Central Council of Jews in Germany sued PETA in 2004 for the campaign, and in 2009, the German Supreme Court banned the images from the country. In November 2012, the European Court of Human Rights in Strasbourg voted to uphold the previous Supreme Court ruling, which had banned the campaign.

Germany's PETA group appealed the European Court's vote to uphold the court ruling, fighting for their right to display their campaign based on the fundamental principles of free speech. The United States Anti-Defamation League and several other American human rights groups continue to condemn the campaign as well.

QUESTION: Is "Holocaust on Your Plate" ethically wrong or a truthful comparison?

WHO: Ingrid Newkirk, the CEO of PETA, ultimately made the decision to release the controversial campaign, and did not address the heated, angry emotions that arose surrounding the images for nearly two years after the campaign's release in 2003. With her decision to run the PR Campaign, her reputation, as well as the reputation of PETA, is at risk of being negatively affected.

Abraham Foxman, the U.S. Anti-Defamation League national director and a Holocaust survivor, is one of many members of the American Jewish community who were highly offended by PETA's campaign.

The Central Council of Jews in Germany represents another sector of the international Jewish community that took great offense to the campaign, suing PETA in 2004 with the support of several human rights groups.

Germany's Supreme Court became involved in the case in 2009, banning the campaign from the country, and the European Court of Human Rights' decision in 2012 to uphold the ruling is still being fought by PETA.

Consumers of media messages, both in the United States and Germany, also play a role in the case, as their perception of "Holocaust on your Plate" images greatly affect their view toward PETA and the organization's main goals. As consumers, the decision on how the case is handled will be a deciding factor on whether or not to support the organization.

WHY: A public relations representative for PETA, alongside the CEO of the company, justified the campaign by describing it on CNN as "The very same mind-set that made the Holocaust possible — that we can do anything we want to those we decide are 'different or inferior' — is what allows us to commit atrocities against animals every single day." PETA maintains that it is making its argument based upon principles of truth. PETA essentially claims that its campaign, although provocative, uses a comparison relating the murder of Jews and animals in a truthful and justified manner.

When examined under a deontological lens, it is arguable that PETA's PR campaign has done nothing wrong — protected under freedom of speech, PETA's communications team and CEO claim their campaign is legal and ethically sound, since it is rooted in fact and historical data, both from the Holocaust and slaughterhouse records. PETA argues that the comparison between the murder of Jews and animals is justified, due to the inherent and quantifiable nature of the slaughtering of innocent lives. However, when considering the case by applying the principles of deontology, the answer could also be argued in simpler, contrasting terms: the mass murder of millions of humans cannot, and *should* not be compared to a chicken or pig, and is inherently wrong.

This case can also be considered from a teleological perspective, placing the argument on a different plane for ethical discussion. There are two main outcomes that may arise from this case: 1) PETA's campaign spreads its pathos-driven message on animal rights successfully, limiting the number of animals consumed by humans, or 2) The campaign angers audiences to a degree that PETA loses the respect and trust that is needed for any form of audience support to ensue. Thus far in the case, the second consequence seems more likely, as the overly emotional, insensitive campaign has not motivated people, but for the most part driven them away.

Germany's High Court stated in 2009 that "Holocaust on a Plate" made "The fate of the victims of the Holocaust appear banal and trivial." The consequences of conveying human suffering to a human audience, whether or not they are rooted in truth, may cause more harm than overall good.

HOW: While PETA's claims may be justified, and the comparison between the murder of humans and animals deemed quantifiable, the harm caused by the campaign overrides the intended message of the PR plan, and should not be used. A mix of legal questioning, high emotional ties, and extremely poor taste make this an ethical case of high stakes and varied opinions, however a decision remains clear: PETA's "Holocaust on a Plate" is ethically wrong. The mass-murder of millions in a catastrophic historical event should not be utilized as a communication tool to gain support for one's organization. The comparison, while arguably similar in quantifiable terms, is disgustingly insensitive and takes advantage of others suffering to make a point.

PETA should utilize a different strategy to convey their message. The CEO of PETA will receive better press, and the overall reputation of the already controversial organization will improve. Stated backlash from numerous human rights groups and the Anti-Defamation League, as well the surely unstated unease of many audience sectors, is not worth a strong emotional response that could drive audience support of PETA.

DECISION: The "Holocaust on a Plate" PR campaign is ethically wrong: a mass-murder of millions should not be utilized as a communication tool to gain support for one's organization. It should not be used to convey PETA's message, no matter how strong the emotional argument.

— by Jill Hamilton, University of Denver

OTHER QUESTIONS: This case applies primarily to strategic communication decisions made by PETA. But it also can be analyzed from the point of view of journalists reporting on the campaign. What are the potential pitfalls of coverage? How do reporters avoid taking sides? Or should they even try?

WHAT THE CODES SAY: Diversity

Diverse faces and voices should be woven into the everyday fabric of the newspaper, but, unless relevant, we don't identify someone's race or ethnicity in a story.

This is particularly important in coverage of crime. We will report suspect descriptions when the information is detailed enough to be useful to people who want to protect themselves or help police find the suspect. We will avoid descriptions that give only the person's race and gender. Describing a suspect as an Asian male in his teens is not enough to distinguish him from plenty of other people in this town. But it may be enough when you can also report height, weight and a clothing description. When in doubt, consult with the editor or managing editor.

Lincoln Journal Star, Nebraska

The race of a speaker in a debate over lunch prices probably is not relevant. The race of a speaker in a debate over busing might be. Similarly, race makes no difference most of the time when neighbors protest a smelly sewer plant — but it's a major element if a black group thinks an all-white city commission ignored its protests because of racism.

Daily Press, Newport News, Virginia

Women and men should not be treated differently. Physical description and familial connections of a woman are appropriate only if a man would be described comparably in similar circumstance. We generally avoid terms that specific gender: e.g., police officer rather than policeman, although such uses as actor/actress and waiter/waitress are acceptable. Phrases that suggest there is something unusual about the gender of someone holding a job (woman lawyer, male nurse) should be avoided. When referring to members of a group, a construction correctly using THEIR is generally preferable to one requiring HIS or HER.

Detroit Free Press

It is our job to reflect the community. Each day's newspaper creates a snapshot of the Tampa Bay area. The snapshot shouldn't overlook minority members. Nor, in an attempt to feature aspects of race, ethnicity or religion should we overstate the differences among us, while ignoring our common ground.

We must not lose the nuances of individuality by casting a community through a high-contrast filter.

Diverse voice should be woven into the everyday fabric of the newspaper.

Tampa Bay Tribune

Use care when identifying transgendered people and use the pronoun that suits the gender they now claim as their identity. For example, a man who dresses as a woman but who has not had a sex-change operation still may prefer to be called a woman. In that instance, we would use the pronouns "she" or "her."

San Antonio Express-News

We do not identify race or ethnic background unless the information is relevant. It may be so:

- In stories involving politics, social action, social conditions, achievement and other matters where race can be a distinguishing factor.
- Where usage has sanctioned the description: black leader, Irish tenor, Polish wedding.
- In reporting an incident that cannot be satisfactorily explained without reference to race. However, the mere fact that an incident involves people of different races does not, of itself, mean that racial tags should be used. And when racial identification is used, the races of all involved should be mentioned.

We do not mention a person's race in describing criminal suspects or fugitives unless the rest of the description is detailed enough to be meaningful. Sketchy descriptions are often meaningless and may apply to large numbers of innocent people.

The Roanoke Times, Virginia

The race of a person in the news won't be reported unless it is clearly relevant to the story or is part of a detailed physical description. If a strong case cannot be made for mentioning race, it should be omitted.

Racially and ethnically derogatory terms are to be treated as obscenities; such a term should be spelled as an initial followed by hyphens, and be used only in quoted material, when it is essential to a story, and with approval of a managing editor.

Detroit Free Press

Reuters recognizes, values and encourages a diverse employment mix. In addition to gender and ethnic origin, the company considers a wide range of backgrounds in terms of experience and knowledge as part of its recruitment and employee development policies. While politics has no place in our newsrooms, diversity does. We welcome the varying perspectives, insights and considerations that diversity of gender, ethnicity, religious, sexual orientation, upbringing, age, marital or parental status, customs and culture bring to the debate about the news we gather. Diversity enriches what we do and there is a place for everyone in the discussion and the exchange of ideas that lead to the best journalism.

Reuters Handbook of Journalism

CHAPTER 9:

Conflicts of Interest

The success of a free press is reflected in the ability of the journalist to honor a primary loyalty to the public. Journalistic principles of truth-telling and independence work together to honor that loyalty. To seek truth and report it as fully as possible, journalists must be independent.

It's important that those who regularly interact with journalists — public relations professionals, public information officials, campaign spokespersons, even advertisers — understand this important component of the journalism culture. It's not that journalists are snobs (though some of them may show that tendency), but that they need to try to remain as impartial as possible.

Journalists must remain free of associations and activities that may compromise their integrity or damage their own or their organization's credibility. (Don't forget: Credibility is what others think of us; ethics is what kind of people we actually are. One is image, the other substance.) Journalists must seek out competing perspectives without being unduly influenced by those who would use their power or position counter to the public interest.

Conflicts of interest occur when individuals face competing loyalties to a source or to their own self-interest, or to their organization's economic needs as opposed to the information needs of the public.

Journalism carries a terrific responsibility in our society. No other profession does what journalism does. No other individuals have the primary and constitutionally protected role of regularly informing and educating the public in a meaningful way on

> It's important that those who regularly interact with journalists — public relations professionals, public information officials, campaign spokespersons, even advertisers — understand this important component of the journalism culture.

significant issues. To abdicate that responsibility, to put awards or friends or self-interest or economic gain ahead of public benefit is unacceptable and unethical.

Editors and reporters in small towns face particularly difficult challenges because of the unique nature of their personal and professional loyalties. They are far more likely than their metropolitan colleagues to be tugged by ties of friendship with sources, commitments to local institutions, and the simple fact that they come face to face with their readers on a daily basis. In rural communities, there tends to be a vacuum in leadership, which often impels communities to draft all competent and willing citizens — including journalists. And the readers have a proprietary interest in the newspaper (not legal, but social). In this setting the journalist may have a responsibility to be a part of the community and may behave in ways that would be a conflict of interest in a larger community.

The cases in this section, while not reflecting the full range of potential conflict-of-interest issues, raise essential questions about obligations and competing loyalties. The accompanying excerpts from codes of ethics provide specific guidelines various news organizations use to guard against conflicts and to ensure journalistic independence. More than half of all the sections in the news media codes reviewed for this project were devoted to conflicts of interest, and we offer a generous sampling of that soul-searching.

Conflicts of Interest: Checklist

Because of the enormous responsibility journalists have to the public, they must be aware of any situations that create a real or perceived conflict of interest. Individual journalists must weigh their obligations against the impact of:

- ☐ involvement in particular activities.
- ☐ affiliation with causes or organizations.
- ☐ acceptance of favors or preferential treatment.
- ☐ financial investments.
- ☐ outside employment.
- ☐ family and friendships.

Newspapers and broadcasters play a dual role in a community, as journalists and as corporate citizens. While these roles are not mutually exclusive, media leaders must guard with vigilance their organizations' stewardship role in society. They also must ensure that their primary obligation to the public is not eroded by other legitimate goals, such as:

- a quest for economic gain.
- the interest of being a good corporate citizen.
- the concern for their own employees.
- the need to be competitive in the marketplace.

In the end, individual journalists would do well to ask themselves:

- Am I being independent?
- Could my action harm my integrity or my organization's integrity?
- Is the mere appearance of a conflict enough to diminish my credibility?
- Am I willing to public disclose any potential conflicts?

Indifference vs. impartiality

As journalists, we know better than to get involved in a story we are covering. But what does that mean, exactly?

Some reporters will say not getting involved means you should always be totally detached — an observer, never a participant.

Yes, reporters should be impartial. They shouldn't take sides. They should avoid even the appearance of conflict of interest.

Yet there's a difference between impartiality and refusing to get involved.

Journalists faced that question in their coverage of Hurricane Katrina in August 2005. In the end, many reporters found themselves siding with the victims.

There's nothing wrong with that. In fact, it's preferable to stony detachment. I'm in favor of showing some humanity, and opposed to getting in the way of those whose real job is to give help.

Let me qualify that. A certain amount of badgering is justifiable and necessary. If aid officials are going to have press conferences to tell us their side of things — and they should; we'd insist on it if they didn't — part of their obligation is to be accountable to their critics.

The media are a conduit for those criticisms. In serving as the public's representative, asking the tough questions, reporters should be impartial. But asking those questions also makes them a part of the story. Involvement is unavoidable. And it's not taking sides to ask the questions that need to be answered.

Getting involved, like most ethical questions, is a matter of degree.

The easiest ethical decision is to avoid covering an organization or an activity in which you — or a spouse, significant other or close friend — have a personal stake or are a regular participant.

But what if it's your home town that's being destroyed? Certainly, you have a personal stake in that story.

And what if you are covering a developing story and find yourself in a position to prevent injury or death?

Doesn't your mere presence as a chronicler of the event change the event itself? Would the story be different if you weren't there — and isn't that a kind of involvement?

Hurricane Katrina was a story in which many reporters decided to get involved. Maybe they couldn't help themselves.

They broke down and cried on the air. They asked angry questions, showing more than the expected journalistic aggressiveness, going beyond assertiveness to emotional anger. And sometimes they did more.

NBC's Kerry Sanders gave food to a very ill 91-year-old man on the floor of the triage center at New Orleans International Airport. Sanders slept at the airport and the next morning reported that people near him had died during the night.

Chris Merrifield, a promotions producer for WWL-TV in New Orleans, waded into chest-deep water to pull a driver through the window of his sinking car.

The station's assistant news director, Chris Slaughter, told *USA Today*: "The kid just reacted. We're proud of what he did. I would hope all of our people would do something like that rather than let someone drown."

So where, exactly, is it written that

reporters should not get involved? It may be one of those things we believe to be so obvious that it doesn't need to be spelled out.

It's not specific in the [1996] SPJ code of ethics, although some code language comes close:

"Professional integrity is the cornerstone of a journalist's credibility."

"Distinguish between advocacy and news reporting."

"Journalists should be free of obligation to any interest other than the public's right to know."

"Avoid conflicts of interest, real or perceived."

"Remain free of associations and activities that may compromise integrity or damage credibility."

But the code of ethics also reminds us to "minimize harm.... Ethical journalists treat sources, subjects and colleagues as human beings deserving of respect."

Sometimes showing that respect comes in the gathering of news, and sometimes it may involve minimizing the harm in the actual unfolding of the news — right there, on the spot.

The code also says, "Show compassion for those who may be affected adversely by news coverage." That could be expanded to say "affected adversely by events."

The question of appropriate involvement, if involvement is ever appropriate, is another of those fine-line ethical issues.

It's more modest and thus nobler to help quietly and behind the scenes than to do it with cameras rolling.

But all of what happened in the Katrina disaster, in New Orleans and elsewhere, was an important part of this huge and historic story, including the media's anger and compassion.

— by Fred Brown, SPJ Ethics Committee, originally published in Quill in 2006

CASES: Conflicts of Interest

CASE STUDY: The Embedded Reporter

WHAT: When the United States ousted the Iraqi army from Kuwait in 1991, it kept reporters far from the front lines of the conflict. By the time the U.S. invaded Iraq in 2003, it was persuaded to allow reporters to be "embedded" with military units. But there were rules: reporters could not drive their own vehicles, military commanders could impose temporary restrictions on electronic transmissions back home, a military public affairs escort might be assigned, datelines would have to follow ground rules of local commanders, bright lights generally would be barred during night missions, embargoes might be imposed, specific troop numbers could not be disclosed, the names of individual soldiers could be released only with their consent. And pictures of wounded or dead soldiers were to be withheld for 72 hours or until the dead soldier's family has been formally notified. In all, the policy and list of rules regarding embedded reporters runs to 13 pages.

Was it possible, within those rules, to offer a journalistically accurate description of a military unit's activities? Given the sometimes extreme nature of the battlefield environment can one retain a detached nature?

QUESTION: Do you surrender your journalistic independence by agreeing to be embedded into a military unit? And therefore should you refuse the opportunity?

WHO: Bill Nemitz, a columnist at the *Portland Press Herald/Maine Sunday Telegram*, returned to his roots as a reporter, going on three tours of duty as an embedded reporter working alongside Maine National Guard Units. Nemitz says it was his idea, approved by his managing editor, Eric Conrad, and Editor Jeannine Guttman, who agreed he should go.

Being an embedded reporter also meant a heightened contact with a stakeholder group other than readers and editors, namely the troops themselves. Nemitz said he began to notice he would find very few soldiers to talk to at the time each day when his stories were posted to the *Press Herald* Web site because, he discovered, they were off at computers reading what he'd written. And some troops became upset that his stories "blew their cover" — not their operational cover, but the reassuring e-mails some troops were sending their families describing conditions in Iraq. Nemitz's reporting sometimes painted a more dangerous picture. Nemitz says he had no choice but to be accurate for his readers' sake. But he also sent a message to the troops by getting their commander to go on the record with a quote saying he always told it like it was to his family.

Only once, in describing a formation used by the troops, did he get after-the-fact criticism from an officer who believed the formation Nemitz reported about was a matter of "operational security" off-limits to reporting. Nemitz said after that he was more conscious of what might constitute "operational security," though he believed sometimes the military's rules about such things "imply the enemy is oblivious."

WHY: For Nemitz, embedding was going to be the best way to capture the local angle of the war story: Maine was facing the largest call-up of its National Guard troops since World War II in support of the Iraq invasion. As Nemitz put it, "If we didn't cover it, they would disappear not to be seen or heard until the deployment was over, or unless something really bad happened."

HOW: Though embedding under the Department of Defense system challenges journalists with the kind of rules normally an anathema to independent reporting, Nemitz says he was always driven by the fact that, even in the confines of the embedded environment, the story was worth doing, worth telling. He says on his three trips, he felt he had unfettered access to anyone in the unit he was covering. He found the unit commander willing to help steer him to the right people to talk to and never felt the commander acted as a gatekeeper.

In one instance he was refused permission to interview a wounded soldier, but that refusal came from an officer of another unit the soldier was with. It affirmed a truth Nemitz said he found on his three visits to Iraq: "Rules are what people who decide them say they are."

"Source cultivation and maintenance," he says, was the key, and, in that way, made reporting as an embedded reporter with military units no different than other reporting assignments. Nemitz added, "If I felt I was being prevented from what I thought was an accurate portrayal I would have gone home."

— *by Irwin Gratz, Maine Public Radio*

CASE STUDY: Reigning on the Parade

WHAT: Frank Whelan, a features writer who also wrote a history column for the Allentown, Pennsylvania, *Morning Call*, took part in a gay rights parade in June 2006 and stirred up a classic ethical dilemma. The situation raises any number of questions about what is and isn't a conflict of interest. Whelan, 56, and his partner of 25 years, Bob Wittman, were the co-grand marshals of a gay pride parade. His newspaper prohibits employees from taking part in "public demonstrations in favor of or opposed to a cause." His editors say Whelan didn't seek their permission to participate in the event. A subsidiary publication co-sponsored the parade, but *Call* editors say they didn't know of Whelan's involvement until they saw a press release. Two days before the parade, they warned him that his role would be a conflict, a breach of the code, and that there would be "consequences" if he participated. Whelan said their roles as grand marshals were a celebration of his and Wittman's long-term relationship.

QUESTION: What should those "consequences" be for Frank Whelan?

WHO: Consider the decision-maker and the parties affected by that person's decision. Put yourself in the position of the editor who must decide how — or whether — to punish Whelan. As for those affected, the major stakeholder obviously is Whelan. Others include his partner, the parade organizers, proponents and opponents of gay rights. The newspaper's reputation is hugely at stake. And of course its readers have a stake in this situation, too, but not nearly as great as the newspaper's.

WHY: The first four principles of the "Act Independently" section of the SPJ code of ethics seem particularly applicable here. It's unprofessional, and unethical, to engage in activities that "may compromise integrity or damage credibility." But there are other questions that should be asked. Is "gay pride" a political cause? Was the parade a demonstration or merely a celebration, intended to advocate or merely to entertain? The newspaper notes that a Web site promoting the parade said naming Whelan and his partner grand marshals "supports the need for Marriage Equality."

> Isn't it better to acknowledge — and disclose — one's interests than to deny them?

A reporter shouldn't be an active advocate for a particular point of view about a subject he's covering. But how far does that go? If a political reporter can cheer for the hometown team, should a sports reporter be able to back a political candidate? How many rights must journalists give up when they accept the idea that they should be detached observers? Would we feel differently about this if it had been an anti-abortion parade? What about an Italian-American reporter marching in a Columbus Day parade?

Isn't it better to acknowledge — and disclose — one's interests than to deny them? Avoiding membership or participation doesn't guarantee objectivity. Some reporters who make a great show in the newsroom of avoiding any ties to anything can be among the most biased in their reporting.

HOW: In this case, you'd want to be fair to a long-time employee — minimizing harm, in other words. Is a suspension in order? Paid or unpaid? A change in assignment, perhaps? Or would that be too harsh? The important thing is to ask the right questions (and by no means is this an exhaustive list), to satisfy yourself that your solution is the best outcome — and to be able to explain it. Put it in writing, to be sure it makes sense.

Whelan, upset by his employer's reaction, took two days off after which the paper told him it would consider that an unpaid suspension. "I basically walked out the door," he said in January 2009, even though he was asked to return after the two days.

Whelan filed three lawsuits: sexual discrimination in violation of a city ordinance, age discrimination and defamation. All three claims were settled out of court, he said. The

Morning Call's owners, the Tribune Co., agreed to pay two years of severance to Whelan and two years of medical benefits for him and his partner, he said.

Morning Call editor Ardith Hilliard, who was editor during the controversy, could not be reached for comment.

—*by Fred Brown and Nerissa Young, SPJ Ethics Committee*

CASE STUDY: Controversy over a Concert

WHAT: Three former members of the Eagles rock band came to Denver during the 2004 election campaign to raise money for a U.S. Senate candidate, Democrat Ken Salazar. John Temple, editor and publisher of the *Rocky Mountain News*, advised his reporters not to go to the fundraising concerts. In a memo to the staff, Temple said:

"Since our longstanding policy precludes all newsroom employees from making political donations, none of us will be able to attend these concerts, or any others that occur this political season. The obvious exceptions are reporters, columnists and photographers covering the concerts, both as entertainment events and political stories."

Some reporters and editors interpreted the directive as implying that their bosses didn't trust them. Some said the only issue should be whether their work is fair and accurate, not about what they do in their off time. At staff meetings requested by the Denver Newspaper Guild, reporters asked all manner of questions, Temple said. Such as: What if my spouse goes, or gives a donation? What if I never cover politics or have a byline in the paper? Why can't we buy tickets to this concert when we can go to concerts by other artists who may then use the money for political donations?

Temple, writing about the situation in two different columns, said a newspaper's first obligation is to its readers. It should avoid anything that might compromise — or appear to comprise — its impartiality and integrity.

QUESTION: Is it fair to ask newspaper staffers — or employees at other news media, for that matter — not to attend events that may have a political purpose? Are the rules different for different jobs at the news outlet?

WHO: In this case, the decision was made by the top executive at the *Rocky Mountain News*. His decision clearly affected his employees, and it was intended to look out for the interests of the newspaper's readers. In Temple's eyes, the public had a major stake in this decision. Also affected, but perhaps not so much, were the entertainers, the Democratic (and Republican) parties and candidate Ken Salazar.

WHY: One of a journalist's biggest challenges is how to put aside personal preferences and prejudices in order to deliver impartial, fair information. Elections raise ethical questions for reporters, and the answer to those ethical questions is usually inflexible: Avoid any display of partisanship, including donating money to candidates, even indirectly. Some media companies discourage employees from participating in partisan politics in any way; some individuals have gone so far as to declare publicly that they do not vote, to avoid even the slightest appearance of bias. That may be going too far, but journalists do give up some of their constitutional rights if they want to practice their profession ethically. Ironically, this is a profession protected by the same First Amendment that grants the right to any citizen to support, by word, deed or cash, the people they'd like to see elected.

HOW: Temple's decision wasn't well-received by many in his staff. Reporters are well aware that some newspaper owners and publishers contribute to political campaigns. Editorial pages endorse candidates. Some members of the public, too, argued that Temple was too concerned with appearances. "I suspect that if and when you and your management put as much thought and effort into changing the reality of political bias on your staff as you do worrying about the image which your staff projects, you won't have to be concerned about either the reality or the image," one reader wrote.

What do you think are appropriate limits — if any — on a journalist's political involvement? Does it differ from job to job? What sort of a policy would you set for your staff if you were managing a media outlet — or yourself, if you were a blog with a staff of one?

CASE STUDY: Writing Checks, Getting Exclusives

WHAT: It's called "checkbook journalism," and it's something serious journalists say is wrong. You shouldn't have to pay your sources for giving you information. And yet sometimes the lines are blurred. Is it legitimate, for example, to buy a murder victim's diary from her family, a diary that might provide clues about whether her former boyfriend stalked and killed her? What about the fairly routine business of flying talk-show guests to New York City so they can appear on your broadcast? When does a journalist cross the line between legitimate newsgathering expenses and, as the SPJ Code of Ethics puts it, "bidding for news"?

On more than one occasion in late 2009 and early 2010, the SPJ Ethics Committee criticized television networks for what the committee felt were clear instances of "checkbook journalism." The circumstances are different, and there's a big difference in the amounts of money involved, but two cases in particular afforded opportunities for a spirited discussion on both a journalistic and humanitarian perspective. We'll look at both cases in this and in the following case study.

The first is the case of David Goldman. Goldman is a New Jersey man whose Brazilian wife, Bruna Bianchi Goldman, took their 4-year-old son, Sean, to Brazil in June 2004 for what was supposed to be a vacation with her family. They never returned. Mrs. Goldman divorced her American husband — though they were still legally married under U.S. law — married a Brazilian lawyer but later died, giving birth, in August 2008. After her death, her family and Brazilian husband took steps to adopt Sean, and

David Goldman stepped up his efforts to win custody of his son. The international custody battle was fought up to the highest levels of both U.S. and Brazilian courts. Finally, in late December 2009, the chief justice of the Brazilian supreme court ruled that Sean should be returned to his biological father, David, by the morning of December 24. That evening, Christmas Eve 2009, NBC News brought the boy and his father to the United States on a chartered Gulfstream jet. Reporter Jeff Rossen and a cameraman were with them on the plane. They did interviews during the flight, and after the plane landed in Orlando, where father and son spent Christmas at Disney World. They then flew to New York, where "Today" show host Meredith Vieira had an exclusive interview with David on December 27, the Monday after the holiday.

From the beginning, NBC had followed this story closely. David Goldman first appeared on NBC's "Dateline" in January 2009. And, while there was widespread interest in what happened to Goldman and his son — there is still a Bring Sean Home Foundation that seeks to resolve "international abductions" — NBC seemed to have a closer relationship to the father than any other news outlet. In fact, NBC said David Goldman had appeared on "Today" 17 times in the year since the story first aired on "Dateline." Not that there's anything wrong with that; any medium in a competitive environment justifiably seeks an edge. And on balance, what NBC did in flying Sean and his father back to the U.S. on Christmas Eve seemed to have much more popular support than criticism. Several online comments on various sites called it "a Christmas miracle." SPJ's Ethics Committee, though, was "appalled"; Chairman Andy Schotz, in a statement, said "The public could rightly assume that NBC News bought exclusive interviews and images, as well as the family's loyalty, with an extravagant gift."

QUESTION: Under what circumstances, if any, should a news organization provide financial assistance to a news source?

WHO: The decision-makers in this case are the people in NBC management who decided to invest tens of thousands of dollars in this story — especially when it came down to chartering the private jet that brought Sean and his father from Rio de Janeiro to the United States. Among the stakeholders in that decision, no one is more affected than the father and son. If the network hadn't flown them out, they might have been stranded in Brazil — or at the very least hounded by international media at their departure from and arrival at commercial airport terminals, and possibly even during the long flight itself.

The family Sean left behind in Brazil also was deeply affected by NBC's decision. The child they had raised for five years had been taken from them by the law and spirited away by a television network. "My heart is empty and broken because our love is missing," said Sean's maternal grandmother, Silvana Bianchi. She called the Brazilian court's custody ruling "a heinous crime." In April 2010 she flew from Brazil to New Jersey to try to see Sean, but a judge denied her immediate access. Maybe later, said David Goldman, but not yet.

Clearly, NBC's reputation is also at stake in this decision. Some saw the trip as a noble humanitarian gesture, an unusual show of empathy from what often are perceived as the

cold-hearted media. From that perspective, the decision greatly helped the network's image. Yet others, no doubt a smaller and less vocal number, saw it as a bad example of callous exploitation. NBC's competitors also were affected; they were kept at arm's length from the drama by NBC's exclusivity agreement. Others with perhaps a lesser stake in the network's action include the Bring Sean Home Foundation and lawmakers such as U.S. Rep. Chris Smith, R-N.J., who sponsored the International Child Abduction Prevention Act of 2009. You may be able to think of others who could be considered stakeholders in this decision.

WHY: In this case, the network's expressed desire to minimize harm, or perhaps to be proactively compassionate toward the Goldmans, conflicts with the journalistic ideals of independence and impartiality. Here are pertinent excerpts from the news release SPJ issued about the situation — a statement that got more coverage, on line and in print, than many SPJ releases get, suggesting a broad public interest in the case:

"By making itself part of a breaking news story on which it was reporting — apparently to cash in on the exclusivity assured by its expensive gesture — NBC jeopardized its journalistic independence and credibility in its initial and subsequent reports. In effect, the network branded the story as its own, creating a corporate and promotional interest in the way the story unfolds. NBC's ability to report the story fairly has been compromised by its financial involvement....

"The news media's duty is to report news, not help to create it. The race to be first should not involve buying — directly or indirectly — interviews, an unseemly practice that raises questions of neutrality, integrity and credibility. 'Mixing financial and promotional motives with an impartial search for truth stains honest, ethical reporting,' [ethics committee chairman Andy] Schotz said. 'Checkbook journalism has no place in the news business.' "

Schotz and SPJ President Kevin Smith called on NBC to explain its decision, "as well as the terms of any deal it made with the Goldman family." And, they added, the network is "ethically bound" to disclose its "active role in the story in each of its future reports on the Goldmans." An NBC spokeswoman did respond by e-mail after the news release, primarily to ask if SPJ would be using remarks made by Goldman's attorney or making similar criticisms of other networks. SPJ also linked to a story about a more formal network response on a Web site called Multichannel News. One of the points NBC made is that the chartered jet already was scheduled to return network staffers from Brazil; the Goldmans merely were invited along. "NBC News has not and will not pay for an interview," the network's statement said.

Some ethics committee members felt SPJ's public criticism should have been held until NBC had had a chance to tell its side of the story. At least one ethics committee member wrote on the ethics blog that he felt it was unfair, and he called the statement "an unwarranted and humiliating pillory of NBC." But other committee members — in a clear example of how different, well-intentioned people can reach different conclusions when presented with the same situation — felt it was important not to wait too long, and NBC already had been given two or three days to respond to a request for a statement.

The main principle at issue here is impartiality. The exchange of money, favors or anything of value inevitably affects the tenor of the news-source relationship. Most journalists understand that they shouldn't accept anything of value from a source; most employers' codes of ethics make that quite clear. Is it, then, equally as wrong for a source to accept anything of value from a journalist? One argument against journalists paying people is that they then might feel compelled to say what they think the journalists want to hear.

Of course, that can happen in the absence of payment, too — merely the opportunity to appear on national television might make some people eager to please. The big three morning shows — and the afternoon shows, too — routinely fly people to New York, feed them, and put them in nice hotels so that they can appear in a broadcast. It's a form of checkbook journalism, even though it's less expensive than a private chartered jet flight from Rio to Orlando. None of the main players in this scenario was in any way destitute. Goldman had had a successful career as a model. If he could not have paid to charter a jet, his case had attracted enough notoriety that some other organization might have donated a corporate aircraft for the flight.

There's also a question of favoritism to consider here. Was NBC being unfair to the family Sean had lived with for five years? Do they matter less because they're Brazilian and not American? You might also want to consider whether the critics of this action, including SPJ, were too quick in their judgment. It probably wasn't good public relations for SPJ, but journalists will argue that they shouldn't base their actions on what the public thinks. The long- and short-term consequences of that attitude certainly merit discussion.

HOW: Obviously, NBC decided that paying to transport a father and his son back to the United States on Christmas Eve was a legitimate, even compassionate thing to do. And it did mention, several times on air, that the flight was an NBC charter. SPJ, although it wasn't a stakeholder in the original decision, became part of the continuing story when it issued its widely circulated statement. Did both organizations achieve the outcomes they hoped for? What do you think?

CASE STUDY: Expensive Home Movies

WHAT: In August 2008, ABC paid $200,000 to the family of a dead Florida toddler for exclusive use of family photos and home videos. The apparent murder of Caylee Marie Anthony had attracted international media attention. Caylee disappeared in June 2008, two months shy of her third birthday. Her body was found six months later, buried near the family home. Caylee's mother, Casey Anthony, was indicted in October 2008 for first-degree murder, but continued to maintain her innocence. One reason for all of the interest in the case is that Casey from the beginning was reluctant to give critical information to authorities. Caylee wasn't reported missing until a month after she was last seen. On July 15, 2008, her grandmother, Cindy Anthony, reportedly called 911 when Casey would not tell her where Caylee had been.

In March 2010, during a pretrial hearing in Orlando, Casey Anthony's attorney revealed that ABC News had made the payment to Anthony's family seven months earlier. ABC, in a statement after the hearing, said the payment was for exclusive rights to "an extensive library of photos and home video for use by our broadcasts, platforms, affiliates and international partners. No use of the material was tied to any interview."

QUESTION: Should ABC have paid for this exclusive access?

WHO: ABC network officials had to approve this expenditure; they're the decision-makers, the moral agents. They are also among the people affected, the stakeholders, because their action drew criticism from journalism ethics watchdogs. The chief stakeholders, though, are the Anthony family. Competing media outlets also have an interest in this decision because of the exclusivity of the agreement; they won't have the same access that ABC has to these scenes from a childhood cut short.

WHY: The SPJ Ethics Committee, as it had in the previous NBC/Goldman case, condemned the payment as another bad example of "checkbook journalism." In this case, though, it was a direct cash payment, not providing an expensive service, as in the Goldman case. "Paying someone while covering them breaches basic journalistic ethics," said Andy Schotz, chairman of the committee. ABC spokeswoman Cathie Levine said the network wasn't paying for an interview, but for exclusive rights to certain materials, which is a common practice for broadcast news organizations. But she also acknowledged that "we should have disclosed it to our audience." In the future, she said, the network would make it a policy to disclose such payments as part of its reporting. Indeed, it could be argued that paying for photographs or other images is no different than paying for a freelance article, or a cell phone picture than an onlooker snapped of a spectacular explosion. But critics of the arrangement with the Anthony family would argue that the difference here is that there's an ongoing relationship with the source of the material — a news relationship that should be free of the influences that money brings. "The public," said the SPJ statement, "can legitimately question a news organization's credibility and doubt whether its reports are fair and accurate."

HOW: ABC defended its contract with the Anthonys and promised to make any similar arrangements in the future part of its future coverage. But apparently that was open to interpretation. ABC did not disclose the $200,000 payment during an interview with Casey Anthony's parents on "Good Morning America," because, said spokeswoman Levine, "we haven't licensed anything from either of them so there was nothing to disclose." She pointed out that there was a disclosure during a "20/20" interview with a former girlfriend of Joran van der Sloot, accused of murdering one woman and suspected in the disappearance of another several years ago. The difference, said Levine, is that "we licensed material from her [the former girlfriend].

There continue to be multiple examples of this questionable practice. In May 2009, ABC paid for plane tickets for Anthony Rakoczy of Pennsylvania to fly to Florida to pick up his daughter and then return home with her after a fake kidnapping attempt. Levine, the ABC spokeswoman, said reporters covered both legs of the trip and disclosed the donated air travel in both stories. Shortly after the Goldman flight from Brazil, CNN, ABC and the *New York Post* bought rights to an image taken by Jasper Schuringa aboard a flight from Amsterdam to Detroit during which a terrorist attempted to set off a bomb hidden in his underpants. Schuringa, a Dutch citizen who was hailed as a hero for overpowering the terrorist, also was criticized for attempting to profit through the sale of his cellphone photos. In June 2010, the *New York Post* published its best estimates of a couple of recent payments for interviews, including "at least $100,000" to Van der Sloot's mother for appearances on "Good Morning America" and "Nightline" and "about $340,000" paid by NBC's "Dateline" for an interview with the mother of the late Michael Jackson. Regardless of what one might think of the *Post*'s own standards, the tone of the report was critical, noting that network policies usually forbid paying for interviews. "One commentator called the no-pay policy TV's equivalent of the 55-mph speed limit," the *Post* said " — a rule no one really pays much attention to."

CASE STUDY: 'A Rude, Terrible Person

WHAT: After a confrontational exchange with President Donald Trump at a post-midterm-election news conference on November 7, 2018, Jim Acosta, CNN's White House reporter, was forced to surrender his "hard pass" press access to the White House. Press Secretary Sarah Sanders defended the revocation, using a disputed video to support her contention that Acosta pushed a young woman aide who was trying to get him to surrender a floor microphone.

While a few journalists felt Acosta overplayed his hand, others came to his defense, and CNN sued in federal court, winning a temporary judgment ordering the White House to restore Acosta's credentials and access. Acosta got his press pass back a little less than two weeks after it was taken from him, and CNN dropped its lawsuit. The White House said Acosta could continue to have access as long as he followed a new set of rules for press conferences, including limiting questions to one at a time.

QUESTION: Should Acosta have been less confrontational with the president? Did he violate the norms of journalistic decorum? Is there even such a thing as journalistic decorum?

WHO: Acosta is the one who made the decision to confront the president, but there's also a decision that can be looked at as a problem of strategic communication. Should the White House have confiscated the reporter's press pass?

Stakeholders: Acosta, obviously, because he couldn't do the job he was assigned to do as long as he was denied access to the White House. CNN also had a lot at stake, and the fact it filed a lawsuit is evidence of the network's concern. The entire White House press corps may have to decide if it wants to fight this precedent, and the new rules for news conferences as well. The White House's image is also deeply involved. The president's supporters may cheer at Sarah Sanders's statements and the denial of access; the president's detractors will see it as further evidence of Trump's autocratic personality. And the public, as consumers of news, has other sources to turn to, but it had been denied CNN's coverage, at least temporarily.

WHY: A journalist's responsibility to act independently is central to any discussion of this incident. Journalists should not be daunted by people in positions of power, including the president of the United States. But they should also treat sources with respect and try to avoid losing their temper.

The White House Correspondents Association and the Society of Professional Journalists were among a number of media organizations issuing statements in support of Acosta, CNN and the lawsuit.

Olivier Knox, president of the correspondents' association, issued a statement saying the WHCA "strongly supports CNN's goal of seeing their correspondent regain a US Secret Service security credential that the White House should not have taken away in the first place." Olivier called it a "disproportionate reaction." "The President of the United States," he added, "should not be in the business of arbitrarily picking the men and women who cover him."

SPJ said the president, who has a record of "constantly demeaning journalists and calling them the enemy of the American people ... now does another disservice by revoking Acosta's White House credentials....

"Politicians denying access to reporters as a way to control who covers them is a violation of the First Amendment and is detrimental to our society and those around the world. We strongly urge the White House to reinstate Acosta's credentials immediately."

But there were some who felt Acosta was out of line, including Al Tompkins and Kelly McBride at the Poynter Institute, who wrote:

> *Jim Acosta's encounter Wednesday at a White House press conference was less about asking questions and more about making statements. In doing so, the CNN White House reporter gave President Donald Trump room to critique Acosta's professionalism.*
>
> *In this time of difficult relations between the press and the White House, reporters who operate above reproach, while still challenging the power of the office, will build credibility.*
>
> *This is in no way a defense of Trump's suspension of Acosta's White House press credentials. Rather, it's a caution to not hand your critic the stick to beat you with. There's no doubt that Trump will continue sowing doubt among his followers about the press' ability to accurately document the administration. Had Acosta phrased his question in a more neutral tone, he likely would have had more information for his audience to digest.*
>
> *Acosta asked the president if Trump had demonized the caravan of Central Americans trekking toward the United States, ending his exchange by stating, "It is not an invasion."*
>
> *If Acosta had asked "What about that seems like an invasion?" he could have both sought an answer and avoided becoming bigger than the event he was covering.*

There also was controversy about the video the White House used to support barring Acosta. After Trump had tried to end Acosta's questioning, demanding that he "put down the mike," a White House staffer moved to take the microphone from the CNN correspondent.

At first Acosta resisted, saying "excuse me, ma'am," but he finally relinquished the microphone and sat down. The president then scolded him from the lectern. "CNN should be ashamed of itself having you working for them," Trump said. "You are a rude, terrible person. You shouldn't be working for CNN."

To support the administration's decision to revoke Acosta's press pass, Ms. Sanders showed a video of the encounter between the reporter and a young woman aide. "We will not tolerate the inappropriate behavior clearly documented in this video," she said. But several reports, relying on sources with expertise in video production, said the clip appeared to have been speeded up, and the result made Acosta's motions appear more violent.

Still, Poynter's McBride and Tompkins said, "Acosta should have handed over the microphone.

"That said, The White House accusation that Acosta manhandled the intern trying to retrieve the microphone is nonsense. It makes us wonder if the White House was looking for an opportunity to pick a fight."

Bob Woodward, famed Watergate reporter and author of many books about the White House through several administrations, was critical of CNN's lawsuit in support of Acosta. And several other journalism companies and organizations, including usually Trump-friendly Fox News, joined the lawsuit as friends of the court — until CNN dropped its court action.

Speaking at a financial conference in Naples, Florida, Woodward said some media figures "have become emotionally unhinged." The proper response to the Trump-driven chaos in Washington is better journalistic diligence, he said. "The remedy isn't suing the administration…. it's more serious reporting about what he's doing."

Woodward essentially supported the argument Poynter had made. He said CNN was falling into Trump's trap by suing him in federal court. "This is negative. Trump is sitting around saying, 'This is great,'" Woodward said.

Tompkins and McBride, the Poynter scholars, concluded: "President Trump deftly used the Acosta incident to play the victim of unfair press treatment. Journalists should not give more fuel to such accusations. Ask tough questions, avoid making statements or arguing during a press event and report the news, don't become the news."

DISCUSSION: Do you agree that Acosta was being too confrontational? Or do you think President Trump presents an unusual adversarial relationship with the press, one that requires a more assertive, even aggressive approach? And, for strategic communicators, what do you think of the White House's defense of its action? How would you have responded?

Mike Keefe, The Colorado Independent. Reprinted with permission.

CASE STUDY: Journalists on the Political Stage

WHAT: Two of the Fox News network's on-air personalities, Jeanine Pirro and the top-rated Sean Hannity, appeared on stage at a November 5, 2018, rally sponsored by the Donald J. Trump for President campaign in Cape Girardeau, Missouri. Hannity was there despite sending out a tweet earlier in the day that declared "I will not be on stage campaigning with the president."

Though apparently brief, the appearances by Hannity and Pirro weren't merely grin-and-waves. Hannity referred to the area set aside for the press with a joke — "By the way, all those people in the back are fake news" — and then, as the mocking cheers and boos faded, repeated a Trump campaign slogan: "Promises made, promises kept." Pirro, in her turn on stage, called Trump "the tip of the spear that goes out there every day and fights for us."

Questions: Is this appropriate behavior for employees of a news medium? If not, what consequences should they face? Does it make a difference if they are opinion journalists rather than reporters?

WHO: Hannity and Pirro made the decision to attend the Trump rally, and to participate in it. Now their employer, Fox News, is faced with a decision about what to do about it, if anything.

Stakeholders: Hannity and Pirro could face discipline, or at least disapproval. Fox has a reputation to uphold, as a source of both news and opinion. The president and his campaign also faced criticism — as well as approval, depending on whether it was coming from the political right or left. And Fox viewers have an interest in seeing how their preferred news source handles issues affecting its image.

WHY: Journalists, according to the principles of the SPJ Code of Ethics, should "act independently." That includes not taking sides in stories they're covering. Hannity and Pirro are in the opinion business, unlike others on Fox who are supposed to be reporters of news — "fair and balanced," to use an old Fox slogan. But the network nonetheless said that what the two opinion hosts did was inappropriate.

The day after the Missouri rally, which was the day of the 2018 midterm elections, the network issued a statement saying "Fox News does not condone talent participating in campaign events." The statement didn't identify Hannity and Pirro by name, referring only — as reported by *The New York Times*'s media columnist Jim Rutenberg — to "an unfortunate distraction" that had "been addressed." Rutenberg wrote that the statement was issued "after in-house complaints from anchors and reporters and a broader social media backlash."

It had been no secret that Fox was supportive of the president's policies. The cable news network was created as a counter to a perceived liberal bias of the mainstream news media, and its opinion-based shows, in particular, were well ensconced in the right of the political spectrum. Still, even the late Roger Ailes, Fox's founder and a former Republican media consultant, strove to maintain a distinction between the GOP and the journalism.

Rutenberg at the *Times* gave an example: When Hannity was invited to be the headliner at a Tea Party event in Cincinnati, Ohio, in 2010, Ailes "forced him to cancel, angry that he had even said yes to such a thing."

HOW: Their employers, without singling out Hannity and Pirro by name, said Fox News "does not condone" their employees ("talent") participating in a political event. It's not clear if there were further consequences for the two opinion hosts.

DISCUSSION: What should be the boundaries for journalists' involvement in politics? Is it OK to register with a political party? What about contributing to a campaign? Does it make a difference if it's a ballot issue or a candidate? Are there different rules for reporters who write about government and politics and, say, business or sports reporters? One would think it would be OK to vote; but some journalists even draw the line at that.

CASE STUDY: The Press Can Be Prickly

WHAT: This is an issue that arises from time to time, affecting journalists and the people who regularly deal with them. Those who seek to have good relationships with the professionals who gather and report the news are understandably interested in being seen in a good light. Sometimes that includes supporting, with donations of time, money or sponsorships, journalism membership organizations such as the Society of Professional Journalists or the Radio Television Digital News Association.

But journalists are a skeptical, even cynical, lot. There's an old, and rather mean-spirited, admonition in the news business that says: "If your mother says she loves you, check it out." Strategic communicators, on the other hand, strive to be of a more convivial nature, always looking for ways to maintain, protect or improve the images they are paid to burnish.

SPJ and RTDNA had for several years cooperated in putting together an annual Excellence in Journalism convention. At the 2018 Excellence in Journalism (EIJ) convention, one of the major events, a panel discussion, was supported by a generous contribution from the Charles Koch Foundation. The foundation is one of many stalls in the stable maintained by Robert and Charles Koch, billionaires widely known for their support of politically conservative causes.

Once this arrangement became widely known, about a month before the convention, there was no shortage of controversy. Some members of the governing bodies of the organizations argued that it would be wrong to accept money from any politically active organization, since journalists go to great lengths to maintain their impartiality. Others argued that to reject money from a family associated with conservative causes would only confirm right-wing criticism that the mainstream media will not even consider ideas that don't fit the media's liberal agenda.

One suggested solution was that only news-media organizations should be accepted as donors to journalistic endeavors. Others said that was too narrow and discriminatory a policy, that generosity should be graciously accepted from anyone who wants to support good journalism.

Question: What's the best policy for journalism organizations to follow in accepting donations from non-journalist organizations?

WHO: The decision makers are those who set policy for journalism organizations, their boards of directors and their executive directors and staff. Also, the organizations with money need to decide if they're willing to support conventions of sometimes prickly journalists.

Stakeholders: Those affected by their decisions are the members of those journalistic associations and journalists generally, as well as the donors who want to support the goals of those organizations (or perhaps, more cynically, simply want to get chummy with potentially adversarial journalists).

WHY: The major principles are journalistic independence and the role of institutions and corporate entities whose primary activity is outside the realm of journalism.

In the EIJ2018 example, some decision-makers were unhappy that an organization associated with the Koch brothers, who have a very conservative political agenda, might be seen as getting something close to an endorsement from the nation's leading journalism membership group. And yet, the Koch foundation didn't attempt to determine the makeup of the panel it was sponsoring. It was to be a discussion of First Amendment and Freedom of Information issues, and beyond that, planning was left to the organizations' people responsible for programming.

The Charles Koch Foundation also supports programs at the Freedom Forum and Newseum, two long-standing supporters of a free press. The National Freedom of Information Coalition has had a Koch Foundation sponsorship for a luncheon at its annual FOI Summit.

And there's the inevitable question of media bias. Would journalists be as upset if a liberal-leaning organization sponsored a major event? Does rejecting a sponsorship from a conservative-leaning organization only confirm the suspicions of many on the political right that mainstream journalism is hostile to conservative views? Should journalism organizations accept financial support only from entities whose primary business is journalism? That would include conservative organizations such as Fox News and Sinclair Broadcasting, both of which were listed as sponsors for EIJ2018, as well as liberal-leaning entities similar to MSNBC.

> Does rejecting a sponsorship from a conservative-leaning organization only confirm the suspicions of many on the political right that mainstream journalism is hostile to conservative views?

DECISION: SPJ put together a task force to consider how such sponsorship opportunities should be handled in the future. It had faced a similar controversy several years earlier, when delegates to a convention found pens or similar souvenirs from the Philip Morris Co. in their goodie bags. The decision then was that it's OK to accept a convention sponsorship if the organization would do the same, say, for a convention of roofing contractors. But alarm bells should sound if it appears the non-journalist sponsors are opening their wallets only because it's a convention of journalists, with their ability to reach large numbers of the general public.

DISCUSSION: As an exercise, see if you can craft a policy for an ethical journalism organization to follow in accepting financial support from other organizations.

WHAT THE CODES SAY: Conflicts of Interest

PRINCIPLE 3: Advertisers should clearly distinguish advertising, public relations and corporate communications from news and editorial content and entertainment, both online and offline.... If consumers are unaware the "news" or "entertainment" they are viewing actually is advertising, they are being misled and treated unethically.

American Advertising Federation

- Act in the best interests of the client or employer, even subordinating the member's personal interests.
- Avoid actions and circumstances that may appear to compromise good business judgment or create a conflict between personal and professional interests.
- Disclose promptly any existing or potential conflict of interest to affected clients or organizations.
- Encourage clients and customers to determine if a conflict exists after notifying all affected parties.

PRSA Code of Ethics

Free airfare or lodging as part of studio, travel or other junkets may not be accepted by employees. Freelance materials resulting from such freebies should not be purchased by the newspaper.

The Arizona Republic, Phoenix

Gifts, favors, free travel or lodging, special treatment or privileges can compromise the integrity and diminish the credibility of food editors and writers as well as their employers. Such offers should be avoided.

Similarly, food editors and writers should not use their positions to win favors for themselves or for others.

Newspaper Food Editors and Writers Association

Meals, transportation and other expenses associated with news gathering will be paid for by The Herald. No transportation, entertainment, food or drink will be accepted. If it is impractical to refuse an item of little or no value, such as a cup of coffee, it can be accepted.

Bellingham (Washington) *Herald*

In declining tickets, gifts and other favors, Ledger-Inquirer staff members should avoid rudeness and self-righteousness. We should express our appreciation and politely decline, explaining that the policy is as much in the would-be giver's interests as our own.

Columbus (Ohio) *Ledger-Inquirer*

Food journalists should not flaunt their titles in hopes of securing favors for themselves, their friends or their relatives. Favors could include restaurant reservations; desirable tables; party invitations or free food and drink.

Food journalists should refuse samples of food, drink or any other product which they don't intend to evaluate for publication.

Association of Food Journalists

Products (books, recordings, videotapes, software and product samples) should not be sold for personal gain. After review, they should be sent to the appropriate public library, given to charitable organizations or sold by the company for charitable purposes. Products such as computer equipment should be borrowed for review and then returned or disposed of as charitable giving.

The Dallas Morning News

Staff members should accept no gifts of value from news sources. For example, a bottle of wine or a box of candy should be returned to the donor with an explanation that it is a violation of Grand Forks Herald policy to accept gifts. Gifts of insignificant value, such as a calendar or a pencil, may be accepted if it would be awkward to return them. Offers of free food and drinks should be politely refused. It may be necessary to accept such offers to avoid being rude or obnoxious, but they should be rare exceptions.

We must remember that many of the kindnesses offered to the Herald and its employees are tendered on the basis of friendship or courtesy and without any self-serving motive. It's important that we avoid appearing rude or narrowly self-righteous in living within the spirit of this policy. We should never assume a stance of outraged innocence. Instead, we should express our appreciation and politely decline, explaining the importance of our policy.

Grand Forks Herald, North Dakota

Staff members are prohibited from accepting gifts or from giving gifts to new sources, potential news sources or those who seek to influence coverage. Exceptions can be made when reporting in countries and cultures in which refusing to accept or provide a modest gift would give offense. When in doubt about the appropriateness of a gift, ask a supervising editor.

The Los Angeles Times

Attendance by news staffers at a party conducted solely for members of the media by news sources is discouraged but not prohibited. For example, there is a good deal of news value in attending political party press functions in Pierre but little news value in attending Bell Telephone's annual Christmas press party in Sioux Falls.

Sioux Falls Argus Leader, South Dakota

Our news staff does not advise or work for politicians or political organizations. We encourage good citizenship by exercising our right to vote in referenda, primaries and general elections, but we do not engage in partisan activity beyond that.

Asbury Park Press, New Jersey

Articles of opinion and analysis shall be clearly identified as such. The publisher's opinions shall be confined to the editorial page except under extraordinary circumstances. Advertisements shall be clearly discernible from editorial copy.

The Orange County Register, California

AP employees must avoid behavior or activities — political, social or financial — that create a conflict of interest or compromise our ability to report the news fairly and accurately, uninfluenced by any person or action….

We do not accept free tickets to sports, entertainment or other events for anything other than coverage purposes. If we obtain tickets for a member or subscriber as a courtesy, they must be paid for, and the member should reimburse the AP….

Employees frequently appear on radio and TV news programs as panelists asking questions of newsmakers; such appearances are encouraged.

However, there is potential for conflict if staffers are asked to give their opinion on issues or personalities of the day. Advance discussion and clearance from a staffer's supervisor are required.

Employees must inform a news manager before accepting honoraria and/or reimbursement of expenses for giving speeches or participating in seminars at colleges and universities or at other educational events if such appearances makes use of AP's name or the employee represents himself or herself as an AP employee. No fees should be accepted from governmental bodies; trade, lobbying or special interest groups; businesses, or labor groups, or any group that would pose a conflict of interest….

Editorial employees are expected to be scrupulous in avoiding any political activity, whether they cover politics regularly or not. They may not run for political office or accept political appointment; nor may they perform public relations work for politicians or their groups. Under no circumstances should they donate money to political organizations or political campaigns. They should use great discretion in joining or making contributions to other organizations that may take political stands.

The Associated Press

Press parking passes and free parking spaces should be used by Post staffers only during the coverage of breaking news, to facilitate deadline reporting and writing, or to gain access to news sites or crime scenes. They are not to be used for all-day free parking.

In general, Post staffers should avoid other forms of free press parking. ... Exceptions are allowed for the coverage of sports events, where parking often is included with press credential and where close proximity to a stadium or arena is an assist for photographers hauling heavy equipment and offers safety and security advantages for staffers leaving arenas late at night.

The Denver Post

Arts organizations commonly provide critics' press passes in pairs. Because a critic's appreciation of a performance or work of art is enriched by viewing and discussing it with someone else, a critic may accept the additional pass for a colleague, spouse, companion or friend with an editor's approval.

The Los Angeles Times

The Inquirer expects to pay for meals served to staff members in press boxes. The sports department should arrange to reimburse professional teams or university athletic departments for these meals.

The Philadelphia Inquirer

Staff members required to attend events where press box facilities are not provided should purchase tickets and be reimbursed by the Free Press. Photographers and reporters assigned to cover sports or political events may use such facilities as review seats, press boxes, press galleries or press rooms which are necessary to cover the event. Access to press boxes or press galleries may be granted to other staff members when the access is necessary to developing information or skills.

Detroit Free Press

The Times, like many other news organizations, does not allow its sportswriters to participate in voting for baseball's Hall of Fame, college football's Heisman Trophy and national rankings in college sports, among other areas. Participation in these polls creates possibilities for conflicts of interest. Similar issues arise in the arts when journalists are invited to vote for awards and prizes in film, literature and other fields.

The Los Angeles Times

... [W]e recognize that our involvement as citizens may sometimes compromise or inhibit our professional responsibilities, and we judge each situation with that in mind. We are particularly conscious of the necessity to avoid personal involvement on either side of an issue about which we would be writing or editing stories for the newspapers.... So we do not prepare publicity or serve on publicity committees for any groups, and we request that all businesses and organizations go through normal newspaper channels in seeking news coverage.

Columbus (Ohio) *Ledger-Inquirer*

Journalists have no place on the playing fields of politics.

The New York Times

Employees may not run for public office or be appointed to any public boards or commission if such service will create a conflict of interest or is exploitation of the employee's connection to The Denver Post. ...

It is not the newspaper's intention to attempt to control private lives, but an employee's involvement in an organization or activity could comprise the individual's professional credibility and the newspaper's.

Therefore, newsroom employees should notify a supervisor of any such potential conflicts so that appropriate assignments or disclosure can be made, if necessary.

The Denver Post

Staff members are not prevented from signing initiative or referendum petitions for state, county or city ballot propositions. But they must recognize that such petitions are public documents and that signing petitions could be interpreted as taking a position on a political issue. As with other potential conflicts of interest, staff members who sign petitions must disclose that fact to their supervisor.

Tacoma Morning News Tribune, Washington

Political activity. Staff members are encouraged, even urged, to exercise their franchise as citizens to discuss matters of public interest and to register and vote in referendums, primaries and general elections. But because the profession requires stringent efforts against partiality and perceived bias, staff members should not be involved in any political activity beyond that.

The Philadelphia Inquirer

Reporters should not comment editorially on stories they are covering and should not write about events in which they're personally involved. Each of us should avoid public involvement in, and expression of opinion about, controversial issues. The editorial page and opinion columns are the places for such expressions. Each of us should be wary of expressing opinions in casual conversation or elsewhere that may then be cited by others as a basis for charging news slanting.

To avoid any appearance of partisanship in any public issue, campaign bumpers and bumper stickers should not be displayed nor should public advertisements or petitions be signed.

The News Journal, Newcastle, Delaware

As Reuters journalists, we never identify with any side in an issue, a conflict or a dispute. Our text and visual stories need to reflect all sides, not just one. This leads to better journalism because it requires us to stop at each stage of newsgathering and ask ourselves "What do I know?" and "What do I need to know?" …

We must also be on guard against bias in our choice of words. Words like "claimed" or "according to" can suggest we doubt what is being said. Words like "fears" or "hopes" might suggest we are taking sides. Verbs like rebut or refute (which means to disprove) or like fail (as in failed to comment) can imply an editorial judgment and are best avoided. Thinking about language can only improve our writing and our journalism.

Reuters Handbook of Journalism

You may not march in special-interest or political demonstration, speak out at public meetings, make monetary contributions to political candidates, PACs or special-interest groups, or engage in other activities in support of a cause or group that would raise questions about the newspaper's impartiality.

The Journal News, White Plains, New York

Do not use the name of the DMN, the paper's stationery or your business cards for personal use (for example, when complaining about poor service at a store). This newspaper's name must not be used directly or by implication in your personal activities.

The Dallas Morning News

As one of the major institutions in the area, The Gazette cannot operate in isolation from the community it serves. Executives on the business side of the paper will, from time to time, be members or directors of appropriate community groups.

The Gazette, Cedar Rapids, Iowa

We do not argue or correct at a public meeting except to challenge a public body's apparent violation of the Freedom of Information law or an attempt to close a courtroom to the public.

The News-Times, Danbury, Connecticut

Adhering to the principles outlined in the [Voice of America] Charter, VOA reporters and broadcasters must strive for accuracy and objectivity in all their work. They do not speak for the U.S. government. They accept no treatment or assistance from U.S. government officials or agencies that is more favorable or less favorable than that granted to staff of private sector news agencies. Furthermore, VOA professionals, careful to preserve the integrity of their organization, strive for excellence and avoid imbalance or bias in their broadcasts.

Voice of America Journalistic Code

CHAPTER 10:

Photojournalism

Some might say that the photojournalist has the toughest job of all when it comes to journalism ethics. Photos and video images tend to generate the most heated of debates within newsrooms. And it's clear that the ire of the public can easily be provoked by a single photo or a short piece of video.

Making ethical decisions about what pictures to take and what to publish or broadcast is no simple matter. The very nature of gathering and reporting the news means that photographers are regularly expected to go into situations involving tragedy, to cover clashes between groups of people, to record the public actions of people who wish to protect their privacy. And photo editors, television producers and others who decide what images the public ultimately will see face equally difficult challenges. The Internet's capacity for seemingly unlimited photo displays has magnified the problem.

The case studies in this section run the gamut, from recording the horrors of violent accidents to revealing the identities of minors; from documenting deplorable behavior to changing images to protect the sensitive.

What the photojournalists did with their camera and in their editing is quite interesting. How and why they decided to do what they did is highly instructive.

Additional photojournalism ethics dilemmas can be found in other chapters of this book, nested within the framework of issues on accuracy and fairness, deception, diversity and privacy.

Photojournalism Checklist

Questions to ask before taking a still or moving image:

- ☐ Am I invading someone's privacy? If so, is it for an appropriate reason?
- ☐ Is this a private moment of pain and suffering that needs to be seen by our readers or viewers?
- ☐ Does this image tell the story I want? Would another be more appropriate?
- ☐ Am I shooting at a distance that is not intrusive or potentially revictimizing individuals?
- ☐ Am I acting with compassion and sensitivity?

Questions to ask prior to publication or broadcast:

- Do I need more information about facts or context?
- Is there information missing from the content of the image?
- What is the news value of the image?
- What is the motivation for publishing the photo or broadcasting the video image?
- What are the ethical and legal concerns?
- Who will be offended? Does such offense outweigh the value of presenting the image?
- What are the possible consequences of using the photo or image?
- How would I react if I were in the picture?
- Can alternative ways to present the information minimize harm while still telling the story in a clear way?
- Will we be able to justify our actions?

CASES: Photojournalism

CASE STUDY: Illegitimate Image

The development of computer technology gives photographers the ability to sharpen, enhance and even fabricate reality. A little knowledge, a computer and the right software allows you to insert your face into the huddle of the Indianapolis Colts, find you a place at the table with the president as he meets with his cabinet, and put you on a movie set with George Clooney. Political campaigns have used the techniques to distort the associations of their opponents.

But what if photojournalists use the same practice? What is the ethical implication when a photojournalist is presented with the opportunity to turn something less than amazing into a Pulitzer-Prize-worthy photo with a few clicks of the computer?

WHAT: Brian Walski, a former staff photographer for the *Los Angeles Times*, digitally combined two photographs taken in Iraq to form one fantastic photo featuring a British soldier gesturing with his gun at an Iraqi civilian man carrying a child. In both original photos, the soldier and civilians are visible; however, in one, the civilians are more in the background than the foreground while the soldier is facing them and looking quite intimidating. In the other original photo, the civilians are more desirably visible while the soldier appears at a distance and is paying less attention to them. The manipulated photo was the only one submitted by Walski and it ran on the front page of the *Los Angeles Times*. An employee at another publication noticed some duplication in the doctored photo and notified top editors at the *L.A. Times* who investigated and then immediately terminated Walski.

> Walski blamed fatigue and stress for what he did.

Question: Is it ethical to alter a photo if it means producing a more compelling image?

WHO: Walski is the moral agent, the original decision-maker, in this scenario. Walski had more than 20 years of photographic experience under his belt, four at the *L.A. Times*, before being let go as a result of what he called a "complete breakdown in judgment." The photograph was widely published by other newspapers throughout the United States, making those unsuspecting publications fall victim to this journalistic crime, tarnishing their reputations and credibility.

WHY: In an apology to his former colleagues, Walski blamed fatigue and stress for what he did. It's a plausible explanation although it overlooks the skill and deliberateness, and amount of time no doubt, it took to manipulate the photo. Those in the news business can certainly identify with the pressure that Walski must have been faced with. It is no secret that the American public has become increasingly more difficult to shock and awe, placing greater expectations and demands on those responsible for drawing in readers. The average reader could argue that since the photo was created using two unaltered photos featuring the same content with just slightly different placement, the alteration was not really a bad offense. What do you think?

HOW: How could publication of a manipulated news photo happen? Editors certainly don't expect their staff photographers to manipulate photos so that they are more pleasing to the eye; but there are plenty of bad examples.

The University of Wisconsin altered the cover photo of its 2001-2002 admissions application by including the photo of an African American male in order to appear to be a more ethnically diverse community. Its goal was to attract, or, perhaps to not deter, any minority students from applying. While the intent may have been defensible, the end did not justify the means. Other examples include instances when photographers or editors:

- swapped heads and bodies to produce more pleasing images
- removed distracting objects such as poles, signs, wires, etc.
- engaged in digital cosmetic surgery
- merged two completely unrelated photographs to produce a scene or situation that never actually occurred.

The latter issue is the big problem. The manipulation of a photograph, even by removing a telephone pole that only interferes in the scene, produces an untrue picture of reality.

Some view these occurrences as outrageous violations of journalistic ethics that others in the profession work so hard to uphold. But does it make a huge difference if someone uses Photoshop if it produces a clearer picture or an image that tells the story better? The National Press Photographers Code of Ethics includes the following guidelines:

- While photographing subjects, do not intentionally contribute to, alter, or seek to alter or influence events.
- Editing should maintain the integrity of the photographic images' content and context. Do not manipulate images or add or alter sound in any way that can mislead viewers or misrepresent subjects.
- Respect the integrity of the photographic moment.

Is there ever an instance when it is all right to alter the content of a photo? You be the judge.

— *by Brittany Daniels and Sara Stone, Baylor University*

The top photo was taken by Tetyana Portyanko and ran Page 1 in The Journal.

*The lower photo was taken by Ron Agnir, chief photographer of the same paper (*The Jornal, Martinsburg, West Virgina*). It ran on Page 1 in* The Register-Herald. *Used with permission.*

CASE STUDY: Too Graphic?

WHAT: A father drives 100 miles from his rural home to Shepherdstown, West Virginia, home of Shepherd University, and shoots his two sons, who are students, in their dormitory parking lot before killing himself. All three are dead at the scene.

The (Martinsburg, W.Va.) *Journal*, the nearest daily newspaper, is 15 minutes from the community, and its photographer is first on the scene. Chief photographer Ron Agnir arrives before the bodies have been covered. He and his assistant, a part-time graphic artist, shoot hundreds of images, and some of those images are transmitted across The Associated Press wire. *Journal* editor Maria Lorensen considers which images to use. Shepherdstown and Martinsburg are close-knit. It is a place where wrecks on the nearby interstate make Page 1.

Meanwhile, at the other end of the state in Beckley, *Register-Herald* editor Carl Antolini is reading the story and looking at the AP photos, which include shots of the bodies before they were covered where bullet holes are plainly seen and shots of the bodies after they are covered. Like his colleague, he works for a newspaper that covers a rural, close-knit area where such a murder would be Page 1. His town also includes a college.

Question: Which photo is least likely to upset readers while capturing the horrific nature of the incident?

WHO: Both editors must consider the effects of the photos on readers. Lorensen must consider the students, family members and friends of the victims who will see the photos and the long-term damage they may do to the community and *The Journal's* credibility. Antolini must consider the shock value on a community not directly connected to the incident but culturally related to it by geography and mores. A college campus shooting is newsworthy wherever it occurs and could happen in his own community.

WHY: Several principles in the Society of Professional Journalists Code of Ethics are in play. The admonition to seek truth and report it is paramount, along with its subordinate guidance to make certain that headlines, news teases, promotional materials, photos, video, audio, graphics, sound bites and quotations do not misrepresent. They should not oversimplify or highlight incidents out of context.

Yet, seeking truth and reporting it must be balanced by minimizing harm. The code encourages journalists to show good taste and avoid pandering to lurid curiosity. Further, it recognizes that gathering and reporting information may cause harm or discomfort. Finally, the code encourages journalists to show compassion for those who may be affected adversely by news coverage.

> What one editor chose not to use in full color on Page 1 because it was too graphic was another editor's choice for Page 1.

HOW: Lorenson chose to run a photo of the partially covered body of one of the victims where two bullet holes plainly could be seen. It was Page 1 above the fold. A photo below the fold showed grieving students. A Page 2 photo, in black and white, showed police officers around the covered body of a victim. Lorensen said she believed the Page 1 photo showed the truth of what happened without being too graphic.

Antolini passed on the photo showing the bullet holes because he said he it was too graphic for his community. Instead, he ran in color and below the fold on Page 1 the photo that his colleague used on Page 2 in black and white. In the color photo, the victim's blood could clearly be seen on the sheet covering his body.

Interestingly, Lorenson said she passed on that photo because the obvious blood on the sheet was too graphic.

This case study illustrates the difficulty in choosing images. What one editor chose not to use in full color on Page 1 because it was too graphic was another editor's choice for

Page 1. Their reasons for the choices were identical — to avoid further traumatizing readers while showing the compelling tragedy in a small college town.

As this case study so well articulates, there is no "right" or "wrong" photograph of a tragedy. Well-intentioned editors in two communities made opposite choices in the interest of protecting readers, and both had sound reasons for their decisions.

It's important to examine images carefully and go through a decision-making process to answer why you are choosing one over another. Going through the process to identify the reasons achieves another principle of the code: Clarify and explain news coverage and invite dialogue with the public over journalistic conduct. Editorials and letters from the editor are good options to explain news coverage contemporaneously.

– by Nerissa Young, SPJ Ethics Committee

CASE STUDY: "An Indelible Photo"

SUMMARY

Seconds after a Northern California jury convicted Richard Allen Davis of murdering 12-year-old Polly Klaas, a press-pool photographer took a picture of Davis, who held up both of his middle fingers. The *San Jose Mercury News* decided to publish the picture of the obscene gesture on its front page accompanied by a "Dear Reader" box soliciting reader response and explaining its reasoning for running the controversial photograph.

Mercury News executive editor Jerry Ceppos told readers that the picture showed Davis' "contempt for the system that convicted him."

"Ever since Davis' arrest, I've wanted to know about the character of a man who could kill Polly Klaas," Ceppos wrote in a front-page column. "Ever since it became clear the jury would convict him, I've wanted to know how he would react, what he's thinking.

"Even though it's unclear who the target of the gesture is, I believe the photograph tells us something about Allen's contempt for the system that convicted him. While the picture is vulgar, it does give us some insight. In fact, I suspect that it will become one of those indelible photographic images that will come to represent a terrible episode in American life."

Ceppos concluded the column, writing, "I'd be interested in your views, too."

More than 1,200 readers responded by fax, phone and mail (this was before most people had e-mail) — 815 were in favor of running the picture and 431 against.

In a subsequent column, Ceppos wrote that he was grateful for the relationship he had fostered with his readers, saying it was clearly "their newspaper." He added that asking for readers' opinions made them "feel part of the newspaper."

Managing editor David Yarnold had suggested the note to readers during a *Mercury News* editors' meeting that included Ceppos, the photo editor and a news editor. Ceppos decided to add the invitation for readers to comment.

"In this case the picture was so jarring and so different from what the *Mercury News* usually does that we felt we owed readers an explanation — on the front page, right under the picture," Ceppos said.

"The key issues were taste and whether this guy should be given such a prominent platform. In the end, we decided that this photograph told us even more than we already knew about the mindset of Richard Allen Davis."

Five other Bay Area newspapers published the photo of the obscene gesture on their front pages. The *Marin Independent Journal* ran the photo on its editorial page with an accompanying editorial. The *San Francisco Chronicle* published the photo on its front page but without an editor's note. The newspaper reported more than 130 negative phone calls, and several readers canceled their subscriptions. The *Sacramento Bee* decided not to publish the photo, allowing the text to convey Davis' message. The *Bee's* drophead read: "Killer flips off camera after verdicts read." Reporter Patrick Hoge referred to the act in his third paragraph, writing, "Silently, menacingly, Davis winked, kissed the air and flashed an obscene gesture with both hands."

Bee executive editor Gregory Favre said that editors who said they published the photo to show "what type of person Davis really is" were looking for an excuse to run it.

"You run that picture for shock value only," Favre told *Editor & Publisher*. "There was no other redeeming value in it. We didn't run it to show that Davis is a despicable, disgusting contemptible human being. What he did spells that out thousands of times more than any picture could ever do."

ANALYSIS

As we have seen many times in this book, reasonable people pursuing the same goal may radically disagree on a course of action. Editors Ceppos and Favre both wanted to tell the story of what happened in the courtroom at a crucial moment in that celebrated trial. They landed on opposite ends of the decision-making spectrum, though both would argue they reported the truth of that story and properly served their readers. Ceppos, and editors at other papers, used the picture to carry the impact. Favre believed words alone would accomplish the task.

While Ceppos could talk himself blue in the face trying to defend Favre's challenge that he was just looking for an excuse to run the picture, the *Mercury News* editor took the best course of action to justify his decision. He held himself and his paper accountable by taking a public stance on why they ran the photo.

The principle of accountability says "Journalists should clarify and explain news coverage and invite dialogue with the public over journalistic conduct."

Ceppos tied his "Dear Reader" column to the photo to explain the paper's decision to run what many would term an offensive picture. This real-time explanation, used judiciously, is an excellent tool of accountability and a key element of the ethical decision-making process.

Additionally, when editors have to write down and publish the how and why of a decision, they are required to be reflective. They know their judgment and logic will be scrutinized in a very public forum. And, knowing that they will likely face dissent from some readers, they must anchor their decisions in a principle that at least will be respected, even if disagreed with.

Ceppos took the additional step of urging readers to give the paper feedback on the decision to publish the photo. The pro and con vote on the use of the picture is interesting, but not nearly as important as the fact that more than 1,200 readers made the effort to respond to Ceppos's invitation.

That invitation and the response to it speak loudly of the importance of news organizations creating an ongoing dialogue with those they serve. Such conversations, whether about dramatic photos or the coverage of complex and controversial issues, help news organizations better understand the communities they serve. Just as importantly, the conversations should help the public better understand the essential role journalism plays in a democratic society. To be sure, disagreements on course of action will continue, but that can be conducted out of mutual respect.

— From the Third Edition, Black, Steele and Barney

WHAT THE CODES SAY: Photo, Video and Other Images

We do not ask people to pose for photos unless we are making a portrait and then we clearly state that in the caption. We explain in the caption the circumstances under which photographs are made. If someone is asked to pose for photographs by third parties and that is reflected in AP-produced images, we say so in the caption. Such wording would be: "XXX poses for photos."

… AP photos must always tell the truth. We do not alter or digitally manipulate the content of a photograph in any way.

The Associated Press

General Policy — Do NOT run photos of the governor, mayor, etc. signing proclamations, receiving plaques, looking at a check or piece of paper, etc. Avoid posed news photos of politicians immediately prior to elections.

St. Paul Pioneer Press and Dispatch, Minnesota

It is insufficient simply to label video or a photograph as "handout." We should clearly identify the source — for example "Greenpeace Video" or "U.S. Army Photo". Similarly, it is essential for transparency that material we did not gather ourselves is clearly attributed in stories to the source, including when that source is a rival organization. Failure to do so may open us to charges of plagiarism.

Reuters Handbook of Journalism

News photographs must not be altered. Photographs that electronically obscure the face of a victim or undercover police officer are exceptions, but the alteration should be clearly explained in the caption.

The Arizona Republic, Phoenix

CHAPTER 11:

Privacy

The public often has a need for information that others, for a variety of motives, would like to keep private. Citizens value knowing about certain activities of public officials, even though the officials may wish to restrict flow of that information. There also is value in the public's knowing about meaningful details of accidents, tragedies and crimes, even though the gathering and distribution of such details might invade someone's sense of privacy.

Such stories highlight the journalist's dilemma in balancing the competing ethical principles of telling the truth while minimizing the harm.

Public discussions that ultimately may bring some benefit often cannot begin without some invasive and harmful disclosure. A story about the spread of AIDS and the failure of society to respond may present this disease as just another abstract threat unless specific names are attached to the story.

Stories that make allegations of criminal activity or unethical behavior, ranging from government corruption to child abuse, are less accurate and potentially unfair if individuals go unidentified. To identify individuals is certain to cause some harm, however.

Crime stories are necessary to inform members of the public of both their own safety and to provide them with information on the performance of those responsible agencies of government. On the other hand, coverage of crime is bound to cause some invasion of privacy.

Harm from privacy invasion is almost certain, but it is more difficult for a journalist to fully identify benefits from an intrusion. That's why it is important even for non-journalists to recognize the primary ethical obligation of journalism is to inform the public by seeking truth and reporting it as fully as possible. That obligation must then be balanced against the obligation to respect individuals and their privacy.

The challenge for journalists is to be courageous in seeking and reporting information, while being compassionate to those who are being covered.

Privacy Checklist

- ☐ How important is the information I am seeking? Does the public have a right to know? A need to know? Merely a desire to know?
- ☐ What level of protection do individuals involved in the story deserve? How much harm might they receive? Are they involved in the news event by choice or by chance?

- How would I feel if I were being subjected to the same scrutiny?
- Do I know the facts of the story well enough? What else do I need to know?
- What can I do to minimize the privacy invasion and the harm? Can I broaden the focus of the story by including more "victims," thereby minimizing harm to a select few? Can I postpone the story without significantly jeopardizing information important to the public?
- Do I need to include other individuals to gain more perspective in the decision-making process?
- Should I be focusing more on the system failure or the big-issue picture instead of focusing intensely on individuals?
- Can I clearly and fully justify my thinking and decision? To those directly affected? To the public?

CASES: Privacy

CASE STUDY: A Rape on Campus. Or Not.

WHAT: On November 19, 2014, *Rolling Stone* published what became one of the most notorious lapses of ethical journalism in recent years. "A Rape on Campus," written by contributor Sabrina Erdely, told the story of a brutal gang-rape at a University of Virginia fraternity house two years earlier. The alleged victim, identified only as "Jackie," was the principal source of the narrative. UVA officials were quoted, too, but the article suggested that school personnel had not done all they could have done to prevent or atone for this and other incidents of sexual harassment.

"A Rape on Campus" created a firestorm of reaction. It was cited as evidence of a toxic and widespread atmosphere of sexual abuse not only at UVA, but also on other campuses and in similar settings around the county.

But almost immediately, questions arose about the article's veracity. Within days, skeptics, including *The Washington Post*, pointed out apparent flaws in the narrative. The *Post's* analysis, published December 5, 2014, just a bit more than two weeks after the original article, revealed information that poked holes in the story.

The day before, on December 4, Erdely herself had called her editors to express concern about certain elements of the story, including the identity of the alleged assailants. "Jackie," the apparent victim, didn't know how to spell the name of the ringleader. And Erdely hadn't talked with "Drew," who was the victim's date that night, nor had she verified details of that night with the three friends "Jackie" had sought out for help immediately after the incident.

On the same day the *Post* published its analysis, *Rolling Stone* published an editor's note effectively retracting its account of the rape.

Questions: What should *Rolling Stone* have done to atone for this major mistake? (And, from a strategic communications perspective, how can it recover its reputation? Similarly, how should university officials respond?)

WHO: This ethical dilemma has multiple stakeholders, principally *Rolling Stone* and its editors, who are also the moral agents responsible for deciding how to proceed. Sabrina Erdely's reputation is also profoundly at risk. The University of Virginia and the Phi Kappa Psi fraternity, whose members and whose house were involved in the story, are major stakeholders. "Jackie's" friends, even though unnamed, are probably known around campus. They're stakeholders, too, as are men on campus who might be viewed as the possible assailants.

There was a broader effect, as well. What began as a powerful tool in raising awareness of a culture of sexual assault and harassment became discredited along with the journalism that produced it.

WHY: This is a situation where the principle of minimizing harm took precedence over a journalist's primary obligation to tell the truth. As Will Dana, the RS managing editor, put it: "Ultimately, we were too deferential to our rape victim; we honored too many of her requests in our reporting.... We should have been much tougher, and in not doing that, we maybe did her a disservice."

There also were several points during the development of the story where questions should have been raised. In effect, "Jackie" assumed editorial control over the reporting. Columbia University's Graduate School of Journalism, asked by *Rolling Stone* to investigate what went wrong, concluded — among many other findings in an exhaustive report — that "Erdely's reporting records and interviews with participants make clear that the magazine did not pursue important reporting paths even when Jackie had made no request that they refrain. The editors made judgments about attribution, fact-checking and verification that greatly increased their risks of error but had little or nothing to do with protecting Jackie's position."

HOW: *Rolling Stone*, as noted above, asked for an independent outside investigation by the well-respected Columbia University Graduate School of Journalism. The magazine gave Columbia's team access to the reporter's notes and drafts of the story. "The authors," they said in their report, "enjoyed the freedom to investigate and write about any subject related to "A Rape on Campus" that they judged to be germane and in the public interest."

The report was printed in *Rolling Stone* on April 5, 2015. Perhaps the most concise statement of what the investigators found is this:

"*Rolling Stone*'s repudiation of the main narrative in 'A Rape on Campus' is a story of journalistic failure that was avoidable. The failure encompassed reporting, editing, editorial supervision and fact-checking. The magazine set aside or rationalized as unnecessary essential practices of reporting that, if pursued, would likely have led the magazine's editors to reconsider publishing Jackie's narrative so prominently, if at all. The published story glossed over the gaps in the magazine's reporting by using pseudonyms and by failing to state where important information had come from."

As for what to do about it, the report had three recommendations for *Rolling Stone* in particular and three more for journalists generally, when they're reporting on rape.

For *Rolling Stone*:
1. Consider banning pseudonyms. They can be a crutch to skirt gaps in reporting.
2. Attempt to verify derogatory information; at least contact the sources of that information as well as the subjects who are criticized.
3. Confront subjects and sources with details of the accounts you've heard.

For all journalists:
1. Balance sensitivity to victims with the need to verify: the perennial conflict between truth-telling and minimizing harm.
2. Corroborate survivor/victim accounts with what's available on the record, for example, hospital records, 911 calls, text messages or cell phone calls.
3. Hold institutions to account for the sufficiency of their response.

The story damaged the cause it was trying to champion. It did indeed raise awareness of sexual assault and of the dangers potential victims face. But as it became discredited and then retracted, it could be used by critics who questioned whether the problem was really as bad as it had been made out to be — and whether some proposed victims were just making stuff up. It was not just a costly embarrassment for *Rolling Stone* but also a cudgel for journalism's critics.

Rolling Stone lost two defamation suits and had to pay millions of dollars in settlements.

In November 2016, a federal jury awarded Nicole P. Eramo, the assistant dean of students at the University, $3 million in damages. She had argued that she had been portrayed as the "chief villain" in the account, indifferent to sexual assault.

Rolling Stone at first appealed, but then in April 2017 both sides agreed to a settlement. Two months later, in June 2017, the magazine agreed to pay the university's Phi Kappa Psi fraternity $1.65 million. *The New York Times* reported that the fraternity originally wanted $25 million in damages and a jury trial.

An investigation by the Charlottesville, Virginia, police found "no substantive basis to support the account alleged in the *Rolling Stone* article.

The magazine formally and finally retracted the article on the day it published the report from Columbia. An editor's note concluded this way:

With its [the report's] publication, we are officially retracting 'A Rape on Campus.' We are also committing ourselves to a series of recommendations about journalistic practices that are spelled out in the report. We would like to apologize to our readers and to all of those who were damaged by our story and the ensuing fallout, including members of the Phi Kappa Psi fraternity and UVA administrators and students. Sexual assault is a serious problem on college campuses, and it is important that rape victims feel comfortable stepping forward. It saddens us to think that their willingness to do so might be diminished by our failings.

Will Dana, *Managing Editor*

The article also was removed from *Rolling Stone's* website.

Further discussion:
- Would you add anything to the recommendations from the Columbia University team?
- Would you continue to use Ms. Erdely as a contributor? Under what conditions?
- As a strategic communicator, is there any further advice you might give the university about how to respond to this situation? What about the fraternity?

To see the report from Columbia University: https://www.rollingstone.com/culture/culture-news/rolling-stone-and-uva-the-columbia-university-graduate-school-of-journalism-report-44930/

CASE STUDY: Covering, or Covering Up, Suicide?

[Jim Pumarlo, who wrote this case study, is the former editor of the *Red Wing Republican Eagle*, where this incident occurred.]

WHAT: The death of Jeff Smith (names have been changed) resonated throughout Red Wing, Minnesota. The 19-year-old hanged himself. The pain was exacerbated by the fact that five years earlier his brother, George, was killed in a car accident. Jeff was survived by his parents and sister.

His death occurred on a Sunday evening in August, and by Monday morning, when the *Republican Eagle* news staff arrived for work, word had spread throughout the community as friends connected on the Internet. The *Republican Eagle* had a longstanding policy of identifying deaths that are the result of other than natural causes.

The policy understandably was not welcomed by all on the premise that suicide often is the result of depression — a sickness. In one case, a family pointed out that the person who took his life was on medication that created a chemical imbalance.

Depression was a significant factor in this suicide. Smith had never gotten over his brother's death and was undergoing treatment for depression.

> Even issues as sensitive as suicide can become a positive force in communities if newspapers treat the subject with respect and care.

By Monday morning, friends already had organized a meeting at the church for family and friends to share stories and console each other. The newspaper reported the suicide in Monday's edition and also included a notice of the gathering.

This story carried extra sensitivity due to the circumstances. A friend of the family, who also was on staff at Goodhue County Mental Health Center, contacted the editor to discuss a way to share with readers — primarily friends of Smith — signs of depression and suicide. It's fairly routine for schools to bring in grief counselors to talk with students in the aftermath of a tragedy. But this death occurred during the summer with no organized opportunity to meet with Smith's peers. Counselors were available Monday afternoon for a brief period at the church, but the need was evident for broader distribution of the message.

It's equally important, the newspaper believed, to be a partner in presenting information that may prevent copycat occurrences. The Mental Health Center specifically requested a story on the signs of depression that may forewarn a suicide. We were sensitive to the fact that we could not write such a story without referring to Smith's death, and we did not want to run the story without the family's awareness — even blessing.

The timing of the story played a role, too. We deemed it important to publish the story before the funeral with the thought that it would help friends visiting the family understand the illness — depression — that led to his death.

Question: As an overall policy, should newspapers identify suicides? In this specific case, should the newspaper detail the circumstances of depression that led to the individual's suicide?

WHO: The final decision of what to publish ultimately rests with the top newsroom editor. But in this case, as with so many stories that deal with challenging and sensitive circumstances, many individuals will be affected. In that regard, it's important to involve as many people — within the newspaper family as well as the community at large — in the decision-making process.

Deadlines often present obstacles to reaching as many people as you'd like. That's why it's instructive for newsrooms to methodically brainstorm — away from the pressure of deadlines — and frame policies for some of the tough decisions that increasingly face newsrooms. For example, what information and photos do you publish from the scenes of fatal accidents? Should you identify high school students who have been suspended from extracurricular activities for violating local school district or state high school league rules? Having a general policy will make it much easier to evaluate these stories as circumstances arise. Policies always should be subject to revisiting and revision based on specific circumstances.

The family was the primary consideration in the pursuit of this story. The newspaper intended to identify suicide as the cause of death, per its policy. But the additional consideration was the broader coverage of linking the youth's death to his struggle with depression caused by the death of his older brother.

This story had a clear impact on the community, too. Smith was an involved and popular high school student. His father worked in retail; and his mother worked in the school district. Grieving is inherent in all deaths, but this one was abuzz throughout the community as people started their work week.

The story could be educational, too, to help readers recognize other individuals who may be suffering depression and susceptible to causing them personal harm.

The newsroom also was under a microscope for how it would handle such a sensitive story. How it approached individuals in gathering the information and how it told the story would likely have an impact on its credibility and ability to collect information for other sensitive stories. The fact that the "cause of death" was a public record took a back seat to how the newspaper dealt with such a challenging story.

WHY: "Is this story news? How should we report it?" These two questions are among the basic five Ws and H for evaluating and writing any news item, and they require extra consideration when dealing with challenging events.

In this case, the suicide was being talked about in the community. It had an impact on people beyond the immediate family. It was news.

Untimely deaths typically generate conversation in a community, and suicides stir even greater emotions. It's standard procedure at most schools to call in counselors in the wake of an untimely death of a classmate, whatever the cause. School was not in session due to summer recess, but that did not stop the buzz. It was the talk of the town among people at work, at the coffee shops and at dinner tables.

The most ticklish issue was sensitivity toward the family. If we approached them for a broader story on their son and brother's depression that led to the suicide, they suddenly were thrust into a broader public discussion beyond what would have occurred with just a short notice on the death. But this untimely death clearly tugged at the community's emotions as evidenced by the decision by friends and mental health advocates to convene a special meeting at the church the day after the death to share memories and help people work through their feelings.

In addition, many in the health care community regard suicide as a national epidemic. The latest statistics identify suicide as the No. 3 cause of death among youths and young adults ages 15 to 24 in the United States. Shedding light on the causes of suicide can be regarded a true public service.

Grieving with death — especially suicide — is difficult enough for immediate family. It can be equally discomforting for friends and co-workers who do not feel comfortable in approaching the family. Publishing the facts can put to rest rumors and make it easier for individuals to approach a family.

HOW: The *Republican Eagle* pursued and published a front-page story complete with a family photo on Smith's struggle with depression that led to his suicide. In the same edition, at the request of the family, we published a column from their pastor on suicide. Primary credit for the story went to the Smiths who were willing to share their story and to the staff at Goodhue County Mental Health Center who helped us hook up with the family. I also wrote a column so readers understood the sensitivity with which we approached this story.

The story had both immediate and long-term impacts.

The interview with the family was published the afternoon of the visitation. The lengthy line of people waiting to visit the family was expected but the story likely played a role. More than one person told us that they initially did not intend to go to the funeral home but changed their minds after the story appeared.

That was not the end of the story, however.

The interview was the start of a broader community response. The family worked with a mental health center to sponsor a forum to help people understand the dynamics of depression and suicide. An overflow crowd filled the municipal theater to hear personal stories from panelists, including local residents. Crisis hot lines were immediately flooded with calls.

A local bank took note of the response and decided to take the discussion to another level as a community service project. A steering committee was formed with representatives from school, youth and health-care professionals. Within a few months, the bank, assisted by a private foundation, brought the founders of the Light for Life Foundation International-Yellow Ribbon Suicide Prevention Program to the community. The national project was started by parents of a suicide victim in Westminster, Colorado.

The steering committee, working with mental-health professionals, conducted school assemblies for each of grades 7-12. Counselors were available to talk. Between the middle school and high school, approximately 60 kids came forward for immediate counseling.

Nearly 150 kids volunteered to work on creating a youth board.

The steering committee also succeeded in getting the school to include discussion of depression and suicide in the health curriculum beginning in eighth grade.

Not all suicides will have such an impact. Not all families of victims will be so sharing of a tragedy. The underlying lesson, however, is that even issues as sensitive as suicide can become a positive force in communities if newspapers treat the subject with respect and care.

Jim Pumarlo, SPJ Ethics Committee
Former Editor, Red Wing (Minnesota) Republican Eagle, 1982-2003

CASE STUDY: 'Naming' a Dilemma

SUMMARY

In July 1994, 7-year-old Megan Kanka of Hamilton Township, N.J., was kidnapped, raped and murdered, allegedly by a neighbor who, unbeknown to the community, was a twice-convicted sex offender.

Less than two weeks after her body was found, New Jersey lawmakers pushed through an emergency measure requiring police to notify communities when certain sex offenders move into a neighborhood. It was called Megan's Law, and it sparked a national drive, fueled by presidential politics, to pass a federal law bearing the same name and intent.

The case also renewed debate among news organizations trying to identify the line that separates their responsibility to the public and their responsibility to vulnerable individuals.

That debate came to focus on the case of E.B., an Englewood, N.J., man who successfully petitioned a federal appeals court in 1996 to prevent authorities from carrying out Megan's Law, which requires police to notify neighbors, day-care centers and schools whenever convicted sex offenders move into a community.

E.B. confessed to the 1969 rapes and gruesome murders of two Virginia boys, one of whom he buried alive. He admitted those crimes in 1976 while in prison and undergoing therapy after molesting three boys in New Jersey. He served his sentence and was released in 1989. He and his wife bought a house and lived in Englewood for more than six years without notice.

Then came Megan's Law and the lawsuit. And then came the Guardian Angels and their leader, Curtis Sliwa.

Unhappy and impatient with the legal processes preventing the wholesale dissemination of names and information, Sliwa's group printed fliers bearing the man's identity and declaring, "E.B., we know who you are." They handed out the fliers in the neighborhood where he lived. A political activist broadcast the man's name on Sliwa's radio show.

At the *North Jersey Herald & News*, a copy editor noted that a story about those events bore E.B's full name. "The copy editor said, 'We've got a story here with a name in it. Do we want to run this?'," *Herald & News* editor Ian Shearn said. "That story was barreling right toward the press. We pulled it."

Thus, one news organization in the area confronted the ethical dilemma of choosing between public information and individual privacy. The involvement of community activists such as the Guardian Angels challenged the media to make independent decisions about identifying E.B. as public support of Megan's Law grew.

From the moment the lawsuit was filed, E.B.'s true identity was available and legally could have been printed and broadcast. It took little research to figure out he was the man who confessed to choking and raping a 14-year-old Petersburg, Virginia, boy and burying him alive, then stabbing a 13-year-old boy 21 times after raping him. The boys lived a block apart.

The state Associated Press tracked down the name quickly, then had to decide what to do with it. The decision: Withhold the name until the courts rule.

"We had the full range of discussion with good arguments on both sides," said Mark Mittelstadt, AP New Jersey bureau chief. "We tried to act responsibly without contributing to the problem. This was a tough one."

John Oswald, managing editor for the *Jersey Journal*, had no trouble figuring out his newspaper would become the first in the state to run E.B.'s real name. With a local peg for the story (the politician who named E.B. on the radio lived in the *Journal's* coverage area), the newspaper's leadership came to a deadline decision.

> Most of the newsroom decision-makers worried about the potential consequences of publishing E.B.'s name in such a charged environment, where the threat of violent vigilantism was thought to be high.

"It seems like a really basic point of information," Oswald said. "We run the names of shoplifters in [nearby] Bayonne. We're not going to run the name of a man who killed two kids — tortured and raped them? I don't see the point of that."

E.B.'s decision to challenge Megan's Law in court made him a public person, Oswald said. The fact that E.B. was trying to derail a law of such national prominence and statewide popularity gave the story all the news value it needed to propel his real identity into the newspaper, Oswald said.

"There weren't great hours of debate going on about it" at the *Journal*, he said, inasmuch as the issue first surfaced on deadline after a television station broadcast E.B.'s name. A small group of *Journal* editors debated the question "for about an hour," Oswald said.

By contrast the Bergen County *Record* convened more than 20 people — editors, reporters, even a former prosecutor now writing about legal affairs — in a meeting editor Glenn Ritt said "eventually turned into a seminar." The discussion lasted about three hours, Ritt said, and yielded a decision to wait until the courts had ruled before deciding whether to release E.B.'s name.

"We didn't want to make an ad hoc policy that we would have to revisit the next time this kind of case came up," Ritt said.

The *Record* did have an opinion, though. In its editorial, "Why we're not naming E.B.," the newspaper said his crimes "were monstrous, and we believe the community has a right to know who he is. But we also believe that in a nation of law, the court should be given time to rule on the case."

For the news organizations involved, the case prompted great soul-searching and few clear answers. "I don't know if there's a right or wrong answer, only the one we came to," AP's Middelstadt said.

ANALYSIS

Even the most difficult of ethical dilemmas *do* have right or wrong answers to them. That's what ethics is about. But few cases have two clear choices.

To publish E.B.'s name strictly for competitive reasons would be ethically unsupportable, since it does not rely on a moral principle. To publish E.B.'s name by caving in to pressure from authorities also would be ethically questionable, since it violates the principle of independence. To make an immediate decision about publishing without considering one's professional duty or the significant consequences of the action is ethically indefensible.

At the same time, there are several possible *right* answers to this dilemma, although they may be grounded in different ethical principles.

Most of the newsroom decision-makers worried about the potential consequences of publishing E.B.'s name in such a charged environment, where the threat of violent vigilantism was thought to be high. They also worried about the swamp they might walk into by journalistically embracing the legislative and legal movement to get more and more information about crime and criminals out to the public.

Those papers that held back on naming E.B. gave strongest weight to the principles of independence and minimizing harm.

Using a different principle, the *Jersey Journal's* John Oswald saw his paper's responsibility as clear: to tell the truth and name E.B. Oswald found no reason to hold back, believing the public benefit of disclosure outweighed any potential of harm.

No matter how courts rule in this and similar cases, news organizations will continue to face similar tough calls when the public's right to know clashes with an individual's right to privacy.

"Where do you stop?" asked Shearn of the *Herald & News*. "Do you print the name and address? Do you print the model of the car? The license plate number? His picture? Do you tell people where he works? Where he drinks? And is the newspaper the venue to do that?"

The difficulty in answering such questions must not deter the effort to make good ethical decisions. News organizations can use the guiding principles of truth-telling, independence and minimizing harm as a moral compass in that decision-making process. And, once a decision has been reached, it is also morally appropriate to go public with your thought process, letting the readers know that the tough calls were not made capriciously. These principles help you recognize and resolve conflicting loyalties to different stakeholders.

Good decisions require some reflection and reasoning. We must not be trapped by our gut reactions when an ethical issue clearly strikes a strong emotional chord. A high-stakes issue deserves attention. To borrow from a time-honored warning: *stop* your reaction; *look* at what you know and what you don't know; and *listen* to what others have to say.

Good ethical decisions are a product of collaborative decision-making, even on deadline. Different voices will raise legitimate concerns and potential alternative actions.

A decision must be made. Make it a justifiable one.

— *This case study originally was written by Keith Woods for The Poynter Institute Web site.*

CASE STUDY: A Controversial Apology

This case involves ethical issues that can be analyzed from both a journalistic and strategic communications perspective. There are questions of telling the truth, minimizing harm, racial dynamics and preserving the image of one of the nation's most prestigious journalism schools.

WHAT: Northwestern University is a private institution of higher education in Evanston, Illinois, just north of Chicago. Its journalism school, Medill, has a host of prominent alumni. Its student newspaper, *The Daily Northwestern*, is independent and student-run.

In November 2019, a campus organization, the College Republicans, invited former U.S. attorney Jeff Sessions to speak. Students gathered to protest. *The Daily Northwestern* sent reporters and a photographer to cover Sessions' speech and the protestors.

About 150 people took part in the demonstrations, according to reports by the Northwestern and Chicago newspapers; some of the demonstrators climbed through open windows and pushed through doors of the building where Sessions was speaking.

After photographs of the speech and protests appeared on line, some of the participants contacted the newspaper to complain. It became a "firestorm," said Charles Whitaker, Medill's dean – first from students who felt victimized, and then, after the Daily apologized for coverage that some students found "traumatizing and invasive," from journalists and others who accused the newspaper of apologizing for simply doing its job.

The episode contributed to the criticism that today's college students are overly sensitive and want to be protected from anything that they don't approve of: "Snowflakes," in the vernacular. Robby Soave, a columnist for right-leaning Reason magazine (slogan: Free Minds and Free Markets), called it "a sniveling, embarrassing apology."

"Is this what students at the country's most prestigious journalism school are learning these days?" Soave wrote. "That self-censorship is the paper's best practice if someone is offended by what's happening in the world?"

Some parts of the 700-word staff editorial (reprinted here) stood out to critics, such as: "While our goal is to document history and spread information, nothing is more important than ensuring that our fellow students feel safe...."

The critics argued that the first part of that excerpt is a much more important journalistic principle than the last part.

The editorial also said the coverage could have been more sensitive: "We know we hurt students that night, especially those who identify with marginalized groups. According to the Society of Professional Journalists Code of Ethics, 'Ethical journalism treats sources, subjects, colleagues and members of the public as human beings deserving of respect'."

But the critics, including professional journalists who were Medill graduates, pointed out that the protestors were involved in a public act in a public place. They shouldn't expect privacy, and if they were concerned about being interviewed, they could always have said no. The coverage was what journalists are supposed to do, they said, and journalists shouldn't apologize for doing their jobs.

QUESTION: Is an apology the appropriate response? Is there something else the student journalists should have done?

WHO: The decision-makers are the students who run the newspaper, especially its top editor. They also have become

Shutterstock

DAILY NORTHWESTERN EDITORIAL FROM NOVEMBER 10, 2019

Last week, The Daily was not the paper that Northwestern students deserve.

On Nov. 5, former Attorney General Jeff Sessions spoke on campus at a Northwestern University College Republicans event. The Daily sent a reporter to cover that talk and another to cover the students protesting his invitation to campus, along with a photographer. We recognize that we contributed to the harm students experienced, and we wanted to apologize for and address the mistakes that we made that night — along with how we plan to move forward.

One area of our reporting that harmed many students was our photo coverage of the event. Some protesters found photos posted to reporters' Twitter accounts retraumatizing and invasive. Those photos have since been taken down. On one hand, as the paper of record for Northwestern, we want to ensure students, administrators and alumni understand the gravity of the events that took place Tuesday night. However, we decided to prioritize the trust and safety of students who were photographed. We feel that covering traumatic events requires a different response than many other stories. While our goal is to document history and spread information, nothing is more important than ensuring that our fellow students feel safe — and in situations like this, that they are benefitting from our coverage rather than being actively harmed by it. We failed to do that last week, and we could not be more sorry.

Some students also voiced concern about the methods that Daily staffers used to reach out to them. Some of our staff members who were covering the event used Northwestern's directory to obtain phone numbers for students beforehand and texted them to ask if they'd be willing to be interviewed. We recognize being contacted like this is an invasion of privacy, and we've spoken with those reporters — along with our entire staff — about the correct way to reach out to students for stories.

We also wanted to explain our choice to remove the name of a protester initially quoted in our article on the protest. Any information The Daily provides about the protest can be used against the participating students — while some universities grant amnesty to student protesters, Northwestern does not. We did not want to play a role in any disciplinary action that could be taken by the University.

major stakeholders, whose reputations — and perhaps even their eventual journalism careers — could be at risk. The protestors are stakeholders, too, as is Northwestern and especially its Medill, which has long had a reputation as one of the nation's leading schools of journalism.

WHY: This is a classic example of the ethical conflict between truth-telling and minimizing harm. In this case, after telling the truth, the student decision-makers sought to atone by attempting to minimize harm.

The *Chicago Tribune*, in a report written by Dawn Rhodes, the paper's higher education reporter, quoted Whitaker, Medill's dean, who cited the pressures the students faced.

In addition to the "firestorm" of criticism from protesters and journalists, Whitaker said, there was the very nature of the contemporary learning environment. "[Y]ou have a group of students who are taking classes in critical race theory, gender studies and who are sympathetic to the notion that media has not always reflected communities of color well," he said.

"Against that backdrop, they do this soul-searching and they come to an ill-considered conclusion that they have somehow done something wrong by practicing journalism."

Part of that academic environment, Rhodes wrote, is the "tightrope student journalists traverse in writing about their own classmates and campuses, managing disagreement about the role and responsibilities of journalism, and confronting the historic failure of a majority white industry to fairly cover people of color and minority communities."

Margaret Sullivan, *The Washington Post's* media columnist, quoted Astead Herndon, national political reporter at *The New York Times*, who said today's generation of journalists instinctively "care about historically marginalized communities and rethink power dynamics." Sometimes, Herndon added, "it is playing out in a raw and uninformed way."

Racial dynamics were at play in the Northwestern case, where many of the protestors and complainers; the newspaper's editor, Troy Closson; and even Northwestern's dean are people of color.

"Being in this role," Closson wrote in a Twitter thread reported by columnist Sullivan, "and balancing our coverage and the role of this paper on campus with my racial identity – and knowing how our paper has historically failed students of color, and particularly black students, has been incredibly challenging to navigate."

HOW: The newspaper decided an apology was appropriate. And then its editor and others on the staff, battered by the ensuing criticism, explained themselves even further. Closson told columnist Sullivan that, in hindsight, parts of the editorial went too far, and that the original coverage was legitimate and in keeping with journalistic principles. "We covered the protest to its full extent and stand by our reporting," he said.

So, as a learning experience, perhaps it had been effective. Dean Whitaker, who had been named to that position just six months before this episode, said he understood why the newspaper's editors "felt the need to issue their mea culpa."

Some students have also faced threats for being sources in articles published by other outlets. When the source in our article requested their name be removed, we chose to respect the student's concerns for their privacy and safety. As a campus newspaper covering a student body that can be very easily and directly hurt by the University, we must operate differently than a professional publication in these circumstances.

Ultimately, The Daily failed to consider our impact in our reporting surrounding Jeff Sessions. We know we hurt students that night, especially those who identify with marginalized groups. According to the Society of Professional Journalists Code of Ethics, "Ethical journalism treats sources, subjects, colleagues and members of the public as human beings deserving of respect."

Going forward, we are working on setting guidelines for source outreach, social media and covering marginalized groups. As students at Northwestern, we are also grappling with the impact of Tuesday's events, and as a student organization, we are figuring out how we can support each other and our communities through distressing experiences that arise on campus. We will also work to balance the need for information and the potential harm our news coverage may cause. We met as a staff Sunday to discuss where our reporting and empathy fell short last week, and we are actively re-examining how we'll address similar situations in the future and how to best move forward.

We hope we can rebuild trust that we weakened or lost last week. We understand that this will not be easy, but we are ready to undertake the reform and reflection necessary to become a better paper. We also welcome any feedback you have about our reporting — that night or otherwise. The feedback that we have already received either directly or via social media has been incredibly helpful for us, and we are working to implement it immediately.

Through our coverage, we know Northwestern students to be passionate, thoughtful and just. Every day, we strive to encapsulate all that you are and all that you deserve.

(The editorial was signed by Troy Closson, Editor in Chief, and seven other editors)

"They were beat into submission by the vitriol and relentless public shaming they have been subjected to since the Sessions stories appeared. I think it is a testament to their sensitivity and sense of community responsibility that they convinced themselves that an apology would effect a measure of community healing.

"I might offer, however, that their well-intentioned gesture sends a chilling message about journalism and its role in society. It suggests that we are not independent authors of the community narrative, but are prone to bowing to the loudest and most influential voices in our orbit."

As for "the swarm of alums and journalists" who were raging on social media, "I say, give the young people a break," Whitaker continued. "Don't make judgments about them or their mettle until you've walked in their shoes."

The *Harvard Crimson*, in a September 2019 news story covering a campus rally that called for eliminating the U.S. Immigration and Customs Enforcement agency, sought comments from ICE officials.

ICE did not respond, but Harvard students and many others did, hundreds of them signing a petition that condemned the Crimson for seeking to get ICE's take on what happened. Some also called on students not to comment to the Crimson unless and until it changes its policies.

But it's a longstanding journalistic principle to cover all angles of a story. As the SPJ Code of Ethics puts it: "Diligently seek subjects of news coverage to allow them to respond to criticism or allegations of wrongdoing."

And, as the *Crimson's* president, Kristine E. Guillaume, said in a prepared statement, "Fundamental journalistic values obligate The Crimson to allow all subjects of a story a chance to comment…. This policy demonstrates a commitment to ensuring that the individuals and institutions we write about have an opportunity to respond to criticisms in order to ensure a fair and unbiased story."

WHAT THE CODES SAY: Privacy

Generally we try to name everyone in a crime serious enough to warrant a story. Names of victims or witnesses may be withheld if there's a legitimate public concern for their safety. We do not name victims of sexual crimes unless they request it. Decisions to publish or withhold a name should be approved by a deputy managing editor. ...

Are we withholding the name of a suspect, victim or witness because of age, safety concerns, the nature of the crime or other privacy concerns? Has a deputy managing editor approved withholding the name?...

Are we writing about an incident only because the suspect is a public figure or connected to a public figure? Does this incident say something about the public figure that the community should know?

The Virginian-Pilot, Norfolk, Virginia

Be certain that any contacts related to a death are handled with care and sensitivity. We seek the cause of death for news obituaries, but that information can be withheld if the family requests it and our editors approve. Discuss with your editor whether we should report suicides, which we would do normally only if it involves a public figure or public suicide.

The Dallas Morning News

In covering allegations of sex crimes, The Times generally does not identify the accusers or potential victims. Exceptions may be made in cases in which they have voluntarily revealed their identities.

The Los Angeles Times

We do not generally identify those who say they have been sexually assaulted, or preteenage children, who are accused of crimes or who are witnesses to them, except in unusual circumstances. Nor do we transmit photos or video that identify such persons. An exception would occur when an adult victim publicly identifies him/herself.

The Associated Press

The Mercury News is sensitive to the privacy of victims of rape and child molestation, and of subjects who clearly would be in physical danger by publication of their names and addresses. There may be circumstances in which we would nevertheless publish such names, but they must be approved by the Executive Editor or Managing Editor.

Ordinarily, consent is implied if a photographer approaches a subject, indicates that he/she is a newspaper photographer and asks for names and other facts. In some circumstances, written releases may be required (at mental health institutions or orphanages, for example).

San Jose Mercury News, California

The newspaper should also respect the reasonable privacy of public figures. Although politicians, government officials and other major community leaders have thrust themselves into the public limelight and in so doing subject themselves to a higher level of public scrutiny, they may also be entitled to keep some aspects of their private lives private. The fact that a politician runs for office does not automatically make that person's life an open book.

Daily Press, Newport News, Virginia

CHAPTER 12:

Source-Reporter Relationships

Sources are the foundation of a journalist's success, developed and nurtured and often protected for the future. The reputation a reporter or newspaper or television station has for protecting sources who provide sensitive information is a part of the continuing dynamic of successful journalism.

At the same time, audiences and conventional wisdom expect sources to be fully identified as a way of assessing and assigning media credibility. Audiences generally have a right to detailed information held by reporters and editors. Only an argument of seeking a greater good, or trying to avoid grievous harm, can justify not identifying the sources of information.

Use of anonymous sources is a decision demanding careful consideration. When an editor decides to keep sources confidential, the editor should recognize that the reputation of the newspaper, station or Web site is being placed on the line, asking audiences to accept the information on faith.

Confidentiality is not the only ethical concern journalists face when dealing with sources. Indeed, the fundamental relationship between journalists and their sources has been subjected to moral scrutiny because it is, by nature, a "use and be used" relationship. Writer Janet Malcolm, in a two-part *New Yorker* series and a subsequent book titled *The Journalist and the Murderer*, leveled the charge that:

> Every journalist who is not too stupid or too full of himself to notice what is going on knows that what he does is morally indefensible. He is a kind of confidence man, preying on people's vanity, ignorance, or loneliness, gaining their trust and betraying them without remorse.... On reading the article or book in question [the source] has to face the fact that the journalist — who seemed so friendly and sympathetic, so keen to understand him fully, so remarkably attuned to his vision of things — never had the slightest intention of collaborating with him on his story but always intended to write a story of his own. The disparity between what seems to be the intention of an interview as it is taking place and what it actually turns out to have been in aid of always comes as a shock to the subject.*

Journalists by and large disagreed with Malcolm's strident point of view. However, her charges did cause some healthy soul-searching within the industry. If nothing else, Malcolm caused journalists to recognize the tenuous nature of the reporter-source relationship. The bottom line is a warning to keep a professional distance or to behave so honorably during the interviewing and the writing that sources are not deceived.

SOURCE: Janet Malcolm, *The Journalist and the Murderer*. New York: Vintage Books, 1990, pp. 3-4.

Source/Reporter Relationships Checklist

- ☐ All else being equal, provide full identity of your news sources. The story is more credible, and future sources will recognize your basic ground rules. Generally, confidentiality should be granted only to protect someone who is relatively powerless or who is in a position to lose the capacity to continue as a solid source of information. In addition, the story should be of overriding public importance.
- ☐ Make sure sources understand the basic ground rules concerning on-the-record, off-the-record, not for attribution, etc. Make those conditions clear before you begin the conversation under those rules.
- ☐ Do not abuse naive news sources, and don't be abused by sophisticated ones. Don't put words in their mouths, but at the same time don't let them dictate to you only the story they want to tell. You're a journalist, not a flack.
- ☐ Before promising confidentiality, try to obtain the same information from sources willing to be quoted.
- ☐ Do not permit "after the fact" requests for confidentiality.
- ☐ Don't let anonymous sources use the cloak of anonymity to attack other individuals or organizations.
- ☐ Make sure you understand your newsroom's policy on confidentiality before promising it to sources. You may need the consent of your editors, and/or you may have to share the source's identity with your supervisor. Professional burdens of trust must expand to include the reporter, editor and sources, always with an eye to the needs of the public.
- ☐ Once you promise confidentiality, keep your promise. Ask yourself how far you and your news organization are willing to go to keep that promise. Are you willing to tell your source that he/she and you are likely to be subpoenaed in case of a libel or invasion-of-privacy suit? Are you willing to go to jail?
- ☐ Always bear in mind the power of the press when dealing with sources. You are in a position to cause harm or benefit. Use that power with great discretion. Do your sources know you are a reporter? Do you and they assume that everything they reveal is fair game for publication?
- ☐ Are you willing to spell out in your news stories the methods you used to gain information from sources and why you may be protecting confidentiality?

CASES: Source-Reporter Relationships

CASE STUDY: A Self-Serving Leak

WHAT: *San Francisco Chronicle* reporters Mark Fainaru-Wada and Lance Williams were widely praised for their stories about sports figures involved with steroids. They turned their investigation into a very successful book, *Game of Shadows*. And they won the admiration of fellow journalists because they were willing to go to prison to protect the source who had leaked testimony to them from the grand jury investigating the BALCO sports-and-steroids scandal (BALCO was a Bay-area business that supplied banned substances to athletes).

Their source, however, was not quite so noble. Attorney Troy Ellerman was using them. He leaked the information, then tried to get a major case against his clients dismissed on the grounds that grand jury information had been leaked.

Ellerman, former commissioner of the Colorado-based Professional Rodeo Cowboys Association, represented two major figures in the BALCO investigation. He had sworn under oath that he was not the source of the leaks that were reported in the Chronicle beginning in late 2004.

But he kept quiet for two years after a federal judge ordered the two reporters jailed for refusing to identify their source for the leaked information. They never did go to jail, because that condition was part of the plea deal that Ellerman agreed to when he finally admitted that he was the source — that he had allowed the two reporters to see transcripts of the grand-jury testimony of San Francisco Giants slugger Barry Bonds and other high-profile figures in the case.

> The reporters knew the identity of someone who was breaking the law.

It was February 2007 when Ellerman finally admitted his role as the leaker, but Williams and Fainaru-Wada still declined to discuss the case.

Question: Should the two reporters have continued to protect this key source even after he admitted to lying? Should they have promised confidentiality in the first place?

WHO: The decision-makers in this case, the moral agents, are Mark Fainaru-Wada and Lance Williams, the two reporters and authors.

The editors who supervised them also have a moral role in this case, and in the decisions that were made. That makes them and their newspaper, the *San Francisco Chronicle*, major stakeholders.

Of course, Barry Bonds and the other star athletes who were implicated have a high investment in the consequences of this case. Troy Ellerman's stake is especially high. Others who could be considered stakeholders include Major League Baseball; the U.S. Attorney's office in San Francisco, which for a time was thought to be the source of the leaks; the rodeo cowboys' association, which fired Ellerman as commissioner after this came to light, and which already had been facing complaints about the way it was run; Ellerman's other clients; and *Chronicle* readers.

WHY: The overriding principle here is a reporter's obligation to keep a promise — and a promise of confidentiality to a source has the legal effect of a contract, the U.S. Supreme Court has said.

On the other hand, a journalist's first obligation is to tell the truth, and concealing a source requires concealing part of the truth. Here, as in the Judith Miller case, where the former *New York Times* reporter was protecting a source who was manipulating her by giving her questionable information, the reporters knew the identity of someone who was breaking the law. They could have identified someone whose identity is a major news story. But they will not. Tim Rutten of the *Los Angeles Times* had this to say:

"To assert any form of journalistic privilege in a situation like that is something far worse than moral obtuseness. Conspiring with somebody you know is actively perverting the administration of justice to your mutual advantage is a betrayal of the public whose protection is the only basis on which journalistic privilege of any sort has a right to assert itself."

Others, though, continued to see the two reporters as First Amendment role models. After the federal court dropped its subpoena intended to force the reporters to reveal their source, Peter Scheer, executive director of the California First Amendment Coalition, told the Associated Press it was one of the best possible outcomes for journalism.

"Ultimately, the reporters did not have to go to jail and they did not have to compromise on ethics," Scheer said, "and that's a good thing. All the press can promise, and it's not a lot, is that we're not going to give you up."

HOW: Different journalists will have different answers to the question of if it's ever permissible to break a promise to a source. Most would say it's never all right. The public may be intensely curious to find out the name of the leaker, but let other reporters go to work on that.

Others, though, would say (in hindsight) that the problem is being too free with unconditional promises of anonymity. In fact, more and more mainstream media outlets are adopting strict rules about confidential sources; more and more are trying to discourage it. And some are saying also that reporters should warn sources that, depending on the situation, there may come a time when it's necessary to reconsider the promise, or to renegotiate it.

One of those times may be when it becomes apparent that a source has lied, or has cynically attempted to manipulate a reporter. It's a lesson in why a compact of confidentiality should not be entered into casually. Promising to protect a source should be a last resort, not a way to break the conversational ice.

CASE STUDY: Keeping a Promise to a Source

Summary

Political campaigns can be full of pitfalls for journalists caught between candidates under stress. In a case in Minnesota, editors of the *Minneapolis Star Tribune* and *St. Paul Pioneer Press Dispatch*, acting under traditional prerogatives, overrode a reporter's promise to a source and disclosed the source's name.

On condition he not be identified, the source, an employee of an ad agency working for the Republican lieutenant governor candidate in Minnesota, had given reporters embarrassing information about the other lieutenant governor candidate in the closing days of the campaign. The hot tip was that the candidate had been arrested nearly 20 years earlier on a shoplifting charge.

Believing the campaign tactic of disclosing information of questionable relevance was a bigger story than the long-ago shoplifting charge, editors at both the *Star Tribune* and the *Pioneer Press Dispatch* independently disclosed the source of the information.

The reporters' source was fired from the agency, took legal action against the newspapers and won a U.S. Supreme Court ruling in 1991 that promises of confidentiality may be legally enforceable under state law.

Despite the court decision, a question still exists about whether the newspaper might not morally justify disclosure of the source's name, despite the promise of its agent (the reporter), and despite legal rulings to the contrary. Editors generally have assumed that even though reporters' assurances to their sources are important, circumstances can justify an overriding of the reporters' judgment. The question of overriding legal consideration when making an ethical call is also important.

Analysis

A number of significant questions are raised in this case:
- Is it reasonable for a reporter to be able to assure a source of confidentiality and expect the news organization to support the promise?
- Should a reporter be required to consult with editors before offering source confidentiality?
- How important should a story be to warrant discrediting the reporter and damaging the news organization's credibility?
- What kind of discussion should take place in the newsroom before a reporter's promise is violated? What weight should the reporter's input have in the discussion?
- Would other stakeholders, particularly the news audiences and the sources, feel the breaking of a promise was justifiable?

The ethical conflict in this case is between two virtues: (1) the right of the source to expect a promise to be kept and (2) the feeling of the editors that the audience needed the information about the source. Audiences' need for that information should be so great that damage done by the breaking of a reporter's (and, hence, the newspaper's) promise is acceptable.

The key ethical question may lie in editors' motives. If their intent was to inform readers about a campaign tactic they considered questionable, justification comes fairly easily. If, however, editors were even subconsciously trying to embarrass a candidate by trying to expose the candidate's agent, ethical justification becomes prohibitively difficult. Generally, any good that may come from embarrassing the candidate will be more than offset by damage to the newspaper's reputation among sources, and probably among readers. Violations of promises have a heavy burden to produce some greater good. In this case, that "good" would be a fully informed readership presumably better able to make a voting decision.

As in other ethics issues, editors are obliged to search their own minds for motives. In their social role, editors can most easily defend an action that places audience interest first and can be justified to the audience. Editors should acknowledge to their readers or listeners that publication of the source's name was not a matter taken lightly, recognizing that future coverage may be at risk because other sources will be reluctant to confide in reporters.

— *from earlier editions, Black, Steele and Barney*

CASE STUDY: Deep Throat, and His Motive

WHAT: The Watergate story is considered perhaps American journalism's defining accomplishment. Two intrepid young reporters for *The Washington Post*, carefully verifying and expanding upon information given to them by sources they went to great lengths to protect, revealed brutally damaging information about one of the most powerful figures on Earth, the American president. They worked diligently on a story others were too indifferent, or too lazy, to pursue, and their reporting eventually forced Richard Nixon to resign, winning them a Pulitzer Prize as well.

The reporters, Bob Woodward and Carl Bernstein, became icons. After their stories broke in the mid-1970s, enrollment increased at journalism schools. They continue to be celebrated decades later for their integrity in never revealing the name of their principal source, "Deep Throat." It was not until that source broke his silence in 2005 that anyone knew "Deep Throat" was Mark Felt, a high-ranking official at the Federal Bureau of Investigation at the time he was talking to *The Post*. And, for some critics, that raised questions.

Question: Is protecting a source more important than revealing all the relevant information about a news story?

WHO: Woodward's and Bernstein's promise to protect "Deep Throat's" identity was fully supported by their executive editor, Ben Bradlee. Together, the three are the major decision-making moral agents in this case.

It was a decision that ultimately affected many stakeholders, most notably Mark "Deep Throat" Felt himself, and of course Woodward and Bernstein, who had made a promise that journalists treat with the highest reverence. President Nixon clearly was a stakeholder, as were others in his administration.

And in this case it also can be argued that the public had a higher stake than it does in many news stories — because of the importance of the information revealed by a source who would not have revealed it had his identity not been kept secret.

WHY: Two major ethical principles are at issue in this very famous case. First is the journalistic credo that granting anonymity to a source is a vow that never should be broken. The other principle, at odds with the first, is that a journalist's primary duty is to reveal information, not conceal it, and often the source of that information is an important part of the story, suggesting a motive or agenda for the leak.

In this case, some critics have held that Felt, who died in late 2008 at age 95, was manipulating *The Post* because he wanted to get even with the president for having passed him over for promotion to FBI director after the death of the legendary J. Edgar Hoover.

One analyst, George Friedman, wrote this for an intelligence and strategic consulting firm called stratfor.com: "This was not a lone whistle-blower being protected by a courageous news organization; rather, it was a news organization being used by the FBI against the president, and a news organization that knew perfectly well that it was being used against the president. Protecting Deep Throat concealed not only an individual, but also the story of the FBI's role in destroying Nixon."

> The source of a leak sometimes is even more interesting than the leaked information, because it may reveal a motive that is less than the epitome of integrity.

HOW: Most journalists consider *The Washington Post's* decision to protect Deep Throat an example of journalism at its finest. Working so hard for so long to keep the promise of anonymity allowed information to be revealed that was critically important to the survival of democracy and its need to correct its flaws. The role of a free press is to reveal those shortcomings, after which a responsive government can — or should — make the needed changes. In this case, the cover-up was perhaps more important than the crime itself, because it uncovered flaws in the presidential character. Nixon's resignation became inevitable — a cathartic moment for the country.

And yet reporters must continue to be very careful about promising anonymity. In some settings — Washington, D.C., in particular — it's almost impossible to get anyone to talk without making such a promise. But in other areas of the country, where bureaucracy and politics are not so entrenched, news executives insist that promising anonymity should be used only as a last resort, not to break the ice at the beginning of an interview. The source of a leak sometimes is even more interesting than the leaked information, because it may reveal a motive that is less than the epitome of integrity.

CASE STUDY: The Dilemma of Anonymity

WHAT: Donald J. Trump, for the first year and a half of his presidency, had definitely been a divisive figure as president. He continued to campaign, holding political rallies that emboldened his base, communicating by hundreds of tweets, preferring that venue to his exceedingly rare formal news conferences, calling the press "the enemy of the people," and often changing his mind and bluntly insulting his opponents.

So when *The New York Times* had an opportunity to print an opinion piece from an official inside the apparently chaotic White House, it agreed to let the author be unnamed. Op-ed page editor James Dao had been contacted a few days earlier by an intermediary for the writer.

The op-ed ran on September 5, 2018, with this editor's note:

> *The Times is taking the rare step of publishing an anonymous Op-Ed essay. We have done so at the request of the author, a senior official in the Trump administration whose identity is known to us and whose job would be jeopardized by its disclosure. We believe publishing this essay anonymously is the only way to deliver an important perspective to our readers.*

The editor's note closed with an invitation for readers to submit questions or comments. And more than 15,000 did.

It was, after all, a top-ranking insider's view reconfirming months of Beltway chatter. And it came hard on the heels of the long-awaited release of "Fear," Bob Woodward's book about White House dysfunction.

The unnamed author of the Times's op-ed said the president's "dilemma — which he does not fully grasp — is that many of the senior officials in his own administration are working diligently from within to frustrate parts of his agenda and his worst inclinations.

"I would know. I am one of them."

The official cited "bright spots" that advanced some long-held conservative goals, such as tax cuts and deregulation. But the overall tone was almost alarmist in its description of President Trump's conduct:

"Meetings with him veer off topic and off the rails, he engages in repetitive rants, and his impulsiveness results in half-baked, ill-informed and occasionally reckless decisions that have to be walked back," the anonymous author said.

Questions: Should the *Times* have agreed to grant anonymity? What should it do if another of its staffers, in the course of other reporting, learns the name of the official?

WHO: The decision to grant anonymity was made by James Dao, the op-ed editor for the *Times*, in consultation with editorial page editor James Bennet and publisher A.G. Sulzberger. They, in addition to being the moral agents responsible for the decision, are also major stakeholders. Perhaps the person with the most at stake, however, is the unnamed author of the opinion piece. Other *New York Times* reporters could be affected, too, particularly if they cover Washington politics, and especially if they learn the identity of the anonymous author. The president and the Trump Administration clearly have an interest in the article and the outcome of the situation.

WHY: The *Times's* editors could have anticipated that publication of the op-ed piece would lead to criticism that it was yet another example of the liberal media "piling on" a president they clearly considered unfit. They also should have considered that they would be placing themselves in a difficult position, by keeping secret the answer to the question all of Washington — and much of the world, for that matter — would immediately be asking: Who wrote this?

Piling on: President Trump's victory in the 2016 election had taken journalists, pollsters and the political establishment by surprise. Polling had predicted a comparatively easy victory for his opponent, Hillary Clinton. And there was good reason to believe the polls. Even before the election, strong evidence — often including actual tapes and photos — emerged about a number of episodes that would have doomed other, more conventional candidates.

But none of it seemed to faze Trump or his fiercely loyal supporters. And the newly inaugurated President Trump never did what most other presidents have done once in office; he did not seek to mend fences with those who did not vote for him. In fact, he continued to campaign — literally; he held frequent political rallies from the beginning of his presidency, all of them designed to appeal to his base, following up on the anti-establishment themes that had gotten him elected.

The mainstream media were confounded by his tweets, his unorthodox negotiating style, his tendency to insult allies and embrace former foes. But the media continued to do what they have always done — look for missteps and scandals and other important, or at least interesting, news stories in the new administration. And while the reporting overall certainly was justified, at times it seemed that there was more a sense of alarm than a sense of good judgment. The traditional media tended to treat all of Trump's indiscretions as equally abhorrent and disqualifying.

Conflict of interest: Once the opinion column had been published, it instantly became a mystery for other media to speculate upon and attempt to solve. Of course, a handful of people at *The New York Times* had the answer to that all-consuming question: Who was "anonymous"? The Times had simultaneously created and then covered up one of the most sensational stories of the Trump presidency. Was that ethical?

Margaret Sullivan, media columnist for *The Washington Post* (and former public editor at *The New York Times*), called it "a quagmire of weirdness: fraught with issues of journalistic ethics and possibly even legal concerns.

"And odd as it is," she continued, "it could get weirder quickly, if New York Times reporters are the ones to break the news of which senior Trump administration official wrote it. (By rights, they ought to — after all, they do have the best potential tipsters on this story, and, handily, right in their own building.)"

It should be noted that the *Times*, like the *Post* and every other reputable major newspaper, maintains a strict boundary between its news and opinion operations. Thus, even NYT Executive Editor Dean Baquet would not have been told the identity of this 21st Century "Deep Throat." That's not to say that someone with Baquet's reportorial skills wouldn't have been able to find out, which put him in rather a difficult position.

HOW: Obviously, the *Times* decided to publish. There remained, at the time of this writing, an open question about what might happen next. What would the newspaper do if one of its reporters who wasn't in on the original discussion nailed down the name of the anonymous writer?

This is one of the major dilemmas of granting anonymity. The newspaper in essence had created an internal conflict of interest. Transparency would have been so much simpler. But then the op-ed might never have run. Was it necessary to run it? Didn't we already know this stuff? Or did it add substantial weight to already growing suspicions?

Times readers had mixed reactions to publication of the op-ed. Most were critical of Trump; others were divided between praise for the anonymous writer's "courage" and condemnation of his or her "cowardice" and secrecy. There were a few who commented on the ethics of the decision to conceal the writer's identity. One reader called the decision "disgraceful." Another said it "sets a very bad precedent journalistically." And another, no doubt reflecting the dilemma that faced the *Times's* opinion editors, said "The Op-Ed is both essential and deplorable."

WHAT THE CODES SAY: Source-Reporter Relationships

When money is paid for information, serious questions can be raised about the credibility of that information and the motives of the buyer and seller. We generally avoid paying for information. Exceptions must be approved in advance by a managing editor.

Detroit Free Press

It is not the newspaper's role to promote; rather it is its role to report news. Sponsored projects — be they a small or large advertiser, charity or foundation — should be given the same consideration as other news stories or news releases and should not be promoted beyond their legitimate news value. When in doubt, see the executive editor or managing editor.

Sioux Falls Argus Leader, South Dakota

Be wary of friendships or romances with sources, particularly public officials or figures. Employees have a right to a life outside the office, but can never totally disassociate themselves from being journalists. Our readers have every right to expect that we make decisions independently of personal relationships. In some cases, reassignment may be necessary to avoid real or perceived conflicts.

Lincoln Journal Star, Nebraska

The Times does not enter into nondisclosure agreements or make deals in exchange for access. When negotiating with Hollywood publicists, for instance, we do not make promises regarding publication, placement, or angle of approach. That such deals are commonplace among entertainment media does not make them acceptable at The Times.

It is permissible to discuss, in general terms, the scope and direction of the coverage we have in mind. It should be clear, however, that the ultimate placement and angle are for reporters and editors to decide.

The Los Angeles Times

If an editorial employee has a close relative or friend working in a political campaign or on a ballot initiative, the employee should refrain from covering or making news judgments about that campaign or ballot proposal and disclose the relative's or friend's involvement to a senior editor.

The Denver Post

Nepotism is contrary to The Gazette's equal opportunity policy and inconsistent with sound managerial practices. Therefore, it is the policy of The Gazette not to hire any relative of a Gazette employee if the employee would participate in the decision to hire the relative or could, directly or indirectly, participate in decisions affecting any of the relative's terms and conditions of employment. ...

Certain staffers — columnists, for example, or those doing first-person pieces — may write about their families without it being a conflict of interest.

The Gazette, Cedar Rapids, Iowa

When information about crime is obtained by the Register, a decision to give that information to authorities will be made in light of the purpose of the reporting and the crime involved. There will be circumstances when such notification is not necessary — for example, when reporting of misconduct by public officials would be frustrated by reporting that investigation. On the other hand, information that a potential crime endangers the person or property of an individual or individuals must be reported promptly to the appropriate public officials. The decision about reporting a crime must be made in consultation with an associate's supervisor and generally will involve the editor, except in circumstances involving an immediate danger to life or property. In that instance, the authorities should be notified immediately.

The Orange County Register, California

---

1. An embargo means we have agreed to hold certain information for release at a predetermined time and date. Embargoes are a fact of life. We respect customary embargoes and those to which we or one of our wire services is a party.
2. We consider an embargo lifted at any point the news becomes public, whether by other announcement or by another news organization breaking the embargo.
3. We reserve the right to make our own decision about respecting an embargo that is unilaterally handed to us. Those that have been traditionally honored (such as release dates on press releases from public agencies with which we routinely do business) should be honored, unless we give advance notice to the contrary.
4. Only senior editors (department heads or above), or their designees, may negotiate or agree to embargoes. Our posture should be to avoid embarrassment when possible.

The Journal News, White Plains, New York

Assist law enforcement authorities only when there is a clear and compelling public interest at stake — and only with approval of the editor or managing editor. Never let cooperation get in the way of holding officials accountable and telling the truth. Take care when cooperating with government and other institutions on public journalism projects. Often, these efforts are worthwhile and in the readers' interests. But they can also compromise our independence.

Lincoln Journal Star, Nebraska

CHAPTER 13:

Being Accountable and Transparent

Ethical journalism means taking responsibility for one's work and explaining one's decisions to the public. That statement from the SPJ Code of Ethics seems innocuous enough. On its face it is perfectly logical. After all, why shouldn't journalists be accountable to their audiences and to each other?

The principle is reasonable, but its execution is problematic.

The code of the nation's largest organization of news professionals says journalists should:

- Explain ethical choices and processes to audiences. Encourage a civil dialogue with the public about journalistic practices, coverage and news content.
- Respond quickly to questions about accuracy, clarity and fairness.
- Acknowledge mistakes and correct them promptly and prominently. Explain corrections and clarifications carefully and clearly.
- Expose unethical practices in journalism, including within their organizations.
- Abide by the same high standards they expect of others.

These are the "standards and practices" that fall under the code's accountability and transparency principle. They define the construct. They make clear that journalism does not exist in a self-interested vacuum, but in an environment of reciprocity. They list the stakeholders, those who have the right to call journalists into account for meeting or falling short of their own and their audiences' expectations. They follow — but do not contradict — the code's principle of independence, suggesting that while seeking independence from the forces of corruption journalists remain inexorably connected to others.

There's a problem, however. Based in part on the existence of a constitutional amendment that says "Congress shall make no law …," American journalism has a long history of cantankerous independence, a resistance to criticism from others and even from within its own ranks. The battles to sustain First Amendment freedoms are instructive. In general, they have resulted in the sense that government can hold journalists accountable for their behaviors — in matters of libel, privacy, copyright, obscenity and the like — only *after* the fact. Prior restraint is another matter altogether. Some journalists have taken this relationship with government to another, more problematic level, arguing that calls for accountability by members of the public and even by other journalists somehow violate the news media's First Amendment privileges.

For nearly three-quarters of a century, journalism organizations have struggled with ways to build accountability and/or enforcement into their codes of ethics. The Society of Professional Journalists is no exception. For a variety of reasons, it has never had an effective enforcement mechanism. Its present code, framed primary by "ideal expectation" guiding principles and positive rather than minimalistic standards and practices, does not lend itself to rigid enforcement. It does, however, address the core issue of accountability by reminding journalists that they can and should be called to judgment by the public and by other professional journalists. (The code wisely avoids issues of accountability to government; after all, it is a code of ethics, not a body of law.)

> American journalism has a long history of cantankerous independence, a resistance to criticism from others and even from within its own ranks.

If journalists decide to hold themselves accountable to the public and peers, what forms does that accountability take? The most obvious might be the several journalism reviews, including the *Columbia Journalism Review* and *Gateway Journalism Review (formerly the St. Louis Journalism Review)*; journals put out by professional organizations: *Quill, IRE Journal, Nieman Reports, The American Editor Masthead*, etc.; trade and academic publications: *Broadcasting and Cable, News Photographer, Communications and Media Studies, Journal of Media Ethics*, etc.

The struggling ombudsman movement (a few dozen of the nation's 1,500 daily newspapers) and the stagger-step press council "movement" come to mind. So do the op-ed pages, the talk shows and the media review sections of the daily press. And of course the nation's hundreds of journalism schools, in which press criticism is flourishing.

All in all, however, the "Calling journalists to judgment" business is of questionable impact on an industry more committed to independence than to accountability.

Going public with our decision-making processes is not always a panacea. Sometimes when audiences better understand why we did what we did, they empathize with our dilemma and lower their lances. On other occasions, our attempts at accountability merely confirm audiences' worst suspicions about how news is made.

It has been said that journalism is not thin-skinned, but that it has no skin at all. If the industry has a serious claim on professionalism, if it seeks to build and sustain bonds with audiences, and if it hopes to retain independence from government control, it will do well to carefully address the notion of accountability. The fourth leg of the SPJ Code of Ethics acknowledges the importance of balancing accountability with the other three principles: seeking and reporting truth, minimizing harm and acting independently.

Celebrity Coverage: When Is It Time to Say Enough?

The death of Princess Diana in early September 1997 was a legitimate news story. After a while, the coverage got a bit overwrought, but the princess was more than just a celebrity. The murder trial of O.J. Simpson, starting much earlier with a memorably bizarre slow-speed police chase, deserved coverage too; probably not as much as it ended up getting, but he had been a star in football and film and had also been a role model.

Then came February 2007, with the death of Anna Nicole Smith and the antics of Britney Spears. The cable television news shows lost their moorings.

Maybe it was because it was February, when winter is old and gray and has worn out its welcome in the major media capitals, when the snow is spattered with grime and reporters are getting cabin fever. But is there really any excuse for serious, responsible media to devote so much attention to people who are famous mainly for being famous?

This pursuit of celebrity is a form of addiction. We know it's not good for us — or for our audiences — but we can't seem to help ourselves. We justify it by saying we're only giving readers what they crave.

Polls in fact show that the public thinks there's too much media attention paid to celebrities. But ratings, circulation figures and visits to Web sites suggest that the public, despite its protestations to pollsters, does indeed pay attention.

At some point, though, enough is enough. How do you tell when you've reached the saturation point? I asked my communication ethics students at the University of Denver what they thought, and how they might structure a policy for handling celebrity news.

The first thing they mentioned was audience. It depends on the demographics of your readers and viewers. Obviously the *Wall Street Journal* will have a different philosophy about celebrity news than will, say, the *New York Post* — because of who their readers are.

Part of the analysis of audience, therefore, involves competition. The voracious appetite of 24/7 news channels seems to demand that all of them drop everything to cover the same dubious events. But was it really necessary for every one of them to broadcast every moment of the judicial determination of what to do with Anna Nicole's earthly remains? Judge Larry Seidlin was a sideshow who muscled his way into the spotlight. Critics suggested he was looking to become the next Judge Judy.

> **Celebrity news: When is it time to say "enough"?**
> - Consider the nature of your audience
> - Cover only significant developments
> - Look for substance and cultural context
> - Sideline the publicity hounds

Responsible media should sideline the Seidlins of the world; do not give them the attention they seek so blatantly. Yes, they're hard to ignore. But don't give them more exposure than is absolutely necessary.

There's some hypocrisy in the way the "responsible" media managed to get these stories before the public; they did it while tsk-tsking at the way other media had gone overboard in their coverage.

One might argue that that approach has a certain validity; excessive coverage can be a news story itself. And it's legitimate to look for broader substance and cultural context in these fluffy stories. My University of Denver students thought it would be worthwhile to seek comments from experts in sociology and mental health about the implications of Britney Spears' decision to shave her head and seek late-night tattoos.

Other possible legitimate stories: What should parents tell their children about these bizarre personalities? Why do they command so much attention? Who are today's legitimate role models, if any?

Cover only the significant developments: The final disposition of Ms. Smith's remains; the determination of the paternity of her newborn. Perhaps short stories on Ms. Spears' repeated returns to rehabilitation were worthwhile for the moral lessons they might contain. The nature of "significant" should be a newsroom discussion.

Ethical decision-making involves, first, recognition of an ethical problem — and excessive celebrity coverage is a problem — and, second, thorough discussion of how to deal with the problem. Different organizations and individuals will have different answers, and different policies. The important thing is to have something in place so you're ready to stand up for your principles and not be swept away in the tide.

— by Fred Brown, SPJ Ethics Committee

CASES: Accountability and Transparency

CASE STUDY: Aaarrghh! Pirates! (and the Press)

SITUATION

Almost one month prior to the release of pop-rock band The Ting Tings' new album, *Sounds From Nowheresville*, all 10 songs from the album were leaked online. Once all figures have been tallied, the leak will likely cause The Ting Tings' record label, Roc Nation, to lose hundreds of thousands of dollars because fans will illegally download the album instead of buy it. Roc Nation scrambled to move the release date up a few weeks to negate the early leak of material.

It is situations like this, though, that have plagued the music industry since Napster first initiated widespread illegal file-sharing in June 1999. The music industry has been limping along ever since, struggling to fight off illegal downloads and sales declines. However, media outlets like *Rolling Stone* and *Billboard*, a music industry publication that covers all breaking music news, are not helping the situation. As collections of songs, studio recordings from an upcoming album or merely unreleased demos, are leaked online, these outlets cover the leak with a breaking story or a blog post. But they don't stop there. *Rolling Stone* and *Billboard* often also will include a link within the story to listen to the songs that were leaked. Considering the news value of this inclusion, it makes sense to include the illegal material, supplementing the copy with the music in question.

Question: Yet, from an ethical standpoint, if *Billboard* and *Rolling Stone* are essentially pointing readers in the right direction — to the leaked music — are they not aiding in helping the Internet community find the material and consume it?

ANALYSIS

Because the digital music community is vast, extending across multiple continents, the consequences of any illegal leak are incalculable. In that same way, providing news coverage of the leak is like playing with an immense fire. With these considerations, then, should music media outlets like *Billboard* and *Rolling Stone* continue to cover music leaks, consequentially perpetuating the cycle, or should they cease to cover these occurrences entirely, as a way to quell the illegality with silence?

Since the introduction of iTunes and the digital music environment, the industry itself has struggled with an outdated business model. Fighting for the mighty dollar, record labels turn to promotion — often times misleading consumers into thinking the majority of albums or song collections can be expected to sound like the catchy single used to promote the album — and subsequently alienate fans and consumers. As an outcry to this discrepancy, in recent years fans have refused to pay for music because it was either overpriced or not in accordance with their sonic expectations. Even so, disappointment or unfair pricing does not justify stealing music and intellectual property. Although the music industry business model is broken, the means of stealing are not justified. As such, this situation, when considered wholly empirically, is a deontological one: fans should not be downloading music leaks — so the act of stealing is clearly wrong.

However, providing media coverage of the leaks' occurrence in the first place is not so clear-cut.

> The ends (coverage) are not justified by the means (illegality).

While there is no policy on media covering a leak, the practice is often to redirect the web traffic centered on the leak instantaneously toward media outlets' websites instead. Therefore, within moments after the leak occurs, *Rolling Stone* or *Billboard* can file a story online about the instance, and if there is a clip of the leaked song or songs included within the copy, search results will include these links near the top and site visits will spike — or at least that is the mentality. Yet this bloodlust-style of driving website traffic does not justify the inclusion of the leaked material, much less covering the news event in the first place. Instead, the free flow of information justifies it, since readers have the right to stay informed if their favorite band, like The Ting Tings, had its album leaked online.

Considering the stakeholders involved in any leak situation, the effects of leaks, which translate to illegally downloaded music and a loss of profit, can largely be attributed to the musicians and record labels involved. Media outlets are also considered, as aforementioned. However, fans also hold some stake in this situation. Ultimately, when a leak occurs, every fan or consumer has the right to choose whether or not to download the new music. Downloading is never forced upon them. Therefore, they have a right to know about whether a leak has occurred because they have the right to choose to benefit from it. They have the right to access all information about the song from *Billboard* or *Rolling Stone*, just short of how to actually download the music — and it is in these organizations' best interest to cover the leak as a newsworthy event, for it would not be proper journalistic practice to ignore something of this magnitude, with so many parties involved.

In this ethical dilemma, one must consider the stakeholders as the foremost priority. The consumers should be considered most highly, since they are essentially driving the industry. Although the Ting Tings' situation is an unfortunate one, it is not the responsibility of the media outlets to protect their recorded music from being leaked. Moreover, the included clips themselves are not downloadable, merely listenable. Ultimately, these songs have already been leaked; *Billboard*, *Rolling Stone*, and similar organizations are empowering readers by providing them the information necessary to make a choice — to illegal download or not to illegally download, that is the question. In this view, the media outlets have a deontological role, as their duty is to provide information and news.

DECISION

While they may be pointing readers toward the leaked music by including clips with the copy, *Billboard* and *Rolling Stone* are not forcing their readers to download it. If anything, these services are providing a best-of-both-worlds solution, allowing the readers to enjoy the leaked music but not place it on their hard drives. This inconvenience — and it is a large inconvenience to visit a website every time fans want to listen to a song — would prevent fans from repeated visits and therefore repeated listens and potentially, in some scenarios like the one of The Ting Tings, promote the music and drive sales. Including a clip of the leaked song in the copy is far from unethical considering the alternatives. The ethics of songs' illegal leaking is an absolute, a right or wrong, deontology — but providing media coverage of the leak is a little bit ethically trickier. With the understanding that covering a leak is like covering any other news event, for the sake and free flow of information and the reader's right to know, including an embedded clip of the leaked song in the copy is purely a means of providing more information. Whether the leak itself is ethical is disregarded at this point; from a teleological standpoint, the ends (coverage) are not justified by the means (illegality). Sorry, Ting Tings, but it is entirely ethical to include the clip in the copy if it is for the betterment of the story and for readers' awareness.

— by Cory Lamz, University of Denver

CASE STUDY: You Don't Know Jack

WHAT: In 2004, a prize-winning journalist at an extremely well-read publication resigned after allegations were brought against him that he fabricated several of his stories, including one that won him a Pulitzer Prize. Jack Kelley made up people who didn't exist, said he witnessed events that he actually never saw, and put others' reputations on the line while doing so. *USA Today*, his employer of 21 years, nominated him for a Pulitzer Prize five separate times, and it was later determined that he fabricated at least part of a story that won him the honor.

> It is important to have an emergency communication plan in place in order to avoid public confusion.

When *USA Today* published its expose' on the situation, the newspaper reported that Kelley fabricated substantial portions of at least eight major stories, lifted nearly two dozen quotes or other material from competing publications, falsely represented what was happening in photographs he ran with his stories, lied in speeches he gave for the newspaper and conspired to mislead those investigating his work. The investigation later found that he had been fabricating stories since 1991.

Kelley quit in January 2004 after admitting to misleading those investigating his work, and a team was formed to investigate all of his stories because the company feared he had plagiarized other pieces. The group reviewed 720 articles, each looked over by two members of the nine-member team. According to the *USA Today* article, Kelley lied about the following:

- Spending a night with Egyptian terrorists in 1997
- Meeting a vigilante Jewish settler named Avi Shapiro in 2001
- Watching a Pakistani student unfold a picture of the Sears Tower and say, "This one is mine," in 2001
- Visiting a suspected terrorist crossing point on the Pakistan-Afghanistan border in 2002
- Interviewing the daughter of an Iraqi general in 2003
- Going on a high-speed hunt for Osama bin Laden in 2003
- Observing the bomber in the 2001 story that won him a Pulitzer Prize

QUESTION: How does the newspaper rectify the situation? (This is a question that can be addressed from both a journalistic and strategic communications perspective.)

WHO: The perpetrator: Jack Kelley, a Pulitzer Prize-winning author who had worked at *USA Today* for his entire 21-year career.

The decision-makers: *USA Today* publisher Craig Moon was ultimately responsible for what was published in his paper. The nine-member investigative team was headed by three former newspaper editors, including Bill Hilliard (former president of the American Society of Newspaper Editors), Bill Kovach (founder of the Committee of Concerned Journalists and former editor of the *Atlanta Journal-Constitution*) and John Seigenthaler (*USA Today's* founding editorial director).

The stakeholders: The public who had read and respected Jack Kelley's stories for many years, the advertisers who trusted that they were investing in a reputable publication, and of course Kelley himself.

WHY: Principles at issue include the fact that Kelley made up stories and then presented them to the public as factual news. Deceit, deception and dishonesty are just a few of the terms that can describe his actions.

There were several issues to consider when *USA Today* discovered his deceit. First, what should the paper do with the offending reporter? Second, what kind of damage control do you conduct in a situation like this? Third, what will be the effect on the public perception of the newspaper? Lastly, how do you go about preventing a similar situation in the future?

If you were *USA Today*, how would you go about handling this reporter's actions? Would you place him on probation while you investigated? How far into the investigation would you fire him? At what point would you let the public know of his indiscretions? Would you make a public apology? What would you say?

HOW: In a situation like this, it is important to have an emergency communication plan in place in order to avoid public confusion. Only specified people should communicate with the public or media on the matter and the employees of the company should be informed on the investigation. In order to keep credibility, it would be imperative for a comprehensive investigation with severe consequences for the reporter in question to be launched.

Legal action would be another possibility for the paper to consider because the employee falsely represented the company by submitting stories he knew weren't true. This would show the public that the newspaper prides itself on news values and takes any breach seriously.

DECISION: *USA Today* asked three journalists with impeccable credentials to head an investigative team that spent weeks reviewing Kelley's work. The three team leaders spent more than 20 hours interviewing Kelley. *USA Today* published the panel's findings in PDF form on the Internet and issued a public apology to its readers and the profession. Kelley was dismissed and, lastly, Hal Ritter, the managing editor of the News section, and Karen Jurgensen, editor, both resigned in the wake of the scandal.

— *Laura Barth and Sara Stone, Baylor University*

CASE STUDY: The Times and Jayson Blair

WHAT: Jayson Blair advanced quickly during his tenure at *The New York Times*, where he was hired as a full-time staff writer after his internship there and others at *The Boston Globe* and *The Washington Post*. Even accusations of inaccuracy and a series of corrections to his reports on Washington, D.C.-area sniper attacks did not stop Blair from moving on to national coverage of the war in Iraq. But when suspicions arose over his reports on military families, an internal review found that he was fabricating material and communicating with editors from his Brooklyn apartment — or within the *Times* building — rather than from outside New York.

Some *Times* staffers, opposed to what they viewed as favoritism by Executive Editor Howell Raines, blamed a star system that allowed Blair to advance unusually fast in an extremely competitive, mostly veteran environment. Blair's former boss, Jonathan Landman, said race played a large part in the African-American writer's ascendancy.

The findings of a 25-member committee headed by Allan Siegal, an assistant managing editor, led to the appointment of a public editor and stricter editorial policies. But staffing changes and higher standards could not change what happened: The *Times*'s reputation was deeply tarnished. Raines and Managing Editor Gerald Boyd resigned in a cloud of mismanagement. Journalism, in general, suffered perhaps the biggest blow to its credibility in U.S. history.

QUESTION: How does the *Times* investigate problems and correct policies that allowed the Blair scandal to happen?

WHO: The consequences of Blair's actions are so broad that it is important to have representatives from all staff levels, as well as journalists outside the *Times* staff, weigh in on corrective steps. Leading this group should be one or several highly ethical consensus-builders who can solicit and synthesize ideas from throughout the profession.

In the case of the *Times*, stakeholders range from the humble retiree who simply reads his paper in the morning, to the power-wielding diplomat who relies on foreign-policy reports to inform her decisions. Journalists, too, lose ground when a colleague lowers the public's value of their work. As a group, the biggest stakeholders are citizens of democracies, which depend on journalists to grow trust in readers with accurate reporting.

WHY: The Blair case raises questions about hiring, management and overall editorial policy. First, there is the issue of relative inexperience in a super-high-stakes newsroom. Is it fair to senior staffers to allow a fresh-out-of-college writer to step into the ranks? More importantly, is it fair to expect such an inexperienced writer, however talented, to produce reporting as sharp as that of a decorated correspondent? While a pure meritocracy allows an individual of any experience level to fill any role, talent in the absence of experience could lead to diminished professionalism: Blair's ability to impress editors with his writing may have led to him feeling that facts are less important than prose.

Second, there is the question of who is responsible for letting Blair go so far. Is it the editor who hired him straight from the University of Maryland? How about successive editors, who, despite their mediocre evaluations, did not object loudly enough to Blair's promotions? Could the executive and managing editors, with their big-picture roles and busy days, truly be responsible for one staffer's malfeasance?

Third, there must be a better way. Is it enough to know what went wrong and tighten the reigns on practices, such as anonymous sources? Or does the *Times* need an auditor, someone it pays for a scolding? Why should an outsider be allowed to make recommendations on better internal practices? Then again, how could an insider, in earshot of the mess itself, lead the committee to fix things?

HOW: The *Times* decided that to remedy the nasty ramifications of the Blair scandal, it would commission an insider, along with others in and outside the *Times* newsroom, to investigate problems and suggest changes. The insider, Siegal, decided the *Times* should hire an outsider (who would be former *Life* magazine editor Daniel Okrent) to suggest further improvements. And *Times* editorial policy changed to reflect a much more cautious, conservative atmosphere concerning staff promotions and, especially, verification of reporting. A notable example of the latter aspect regards anonymous sources. In terms of staffing, the *Times* went so far as to require written evaluations for any candidates transferring between posts.

A particularly difficult aspect of the fallout, although one welcome by staffers who felt marginalized, was the dual resignation of Raines and Boyd. That development, at least in the view of Publisher Arthur Sulzberger, was for the greater good of the *Times*. Symbolically, their departures made it possible for observers to view the *Times* as a reformed institution.

— By Adrian Uribarri, SPJ Ethics Committee

Another question: This case can also be analyzed from the perspective of the people responsible for upholding the *Times*'s image.

CASE STUDY: And the Winner Is . . .

WHAT: The 2000 presidential election was riddled with controversy. Mistakes were made on both sides of the political spectrum, from indiscretions to straight-up unlawfulness. But the biggest offenders on Election Day itself were not the candidates, George W. Bush and Al Gore, or their supporters. The biggest offenders were the members of the media.

Prior to Election Day, the race was tight, with Bush in the lead in the state-by-state race, and Gore an extremely close second. Every vote counted, at least in the "trifecta." That's what the three states were called that hung the election in the balance: Pennsylvania, Michigan and Florida. If the trailing Gore could win these three, he could take the lead and the Oval Office. But if Bush could retain even one of these states, the presidency was his.

As time ticked on, it became clear that everything would come down to the Sunshine State. Gore decided to end his 18-month campaign in Florida, where Gov. Jeb Bush was busy making calls to his fellow Republicans throughout the state. The stakes were unbelievably high, while the voting differentials were low. Numbers were close, and it became clear that the voters in Florida would decide the presidency.

At 7 p.m. Eastern Time on Election Day, the portion of Florida lying in the Eastern Time Zone closed its polls. The VNS, or Voter News Service, had gathered information in exit polls at precincts throughout the Eastern Time Zone and used it to arrive at its prediction that Al Gore had won Florida. The portion of the Florida population residing in the Central Time Zone area of the state still had another hour of voting. But VNS did not wait for those Central Time exit polls to close before submitting their projected winner to the television networks. Their rush to get the information on air turned out to be a mistake that would cost the media a lot of credibility.

At 6:49 p.m. Central Time, the radio crackled the false message over the airwaves that Al Gore was the projected winner of the state of Florida. In the ensuing minutes, seconds even, other networks picked up this news flash and ran with it. And within the next 11 minutes, two-thirds of all voters in Florida's western Panhandle heard about it.

Before the incorrect information could be retracted, the voting lines closed at 7 p.m. Central Time. People only had to arrive by 7 p.m. to be allowed to vote. They could wait in line for as long as it took. So the polls themselves wouldn't have closed until every person who arrived had been allowed to vote. But when last-minute voters on the way to their voting stations heard the news, their feeling of ineffectiveness was overwhelming. Many voters reported that they turned around and went home.

Some 187,000 registered voters in the Florida Central Time Zone didn't vote in the Bush v. Gore election. Perhaps a number of them chose not to vote out of pure disinterest. But many didn't vote due to the false "winner announcement" heard over the radio. A Yale study estimates a loss of 10,000 votes for Bush due to the blunder. Another study, done by a Washington, D.C.-based firm, puts the loss at about 11,500 votes. It estimates that 28,050 voters were discouraged from voting due to the premature announcement, and that 64 percent of those voters were planning on voting for Bush.

> The competition to be first in calling a winner in an election may, in fact, affect the outcome.

The VNS, as well as various news networks, later apologized for their error. But hardly any of the network heads were willing to accept the impact their mistake had made on the integrity of the presidential election. ABC News President David Westin said: "There was no point during the evening when it was likely or even possible that voters would decide not to vote simply because of the erroneous projection of the presidential race in Florida." Clearly Mr. Westin underestimated the power of the media, because, as one dissuaded Florida voter put it, "You know, a lot of people take the news as gospel."

Question: Did the news media's early and erroneous release of the Bush vs. Gore presidential race affect voters before the polls closed? And, on a larger scale, does the race to beat out competitors affect the trustworthiness of news networks? Does the race to be first result in guesswork journalism?

WHO: NBC was the first network to announce the false report of Gore's Florida victory. What would you have done as a reporter for another news network? Would you have borrowed the story and run with it, even though you knew the Central Time polls wouldn't close for at least another 11 minutes?

Pretend you're a Florida voter on your way to the polls. Traffic is jammed, you're tired from a long day of work and the lines at the polls will undoubtedly be long. You hear over your car radio that Gore has already won Florida. Would you continue to the polls to cast your vote anyway? Or would you take the news for truth, turn your car around and head on home for dinner?

WHY: A similar situation occurred in the 1980 election, 20 years earlier, in the race between Ronald Reagan and Jimmy Carter. President Carter's approval ratings had been so low that, come November, he didn't appear to stand a chance. When projections showed Reagan's incredible advantage, Carter chose to concede before many West Coast voters ever made it to the polls.

The erroneous VNS projections caused a similar effect in 2000. Many voters on the West Coast, operating on a later schedule than their fellow Americans in the East, voted, or opted not to vote, based on false information.

Thus, because of technology and our incredible ability to communicate over entire continents, the integrity of the presidential election has greatly suffered.

HOW: Why would the VNS report false information? Do you think the error was malicious? Or do you think it was simply a case of competitive journalism gone awry?

Think of ways that this situation could have been avoided. Possible examples might include better fact checking or a wider range of sources.

Also, consider the incredible effect that the news media can have on individuals, both large-scale and small-scale. How can you, as a journalist, work to avoid involvement in rapacious reporting? Does news need to be confirmed as 100 percent accurate before being reported?

Since the 2000 election, the news media have made strides to avoid repeating their blunder. They no longer will rely on the VNS. In fact, the VNS has disbanded. News networks will now take their own polls, and they will be much more careful about estimating races that are too close to call. But the news business is still a race against time. As CBS News Vice President Linda Mason said, "If we hit 270 [electoral college votes], if anybody gets to 270, we're certainly going to estimate the president."

ANALYSIS

The VNS made a mistake by failing to include absentee voters and in relying on antiquated computer software programs to create inaccurate information. Complete accuracy is needed before information is presented to the public. And that's simply not the case here. News and truth must be synonymous.

In spite of tabloids, blogs and various other non-reliable sources, people still look to the mainstream media for their news, their truth. As a practitioner of journalism, you have a duty to report the truth. Of course, you have a duty — not to mention a financial urgency — to report it in a timely manner. Old news doesn't sell papers. But if timeliness and the urge to beat out competitors come at the cost of telling the truth, it's not worth it. Your career can end over mistakes like that. Entire nations can be jeopardized with mistakes like that.

(Postscript: Since the 2000 election, the news media have made strides to avoid repeating their blunder. The VNS has disbanded. News networks will now take their own polls, and they promise to be much more careful about estimating races that are too close to call.)

— by Elizabeth Suggs and Sara Stone, Baylor University

CASE STUDY: CIA Crack Contra-versy

SUMMARY

The reprint of the *San Jose Mercury News* series "Dark Alliance" hit the desks of newspapers across America in the summer of 1996 with an unusual greeting from executive editor Jerry Ceppos. His letter began, "Dear Editor: At first I found the story too preposterous to take seriously."

Ceppos, it turned out, wasn't alone.

Several of the nation's largest newspapers criticized the *Mercury News*'s three-part series, challenging its findings and questioning the motives and skills of its author, investigative reporter Gary Webb.

The series alleged that two Nicaraguan drug dealers with connections to the CIA-backed Contra army — along with a Los Angeles drug dealer — had "opened the first pipeline between Colombia's cocaine cartels and the black neighborhoods of Los Angeles, a city now known as the crack capital of the world." (The series called one of the Nicaraguans "the Johnny Appleseed of crack cocaine.") The drug dealers funneled "millions in drug profits" to the Contras, the newspaper reported, adding that the ring "helped spark a crack explosion in urban America." All this took place at the same time the guerrilla army was being funded and advised by the CIA, the series reported. The Mercury News never flatly asserted that the CIA was behind any drug dealing or was even aware of it.

In his letter to editors Ceppos wrote, "A drug ring virtually introduced crack cocaine in the United States and sent the profits of the drug sales to the U.S.-government supported Contras in Nicaragua. All the while, our government failed to stop the drug sales. ... In quiet, reasoned articles, Webb proved the case."

The Los Angeles Times didn't think so. Nor did *The Washington Post* or *The New York Times*, among other newspapers, which debunked the series. In October 1996, the *Mercury News* responded by publishing its own analysis of the series and its criticism. The lengthy piece was written by a reporter not connected to the original series.

Numerous issues surfaced regarding the series: the conduct of the reporter and editors, the role of the Internet and reaction from other media outlets.

Consider:
- The series did not establish a firm link between the CIA and drugs. Yet a logo that ran on the *Mercury News*' Web site — and in the reprints — depicted a man smoking a crack pipe superimposed over the CIA seal. The logo did not appear in the newspaper. The logo was removed from the Web site only after a critical story appeared in *The Washington Post*. Ceppos told *American Journalism Review* that the logo was the newspaper's "main regret."
- The stories ignited anger and outrage, particularly in the African-American community At first, when the series received a muted response, many black leaders suggested that if these sorts of suspicions had been raised concerning any other community, there would be widespread calls for congressional investigations and demands for government action. "People in high places were winking

and blinking, and our children were dying," said U.S. Rep. Maxine Waters, a Los Angeles Democrat.
- According to *American Journalism Review*, Ceppos didn't read the entire series before it ran.

Critics of the series argued that the *Mercury News* had irresponsibly fanned suspicions about a government conspiracy to destroy black neighborhoods. Supporters, meanwhile, said that although some aspects of the newspaper series may have been hyped, the general thesis—that drug dealers associated with the Contras sold cocaine in South-Central Los Angeles at about the time the crack explosion began—should not have been brushed aside.

The *Washington Post, L.A. Times* and *New York Times* led the charge in dismantling the series, though not all media reaction was unfavorable.

The *L.A. Times's* three-part condemnation of the series covered six and a half pages—more than the *Mercury News*'s original pieces. In its 5,000-word attack, *The Washington Post* called the series "weak on evidence." *Post* ombudsman Geneva Overholser wrote that the *Mercury News* series was "seriously flawed ... reported by a seemingly hotheaded fellow willing to have people leap to conclusions his reporting couldn't back up." However, Overholser also called the *Post*'s attack a "case of misdirected zeal" and concluded that "the *Post* (and others) showed more passion for sniffing out the flaws in San Jose's answer than for sniffing out a better answer themselves."

> Numerous issues surfaced regarding the series: the conduct of the reporter and editors, the role of the Internet and reaction from other media outlets.

After re-examining "Dark Alliance" with seven *Mercury News* reporters and editors, Ceppos acknowledged in a May 1997 column that the series had "shortcomings," was "oversimplified" and fell short of his journalistic standards.

"... We fell short at every step of our process, in the writing, editing and production of our work," Ceppos wrote in the column, which appeared on the front page of the Mercury News's Sunday opinion section. "Several people here share that burden .... But ultimately, the responsibility was, and is, mine."

Ceppos wrote that the *Mercury News* presented only one interpretation of complicated, sometimes conflicting evidence; oversimplified the complex issue of how the crack epidemic in America grew; created impressions, through imprecise graphics and language, that were open to misinterpretation; and failed to label the amount of money involved in the drug ring as an estimate.

The reporter, Gary Webb, who was reassigned to a *Mercury News* bureau in Cupertino, California, and instructed not to report further on the case, has stood by his story. In an interview with *The Washington Post*, Webb called Ceppos' column "very bizarre" and in some cases "misleading." He added: "I'm not happy about it at all. It's rather nauseating." Webb resigned from the *Mercury News* in December 1997 and took a state government job. His book, also titled *Dark Alliance*, was published in the fall of 1998. Unable to find another job in daily journalism, Webb committed suicide in December 2004.

ANALYSIS

Two keys to judging this story lie in the motives and competency of both the reporter and the *Mercury News* editors. If Gary Webb's purpose was to attract readers and draw attention to himself with only sketchily supported declarations, the story would be difficult to defend, because a reporter's conviction that the truth is being told is a bedrock necessity of journalism. Similarly, then, the conviction must be supported by solid reporting.

Assuming his sincerity and some substantive competence, the arena in which Webb was operating is a particularly secretive one, meaning that an intense search for story information is only the first step in the truth-telling process. Others must come forward with their information once the first step is taken. If, after conducting serious, professional fact-gathering, Webb had a high level of confidence in his thesis about the drug explosion and its victims, his only course was to start the public discussion. If the story as far as he could take it had merit, it could attain a life of its own as more information was disclosed.

Webb certainly started the discussion, but its direction might be questioned. It would appear that the media critics cited above looked more at his methods and information than at either confirming or discrediting the story per se. This could certainly raise the question of whether journalists are not sometimes more conditioned to protect icons — often their sources — than to provide information the public needs. While it is important to ask publicly whether the story was solid, the emphases of the critics suggest they were more intent on disciplining a rogue colleague than on seeking truth themselves. Nevertheless, journalists calling colleagues to account is a healthy practice.

Because of the secretive nature of both drug dealers and the Central Intelligence Agency, and because the minority community portrayed as victims of the drug explosion sees itself as neglected by the media, the agenda raised by Webb has inherent value. However, partial repudiation of its own story and reporter suggests the Mercury News was not as persuaded as Webb that his information and conclusions were sound. It is interesting to note that the newspaper waited until external criticism reached a crescendo before conducting its own self-examination; a bit more front-end editing and soul searching probably would have been more productive than the post hoc scrambling Ceppos and others engaged in. That said, public accountability remains a valuable component of the entire journalistic enterprise.

As is often the case, perhaps the whole truth of the "Dark Alliance" will never be told. Yet the story ran, seeking to illuminate dark corners, and the reporter's own newspaper and other media called the account into question.

Some questions that could be asked in the production of this and related news stories:
- What standards of fairness should apply to public discussion about government agencies? Does their power to control information about themselves (particularly

the more secretive agencies, such as the CIA) require a different standard of fairness as we engage the public in an open discussion?
- Is there any justification, such as marketing, for including elements in your promotional material that were not fully supported by the story itself (the CIA logo on the Web page and in reprints)? Should newsrooms and marketing departments be held to the same standards of truth-telling, fairness and accuracy?
- How morally defensible is it to present a united front (the newspaper defending its reporter) against outside criticism when members of your own staff may agree with some of the critics?
- What level of proof should a reporter have before drawing conclusions about such matters as a vague connection between the CIA and a drug explosion in a minority neighborhood?
- What level of proof would justify inciting an African-American (or any other) neighborhood's anger against a government agency, as was done in this case? Can discussion born of public anger be considered healthy?

— from earlier editions, Black, Steele and Barney; edited by Elizabeth K. Hansen

CASE STUDY: Nasty Swamp Creatures

WHAT: Polling consistently shows that the American electorate has a generally low opinion of politicians — especially politicians as a group, as in low ratings for Congress — and a promise to "drain the swamp" was an effective tool in Donald Trump's presidential campaign. But individual politicians are not always held in high regard, either.

It may be due to the way political campaigns are run. They're nasty and they're negative. And that may be due, in part, to what was supposed to be a political reform.

Political Action Committees, or PACs, were conceived of as independent groups, as a way to blunt the influence of big donors on the way governance is done. They were organized around issues, or at least some of them were, and that caused problems from the beginning of the "reform." PACs essentially created litmus tests to assess which candidates they would support, often based on an issue the PAC was passionate about: gun rights, say, or the right to an abortion.

Those PACs still try to influence election outcomes, of course, but there also is a large group of PACs formed specifically to support candidates — without working directly with the people they are trying to get elected. Federal law prohibits such collaboration.

Question: Can anything be done to change the negative tone of political advertising?

WHO: Campaign managers are the front-line decision-makers, but it's currently not legal for them to work directly with the PACs that provide advertising money. Ultimately, it may be that only Congress can make the decisions and write the laws that will defang the nastiness of political season.

Stakeholders: Candidates for political office, their campaign staffs, and the political action committees that support them — albeit at arm's length — are the most affected. But so is the American electorate, a majority of whom profess to be disgusted with the tone of attack ads. And television stations, in particular, make a great deal of money from political advertising. The ad rates are higher than for regular advertisers, and the money is usually paid up front.

WHY: This is a situation where telling the truth also would minimize harm. But perhaps more than any other of the main principles in the SPJ and other communicators' codes of ethics, this has to do with accountability and transparency.

Under federal election law, it's illegal for political candidates or anyone associated with their campaigns to "coordinate" with the super PACs that would like to see them elected. As a result, most political advertising the public sees explains in often sinister tones what's wrong with the opposition candidate, rather than upbeat advertising explaining what's good about the candidate the advertiser wants to see elected.

Since both sides typically do this, what the public sees is mainly negative about everyone who's running. Political operatives protest that negative advertising works. But if everybody does it, and somebody always wins, does that mean the ads are effective, or is it simply that the major effect is to keep people from voting?

Although working together is prohibited by the law and Federal Election Commission rules, there are ways around that supposed firewall. One way is the strategic leak. The online magazine Slate explained how this works in an article during the 2016 presidential primaries.

The trick is to "leak," to a news media outlet, internal campaign communications — emails, tweets, memos, etc. — that provide information on what messages the campaign wants to stress, what audience it wants to reach, how much money it figures would have to be spent; in other words, all manner of useful information that can provide guidance to a helpful PAC that has millions of dollars it's just itching to spend.

Slate found one particularly blatant example:

"The award for the most shameless flouting of the FEC rules, though, probably goes to Carly Fiorina's friends, who earlier this year changed the name of their super PAC from 'Carly for America' to 'Conservative, Authentic, Responsive Leadership for You and for America' as not to violate the rule barring an independent group from using a candidate's name in their own. The super PAC opts for an acronym on its signs and other campaign materials: 'CARLY for America.' We're sure that's just to save on printing costs."

DECISION: Maybe such deceptive workarounds wouldn't be necessary if collaboration were legal. If the candidates, and the ads that support them, were allowed to work together, maybe there would be more about each candidate's good qualities, and less about what a horrid troll the other candidate is. Maybe that would lead to more people appreciating that some politicians actually do work in the public interest. Maybe there would be less cynicism, and more reason for trust and hope in the institutions of governance. Maybe more people would vote. Or maybe it would just mean that the influence of big money would be worse than ever.

DISCUSSION: This is a problem especially for students who are considering a career in one of the strategic-communications fields. It has to do with advertising, public relations and campaign management. The idea of doing away with this artificial wall between politician and PAC might be one solution. Or it might not. What are your thoughts? Is there another way to make political campaigns more positive and less negative?

WHAT THE CODES SAY: Accountability and Transparency

PRINCIPLE 4: Advertisers should clearly disclose all material conditions, such as payment or receipt of a free product, affecting endorsements in social and traditional channels, as well as the identity of endorsers, all in the interest of full disclosure and transparency.

PRINCIPLE 8: Advertisers and their agencies, and online and offline media, should discuss privately potential ethical concerns, and members of the team creating ads should be given permission to express internally their ethical concerns.

American Advertising Federation

- Be honest and accurate in all communications.
- Act promptly to correct erroneous communications for which the member is responsible.
- Investigate the truthfulness and accuracy of information released on behalf of those represented.
- Reveal the sponsors for causes and interests represented.
- Disclose financial interest (such as stock ownership) in a client's organization.
- Avoid deceptive practices.

PRSA Code of Ethics

All staffers are encouraged to cooperate with and become familiar with operations in circulation, production, advertising and other departments of The Dallas Morning News. Any advertiser request for stories or photos should be routed through the managing editor's office to avoid any appearance or perception of pressure on this staff. However, any person inside or outside of The Dallas Morning News is encouraged to offer story or photo ideas to the news department, and they should be received courteously.

The Dallas Morning News

If there is a mistake or an injustice, do not cover it up or ignore the situation. Failure to correct it or report promptly to the next higher supervisory level may result in disciplinary action, including termination.

Deseret News, Salt Lake City

To be trusted in the community, we have to be seen as decent, caring and courteous people. That means listening, acknowledging when we're wrong and taking action to correct our mistakes. …

We do not, under any circumstances, expect staffers to tolerate abusive language or behavior from readers or sources. If a caller's language becomes abusive, politely tell him or her that you want to hear him out but that you can't listen to such language. If the language persists, politely ask him to call back when he's calmer, tell him you are going to hang up, and say "goodbye" as you do so. Never end a call unannounced, slam a receiver down or use profanity or obscenity in any telephone conversation, no matter what the provocation. Get out of the conversation or situation, and inform your supervisor immediately as to what has happened.

The Roanoke Times, Virginia

The Register will not give favored treatment in news to anyone. It will report matters regarding itself or its personnel with the same vigor and candor as it would other institutions or individuals.

The Orange County Register, California

We want a dialogue with our readers; they, too, have a stake in this newspaper. It shall be the policy of our editors and staff members to encourage the maximum amount of public participating in bringing all points of view before our readers.

The Honolulu Advertiser

Dow Jones takes this code of conduct very seriously. All employees of Dow Jones are responsible for compliance with all aspects of this code. All new employees shall be required to read this code at the outset of their employment and to attest in writing that they have done so. In addition, all Dow Jones employees shall be required each year to provide a written attestation that they have read and abided by this code during the previous calendar year.

The matters addressed by this code are sufficiently important that any lapse in judgment within the areas covered here may be considered serious enough to warrant discipline up to and including dismissal.

Dow Jones & Company (publishers of the *Wall Street Journal*)

For the sake of accuracy, there is nothing wrong with reading back a quote to the individual who said it to make sure you have it straight.

Reading back an entire story or the gist of it to a source is perilous and ordinarily should be avoided. Any exceptions should be discussed in advance with a supervising editor and should be done only to ensure accuracy. In such cases, reporters should make clear to the source in advance that, whatever the objections, the newspaper will have ultimate control over the final wording and publication.

The Journal News, White Plains, New York

Allowing a source or a subject to see a proposed story before publication in the newspaper is a relatively rare practice among journalists. There is no intrinsic journalistic reason for that reluctance. In fact, pre-publication review of stories or parts of stories should be considered a helpful and useful part of the newsgathering process.

There is no obligation on the part of the reporter or the newspaper at any time to allow a pre-publication review. At the same time, the idea should not be rejected out of hand.

Daily Press, Newport News, Virginia

Stories should not be shown to sources or people outside the newsroom prior to publication.

However, it is sometimes acceptable to allow a source to review portions of stories for purposes of accuracy. For example, an engineer might be sought to review a technically descriptive passage in an environmental story that details how sewer piping allows toxic chemicals to flow into public waters.

Such exceptions should be approved beforehand by the Managing Editor/News.

The Denver Post

Because these Principles embody the highest standards of professional conduct, the Gannett Newspaper Division is committed to their adherence. They have been putting in writing specifically so that members of every Gannett Newspaper Division newsroom know what the Division stands for and what is expected of them. The public will know, too.

Gannett Newspaper Division

The guidelines also are intended to inform the public of the standards by which The Journal Gazette gathers and publishes information. Under this principle, the public has a right to expect a newspaper to remain free from influences, and the appearance of influences, that might affect what is reported. The guidelines represent a pledge by The Journal Gazette and its staff to maintain and cultivate public confidence.

The Journal Gazette, Fort Wayne, Indiana

No employee or director who in good faith reports a violation of this Code will suffer harassment, retaliation or adverse employment consequences. An employee who retaliates against someone who has reported a violation in good faith is subject to discipline up to and including dismissal.

ProPublica

The Times expects its editorial staff to behave with dignity and professionalism. We do nothing while gathering the news that we would be ashamed to see in print or on television. We do not let the behavior of the pack set standards for us.

The Los Angeles Times

In the end, the simplest rule of thumb for ethical decision-making is this: Don't do anything you wouldn't want to explain on the front page of the paper.

Lincoln Journal Star, Nebraska

WHAT THE CODES SAY: Use of Social Media

Anyone who works for the AP must be mindful that opinions they express may damage the AP's reputation as an unbiased source of news. They must refrain from declaring their views on contentious public issues in any public forum, whether in Web logs, chat rooms, letters to the editor, petitions, bumper stickers or lapel buttons, and must not take part in demonstrations in support of causes or movements.

The Associated Press

Many Denver Post reporters and columnists already blog. Blogs allow readers to connect with us on a more personal level, and they help us in building an online audience. We encourage blogging, but we also realize it presents many of the same ethical issues inherent in traditional newspaper journalism, as well as some new issues. The Denver Post's ethics policy provides ample guidance as we provide different kinds of content via the internet. The policy's requirements of accuracy, fairness, independence and disclosure will continue to guide everything we do, including blogging....

Nothing may be published under the Denver Post name, or on its internet sites, unless it has gone through an editing and/or approval process. While blogs are more often written in an informal and personal style, everything that is posted to a blog must be factual and fair. Maliciously and inaccurately attacking private citizens or public officials is prohibited, and any criticism of public officials needs to meet the same standards of fairness as in print....

A staff member who writes a personal blog or who writes for a non-Denver Post internet site should generally avoid writing about topics, institutions or organizations they cover for The Denver Post. This helps to prevent any confusion between professional and personal activities. No personal blog should imply the endorsement of The Denver Post and no Denver Post photograph, video, text or audio may be used on a personal blog without permission from The Denver Post.

Staff members who post comments on internet chat sites, web pages or the blogs of others should use their names and avoid using pseudonyms. We do not publish stories anonymously in the paper, and we should not blog or post online anonymously.

The Denver Post

- Social networking sites are a legitimate and useful way for 21st century journalists to expand and maintain their list of contacts.
- Employees should feel free to join and to utilize these sites. However, as with all other rules and guidelines set forth in this ethics and practices policy, maintain your independence, remain free of obligations to news sources, newsmakers and people on your social network and always act with discretion and integrity.

San Antonio Express-News

The Internet's unique characteristics do not lower the standards by which we evaluate, gather and disseminate information.

Material gathered online should be verified.

Material disseminated online should be solidly confirmed.

The ability to change information around the clock does not lessen the need for accuracy.

Tampa Bay Tribune

Internet communications. Inquirer journalists should mention their Inquirer affiliation only in communications relating to their Inquirer duties. Freelance contributors may mention The Inquirer only when pursuing an Inquirer assignment, and they should make their freelance status clear.

Everyone should keep in mind that the Internet is a public forum. Therefore, people mentioning their Inquirer affiliation should be very careful not to express opinions that would compromise their impartiality in covering the news.

The Philadelphia Inquirer

All written communications, including email, must be carefully written, keeping in mind that they may have to be disclosed in litigation or will otherwise become public.

Hearst Newspapers

All our standards for accuracy, sourcing, taste and avoidance of conflict of interest apply to work posted on The Roanoke Times Online.

However, the digital medium gives us space to post the complete text of something in the news, a court decision, speech or manifesto, for instance. These are posted as resource materials, not news stories, and will be presented verbatim.

But before we post any document on our Web site, it must first be read in its entirety by an appropriate staff member. If there are occasional objectional words in the document, it should be left unchanged, but a note about the offensive language should be posted at the top. If a document contains a great deal of potentially offensive language, it should not be posted without the approval of a senior editor, and a note should be posted at the top.

The Roanoke Times, Virginia

Make certain any electronic communication is genuine and verify all material gathered online unless it is known to be from a credible source. Material disseminated online should be solidly confirmed and all normal standard for fairness apply. Before we post any document on our Web site, it must first be read in its entirety by an appropriate staff member.

Lincoln Journal Star, Nebraska

Journalists may not work for people or organizations they cover or who are regular subjects of Times coverage. Blogs and social media have created potential quandaries for staff members who want to express themselves through those channels. No matter how careful staff members might be to distinguish their personal work from their professional affiliation with The Times, outsiders are likely to see them as intertwined.

As a result, any staff member who seeks to create a personal blog must clear it with a supervisor; approval will be granted only if the proposed blog meets The Times' journalistic standards. When approval is granted, staff members should take care not to write anything in their blogs that would not be acceptable in Times publications. Staff members should observe the same principle when contributing to blogs other than their own or to social media.

The Los Angeles Times

Recently, the National Advertising Division (NAD), the industry's self-regulatory arm, and the Electronic Retailing Self Regulation Program (ERSP) have taken a number of self-regulatory actions when a company is either sponsoring a site or paying for product review by bloggers without a clear, conspicuous and meaningful disclosure of that fact.

The Federal Trade Commission, the chief federal regulator of advertising, has also amended its Endorsement and Testimonial Guides to require bloggers to disclose when they are paid by a company, and when they work for the company whose product is being blogged, also when they are given the product free of charge.

American Advertising Federation

APPENDIX

A History of the SPJ Code of Ethics

1926 version:

(Editors' Note [original]: These Canons of Journalism were drawn up and adopted by The American Society of Newspaper Editors in their annual conventions of 1924 and 1925. The 1926 convention of Sigma Delta Chi, sitting at Madison, Wisconsin, in November, officially adopted the Canons in behalf of the fraternity.)

The primary function of newspapers is to communicate to the human race what its members do, feel and think. Journalism, therefore, demands of its practitioners the widest range of intelligence, of knowledge, and of experience, as well as natural and trained powers of observation and reasoning. To its opportunities as a chronicle are indissolubly linked its obligations as teacher and interpreter.

To the end of finding some means of edifying sound practice and just aspirations of American journalism, these canons are set forth:

I. Responsibility – The right of a newspaper to attract and hold readers is restricted by nothing but considerations of public welfare. The use a newspaper makes of the share of public attention it gains serves to determine its sense of responsibility, which it shares with every member of its staff. A journalist who uses his power for any selfish or otherwise unworthy purpose is faithless to a high trust.

II. Freedom of the Press – Freedom of the press is to be guarded as a vital right of mankind. It is the unquestionable right to discuss whatever is not explicitly forbidden by law, including the wisdom of any restrictive statute.

III. Independence – Freedom from all obligations except that of fidelity to the public interest is vital.
  1. Promotion of any private interest contrary to the general welfare, for whatever reason, is not compatible with honest journalism. So-called news communications from private sources should not be published without notice of their source or else substantiation of their claims to value as news, both in form and substance.

2. Partisanship, in editorial comment which knowingly departs from the truth, does violence to the best spirit of American journalism; in the news columns it is subversive of a fundamental principle of the profession.

IV. Sincerity, Truthfulness, Accuracy – Good faith with the reader is the foundation of all journalism worth of the name.
1. By every consideration of good faith a newspaper is constrained to be truthful. It is not to be excused for lack of thoroughness or accuracy within its control or failure to obtain command of these essential qualities.
2. Headlines should be fully warranted by the contents of the articles which they surmount.

V. Impartiality – Sound practice makes clear distinction between news reports and expressions of opinion. News reports should be free from opinion or bias of any kind.
1. This rule does not apply to so-called special articles unmistakably devoted to advocacy, or characterized by a signature authorizing the writer's own conclusions and interpretation.

VI. Fair Play – A newspaper should not publish unofficial charges affecting reputation or moral character without opportunity given to the accused to be heard; right practice demands the giving of such opportunity in all cases of serious accusation outside judicial proceedings.
1. A newspaper should not invade private rights or feeling without sure warrant of public right as distinguished from public curiosity.
2. It is the privilege, as it is the duty, of a newspaper to make prompt and complete correction of its own serious mistakes of fact of opinion, whatever their origin.

VII. Decency – A newspaper cannot escape conviction of insincerity if while profession high moral purpose it supplies incentives to base conduct, such as are to be found in details of crime or vice, publication of which is not demonstrably for the general good. Lacking authority to enforce its canons, the journalism here represented can but express the hope that deliberate pandering to vicious instincts will encounter effective public disapproval or yield to the influence of a preponderant professional condemnation.

(Editors' Note [original]: The A.S.N.E. adopted the above Canons of Journalism at their 1924 convention, and their 1925 convention voted to add the following paragraph):

To its privileges under the freedom of American Institutions are inseparably joined its responsibilities for an intelligent fidelity to the Constitution of the United States.

1973 version:

(First revision since 1973; adopted by the 1973 national convention of The Society of Professional Journalists, Sigma Delta Chi. References to "newspapers" are replaced by "media" or "mass media." Much of the language is similar to 1926; Casey Bukro wrote this version.)

The Society of Professional Journalists, Sigma Delta Chi, believes the duty of journalists is to serve the truth.

We believe the agencies of mass communication are carriers of public discussion and information, acting on their Constitutional mandate and freedom to learn and report the facts.

We believe in public enlightenment as the forerunner of justice, and in our Constitutional role to seek the truth as part of the public's right to know the truth.

We believe those responsibilities carry obligations that require journalists to perform with intelligence, objectivity, accuracy and fairness.

To these ends, we declare acceptance of the standards of practice here set forth:

RESPONSIBILITY: The public's right to know of events of public importance and interest is the overriding mission of the mass media. The purpose of distributing news and enlightened opinion is to serve the general welfare. Journalists who use their professional status as representatives of the public for selfish or other unworthy motives violate a high trust.

FREEDOM OF THE PRESS: Freedom of the press is to be guarded as an inalienable right of people in a free society. It carries with it the freedom and the responsibility to discuss, question and challenge actions and utterances of our government and of our public and private institutions. Journalists uphold the right to speak unpopular opinions and the privilege to agree with the majority.

ETHICS: Journalists must be free of obligation to any interest other than the public's right to know the truth.
1. Gifts, favors, free travel, special treatment or privileges can compromise the integrity of journalists and their employers. Nothing of value should be accepted.
2. Secondary employment, political involvement, holding public office, and service in community organizations should be avoided if it compromises the integrity of journalists and their employers. Journalists and their employers should conduct their personal lives in a manner that protects them from conflict of interest, real or apparent. Their responsibilities to the public are paramount. That is the nature of their profession.
3. So-called news communications from private sources should not be published or broadcast without substantiation of their claims to news value.
4. Journalists will seek news that serves the public interest despite the obstacles. They will make constant efforts to assure that the public's business is conducted in public and that public records are open to public inspection.

5. Journalists acknowledge the newsman's ethic of protecting confidential sources of information.

ACCURACY AND OBJECTIVITY: Good faith with the public is the foundation of all worthy journalism.
1. Truth is our ultimate goal.
2. Objectivity in reporting the news is another goal, which serves as the mark of an experienced professional. It is a standard of performance toward which we strive. We honor those who achieve it.
3. There is no excuse for inaccuracies or lack of thoroughness.
4. Newspaper headlines should be fully warranted by the contents of the articles they accompany. Photographs and telecasts should give an accurate picture of an event and not highlight a minor incident of out context.
5. Sound practice makes clear distinction between news reports and expressions of opinion. News reports should be free of opinion or bias and represent all sides of an issue.
6. Partisanship in editorial comment that knowingly departs from the truth violates the spirit of American journalism.
7. Journalists recognize their responsibility for offering informed analysis, comment and editorial opinion on public events and issues. They accept the obligation to present such material by individuals whose competence, experience and judgment qualify them for it.
8. Special articles or presentations devoted to advocacy or the writer's own conclusions and interpretations should be labeled as such.

FAIR PLAY: Journalists at all times will show respect for the dignity, privacy, rights and well-being of people encountered in the course of gathering and presenting the news.
1. The news media should not communicate unofficial charges affecting reputation or moral character without giving the accused a chance to reply.
2. The news media must guard against invading a person's right to privacy.
3. The media should not pander to morbid curiosity about details of vice and crime.
4. It is the duty of news media to make prompt and complete correction of their errors.
5. Journalists should be accountable to the public for their reports, and the public should be encouraged to voice its grievances against the media. Open dialogue with our readers, viewers and listeners should be fostered.

PLEDGE: Journalists should actively censure and try to prevent violations of these standards, and they should encourage their observance by all newspeople. Adherence to this code of ethics is intended to preserve the bond of mutual trust and respect between American journalists and the American people.

1987 version:

(Incorporates changes made in 1984 and 1987; they are indicated by italics. The pledge, in particular, is new and eliminates the admonition that journalists should "actively censure" breaches of the code.)

The SOCIETY of Professional Journalists, Sigma Delta Chi, believes the duty of journalists is to serve the truth.

We BELIEVE the agencies of mass communication are carriers of public discussion and information, acting on their Constitutional mandate and freedom to learn and report the facts.

We BELIEVE in public enlightenment as the forerunner of justice, and in our Constitutional role to seek the truth as part of the public's right to know the truth.

We BELIEVE those responsibilities carry obligations that require journalists to perform with intelligence, objectivity, accuracy and fairness.

To these ends, we declare acceptance of the standards of practice here set forth:

RESPONSIBILITY: The public's right to know of events of public importance and interest is the overriding mission of the mass media. The purpose of distributing news and enlightened opinion is to serve the general welfare. Journalists who use their professional status as representatives of the public for selfish or other unworthy motives violate a high trust.

FREEDOM OF THE PRESS: Freedom of the press is to be guarded as an inalienable right of people in a free society. It carries with it the freedom and the responsibility to discuss, question and challenge actions and utterances of our government and of our public and private institutions. Journalists uphold the right to speak unpopular opinions and the privilege to agree with the majority.

ETHICS: Journalists must be free of obligation to any interest other than the public's right to know the truth.
1. Gifts, favors, free travel, special treatment or privileges can compromise the integrity of journalists and their employers. Nothing of value should be accepted.
2. Secondary employment, political involvement, holding public office, and service in community organizations should be avoided if it compromises the integrity of journalists and their employers. Journalists and their employers should conduct their personal lives in a manner that protects them from conflict of interest, real or apparent. Their responsibilities to the public are paramount. That is the nature of their profession.
3. So-called news communications from private sources should not be published or broadcast without substantiation of their claims to news values.
4. Journalists will seek news that serves the public interest despite the obstacles. They will make constant efforts to assure that the public's business is conducted in public and that public records are open to public inspection.

5. Journalists acknowledge the newsman's ethic of protecting confidential sources of information.
6. *Plagiarism is dishonest and is unacceptable. (added in 1984)*

ACCURACY AND OBJECTIVITY: Good faith with the public is the foundation of all worthy journalism.
1. Truth is our ultimate goal.
2. Objectivity in reporting the news is another goal *that* serves as the mark of an experienced professional. It is a standard of performance toward which we strive. We honor those who achieve it.
3. There is no excuse for inaccuracies or lack of thoroughness.
4. Newspaper headlines should be fully warranted by the contents of the articles they accompany. Photographs and telecasts should give an accurate picture of an event and not highlight a minor incident of out context.
5. Sound practice makes clear distinction between news reports and expressions of opinion. News reports should be free of opinion or bias and represent all sides of an issue.
6. Partisanship in editorial comment that knowingly departs from the truth violates the spirit of American journalism.
7. Journalists recognize their responsibility for offering informed analysis, comment and editorial opinion on public events and issues. They accept the obligation to present such material by individuals whose competence, experience and judgment qualify them for it.
8. Special articles or presentations devoted to advocacy or the writer's own conclusions and interpretations should be labeled as such.

FAIR PLAY: Journalists at all times will show respect for the dignity, privacy, rights and well-being of people encountered in the course of gathering and presenting the news.
1. The news media should not communicate unofficial charges affecting reputation or moral character without giving the accused a chance to reply.
2. The news media must guard against invading a person's right to privacy.
3. The media should not pander to morbid curiosity about details of vice and crime.
4. It is the duty of news media to make prompt and complete correction of their errors.
5. Journalists should be accountable to the public for their reports, and the public should be encouraged to voice its grievances against the media. Open dialogue with our readers, viewers and listeners should be fostered.

PLEDGE: *Adherence to this code is intended to preserve the bond of mutual trust and respect between American journalists and the American people.*

The Society shall – by programs of education and other means – encourage individual journalists to adhere to these tenets, and shall encourage journalistic publications and broadcasters to recognize their responsibility to frame codes of ethics in concert with their employees to serve as guidelines in furthering these goals.(amended in 1987)

1996 version:

This was a thorough rewriting of the code and took more than two years. The first proposal offered by an expanded ethics committee didn't get a favorable reception at the 1995 SPJ national convention. The committee was told to try again. This version was accepted to a standing ovation. A disclaimer legal note at the bottom was added in 2009, at the urging of SPJ's attorneys. A very similar version is part of the 2014 Code, and you can read it there.

Preamble

Members of the Society of Professional Journalists believe that public enlightenment is the forerunner of justice and the foundation of democracy. The duty of the journalist is to further those ends by seeking truth and providing a fair and comprehensive account of events and issues. Conscientious journalists from all media and specialties strive to serve the public with thoroughness and honesty. Professional integrity is the cornerstone of a journalist's credibility. Members of the Society share a dedication to ethical behavior and adopt this code to declare the Society's principles and standards of practice.

Seek Truth and Report It

Journalists should be honest, fair and courageous in gathering, reporting and interpreting information.

Journalists should:
- Test the accuracy of information from all sources and exercise care to avoid inadvertent error. Deliberate distortion is never permissible.
- Diligently seek out subjects of news stories to give them the opportunity to respond to allegations of wrongdoing.
- Identify sources whenever feasible. The public is entitled to as much information as possible on sources' reliability.
- Always question sources' motives before promising anonymity. Clarify conditions attached to any promise made in exchange for information. Keep promises.
- Make certain that headlines, news teases and promotional material, photos, video, audio, graphics, sound bites and quotations do not misrepresent. They should not oversimplify or highlight incidents out of context.
- Never distort the content of news photos or video. Image enhancement for technical clarity is always permissible. Label montages and photo illustrations.
- Avoid misleading re-enactments or staged news events. If re-enactment is necessary to tell a story, label it.
- Avoid undercover or other surreptitious methods of gathering information except when traditional open methods will not yield information vital to the public.
- Use of such methods should be explained as part of the story.
- Never plagiarize.
- Tell the story of the diversity and magnitude of the human experience boldly, even when it is unpopular to do so.

- Examine their own cultural values and avoid imposing those values on others.
- Avoid stereotyping by race, gender, age, religion, ethnicity, geography, sexual orientation, disability, physical appearance or social status.
- Support the open exchange of views, even views they find repugnant.
- Give voice to the voiceless; official and unofficial sources of information can be equally valid.
- Distinguish between advocacy and news reporting. Analysis and commentary should be labeled and not misrepresent fact or context.
- Distinguish news from advertising and shun hybrids that blur the lines between the two.
- Recognize a special obligation to ensure that the public's business is conducted in the open and that government records are open to inspection.

Minimize Harm

Ethical journalists treat sources, subjects and colleagues as human beings deserving of respect.

Journalists should:
- Show compassion for those who may be affected adversely by news coverage. Use special sensitivity when dealing with children and inexperienced sources or subjects.
- Be sensitive when seeking or using interviews or photographs of those affected by tragedy or grief.
- Recognize that gathering and reporting information may cause harm or discomfort. Pursuit of the news is not a license for arrogance.
- Recognize that private people have a greater right to control information about themselves than do public officials and others who seek power, influence or attention.
- Only an overriding public need can justify intrusion into anyone's privacy.
- Show good taste. Avoid pandering to lurid curiosity.
- Be cautious about identifying juvenile suspects or victims of sex crimes.
- Be judicious about naming criminal suspects before the formal filing of charges.
- Balance a criminal suspect's fair trial rights with the public's right to be informed.

Act Independently

Journalists should be free of obligation to any interest other than the public's right to know.

Journalists should:
- Avoid conflicts of interest, real or perceived.
- Remain free of associations and activities that may compromise integrity or damage credibility.
- Refuse gifts, favors, fees, free travel and special treatment, and shun secondary employment, political involvement, public office and service in community organizations if they compromise journalistic integrity.

- Disclose unavoidable conflicts.
- Be vigilant and courageous about holding those with power accountable.
- Deny favored treatment to advertisers and special interests and resist their pressure to influence news coverage.
- Be wary of sources offering information for favors or money; avoid bidding for news.

Be Accountable

Journalists are accountable to their readers, listeners, viewers and each other.

Journalists should:
- Clarify and explain news coverage and invite dialogue with the public over journalistic conduct.
- Encourage the public to voice grievances against the news media.
- Admit mistakes and correct them promptly.
- Expose unethical practices of journalists and the news media.
- Abide by the same high standards to which they hold others.

2014 version:

See Chapter One for a full copy and thorough discussion of the current code. The 2014 SPJ Code of Ethics contains very few changes from the 1996 version, except that it concentrates entirely on abiding principles and eliminates most references to specific information-delivery technologies. A disclaimer at the end is almost identical to an addition made to the code in 2009.

ACKNOWLEDGMENTS

The Society of Professional Journalists has long been a leader in journalism ethics, but didn't publish its first ethics handbook/textbook until 1993, six years after former national president Carolyn Carlson decided to make it a priority.

The original authors, whose work still comprises a major part of this fifth iteration of the book, are Jay Black, professor emeritus at the University of South Florida; Bob Steele, since retired from the Poynter Institute; and Ralph Barney, professor emeritus at Brigham Young University. Their checklists of ethical criteria, for instance, are included for all of the major categories of ethical scenarios. They were responsible for the first three editions of the text, then called *Doing Ethics*, and the revisions and editions to the fourth and fifth editions would not have been possible without the foundations laid by these three celebrated media ethicists.

The Society of Professional Journalists Foundation, which provides educational and financial support to SPJ, is the principal driver behind the current project, and is responsible for bringing it to fruition. Fred Brown, a former SPJ national president, longtime ethics committee member and now a member of the foundation board, edited and wrote much of this fifth edition.

Brown has a lot of people to thank for helping this effort see the light of day. Especially:

- Yvette B. Walker, assistant dean of the Gaylord College of Journalism and Communication at the University of Oklahoma, who painstakingly copyread the text and double-checked links to various codes of ethics and other outside sources, a daunting but extremely important task, and very much appreciated.
- Larry Messing, Tony Peterson, Billy O'Keefe, Monica Williams and former executive director Alyson Bethel McKenzie at SPJ headquarters, took time during a turbulent period to give attention to this effort.
- Paul Fletcher, a former SPJ national president trained in the law, generously contributed Chapter 4, comparing and contrasting media law and media ethics.
- Two former chairs of the SPJ Ethics Committee, Kevin Z. Smith and Andy Schotz, and the chair at the time of this writing, Lynn Walsh, provided leadership and guidance. Schotz, in particular, assigned, coordinated and wrote case studies.
- Other SPJ members, including several who serve or have served on the ethics committee, contributed case studies and editing: Irwin Gratz of Maine Public Radio and president of the SPJ Foundation; Casey Bukro, retired from the *Chicago Tribune*; Adrian Uribarri of the *Orlando Sentinel*; Jim Pumarlo, media

consultant and former editor of *The Red Wing Republican Eagle* in Minnesota; Gordon "Mac" McKerral, a former national president; Elizabeth K. Hansen, Eastern Kentucky University; Nerissa Young, Marshall University; Sara Stone, Baylor University, and her former students, Laura Barth, Brittany Daniels, Amber Orand, Robbie Rogers and Elizabeth Suggs.

- Winston & Strawn, a leading Chicago law firm, shared its research on, and online links to, publicly available media codes of ethics.
- Brown's media ethics students at the University of Denver provided energy and inspiration, especially Chloe Barrett, Jill Hamilton, Cory Lamz and Selene McConachy, who contributed case studies (and of course got A's in class for them).
- Brown's colleagues in the Department of Media, Film and Journalism Studies at the University of Denver, especially the department chair, Dr. Lynn Schofield Clark, and technology wizard Ethan Crawford.
- Mike Keefe, Pulitzer Prize-winning cartoonist and Brown's former colleague on The Denver Post's editorial page, who generously contributed two of his most current creations from The Colorado Independent.
- And none of this would have been possible without the spousal indulgence, support, intellectual challenge and love of Mary Clara Ames Brown.

BIBLIOGRAPHY

Other Codes of Ethics

Dozens of media organizations have made their codes of ethics accessible to the public online. It's not particularly helpful to list them in a printed publication, because it requires retyping what amounts to url codes. But for a comprehensive list, with live links updated as necessary, go to **spj.org/ethics** (or more directly, **spj.org/ethicscode-other.asp**).

Footnotes by Chapter (where applicable)

Chapter 1: Ethical Thinking

On ethics and morality: Black, Jay, and Bryant, Jennings. *Introduction to Media Communications*, Fourth Edition, pp. 540-541. Madison: Brown & Benchmark, 1995. Gert, Bernard. *Morality: Its Nature and Justification*, Revised Edition. Oxford University Press, 2005

A regularly updated resource of the history of moral reasoning and current writings: Stanford Encyclopedia of Philosophy: https://plato.stanford.edu/

Chapter 2: The Role of the Journalist

Black, Jay; Steele, Bob and Barney, Ralph. *Doing Ethics in Journalism*, Third Edition (1997), pp. 12-23. Boston: Allyn & Bacon

Chapter 3: Codes of Ethics and Beyond

Meyer, Philip. *Ethical Journalism: A Guide for Students, Practitioners, and Consumers.* New York: Longman (1997).

Black, et al.; *Doing Ethics in Journalism*, Third Edition (1997), pp. 24-50.

Chapter 4: Ethics and the Law

"Unwarranted publishing of the names of permitted owners just encourages gun owners to skip the permitting." Source: Julie Moos, https://www.poynter.org/reporting-editing/2012/where-the-journal-news-went-wrong-in-publishing-names-addresses-of-gun-owners/Dec. 26, 2012.

Richard Jewell and the Atlanta Olympics bombing. Source: Ronald Ostrow, http://www.columbia.edu/itc/journalism/j6075/edit/readings/jewell.html, June 13, 2000.

Stephen Hatfill and the anthrax mailings. Source: Donna Shaw, American Journalism Review, http://ajrarchive.org/Article.asp?id=4042. Feb/March 2006.

Shield laws and protecting sources: Source: Paul Fletcher, Forbes.com, https://www.forbes.com/sites/paulfletcher/2017/11/29/sessions-testimony-prompts-new-federal-shield-law-bill-protecting-journalists/#1ed665d04912, Nov. 29, 2017.

History of the Freedom of Information Act. Source: Bert Bostrom, *Talent, Truth and Energy*, chapter 5.

Using the SPJ Code of Ethics in Hulk Hogan's lawsuit against Gawker: Source: Peter Sterne, Politico,

https://www.politico.com/media/story/2016/03/journalism-group-responds-to-invocation-of-its-ethics-code-in-hogan-v-gawker-004421, March 10, 2016.

Chapter 5: Accuracy and Fairness

Satire as Journalism and John Oliver's dealings with whistle-blower Edward Snowden:

Bilton, Nick, et al. "The New Establishment 2015." The Hive, Vanity Fair, Sept. 9, 2015, www.vanityfair.com/news/photos/2015/09/new-establishment-list-2015.

CBS This Morning. "John Oliver: I'm Not a Journalist." YouTube, Oct. 30, 2015, www.youtube.com/watch?v=1lFoyDOi-Ww.
CNNMoney. "Why Snowden Chose John Oliver." YouTube, YouTube, April 8, 2015,

www.youtube.com/watch?v=zpYW1fpuyNA.

Fusion. "John Oliver to Jorge Ramos: 'I'm Not a Journalist.'" YouTube, May 12, 2015,

www.youtube.com/watch?v=l17TPkXGVCo&t=192s.

Last Week Tonight. "Journalism: Last Week Tonight with John Oliver (HBO)." YouTube, Aug. 7, 2016, www.youtube.com/watch?v=bq2_wSsDwkQ.

"Satire." Merriam-Webster, Merriam-Webster, www.merriam-webster.com/dictionary/satire.

"What Is Journalism? Definition and Meaning of the Craft." American Press Institute, Oct. 9, 2013, www.americanpressinstitute.org/journalism-essentials/what-is-journalism/.

Chapter 6: Deception

Bok, Sissela. *Lying: Moral Choice in Public and Private Life*. New York: Vintage Books, 1999.

Chapter 7: Minimize Harm

Las Vegas shooting: References
Waxman, Olivia B. "Las Vegas Was the Deadliest Shooting in Modern U.S. History. Here's Why 'Modern' Is So Important." *Time Magazine*, 4 Oct. 2017. http://time.com/4968108/las-vegas-deadliest-shooting-modern-us-history/ Accessed January 19, 2018.

Chapter 11: Privacy

To see the report on Rolling Stone's "A Rape on Campus" story from Columbia University's Graduate School of Journalism: https://www.rollingstone.com/culture/culture-news/rolling-stone-and-uva-the-columbia-university-graduate-school-of-journalism-report-44930/

Chapter 12: Source-Reporter Relationships

Malcolm, Janet. *The Journalist and the Murderer*. New York: Vintage Books, 1990, pp. 3-4.

Other Useful Books and References

Bauerlein, Mark, *The Dumbest Generation: How the Digital Age Stupefies Young Americans and Jeopardizes Our Future (or Don't Trust Anyone Under 30)*. New York: Penguin Group (USA), 2008.

Bivins, Thomas H. *Mixed Media: Moral Distinctions in Advertising, Public Relations and Journalism*. Mahwah, N.J.: Lawrence Erlbaum Associates, 2004.

Black, Jay, and Roberts, Chris. *Doing Ethics in Media: Theories and Practical Applications*. New York: Routledge, 2011.

Bugeja, Michael. *Living Media Ethics: Across Platforms*. New York: Routledge, 2018.

Christians, Clifford; Fackler, Mark; Brittain, Kathy McKee; Kreschel, Peggy J.; and Woods, Robert H. *Media Ethics: Cases and Moral Reasoning*, 10th edition. Oxfordshire, UK: Taylor & Francis Group, 2016.

Christians, Clifford; Fackler, Mark; and Ferre, John P. *Ethics for Public Communication*. Oxford University Press, 2011.

Cooper, Stephen D. *Watching the Watchdog: Bloggers as the Fifth Estate*. Spokane: Marquette Books, 2006.

Day, Louis A. *Ethics in Media Communications: Cases & Controversies*, 5th edition. Belmont, California: Wadsworth Publishing Co., 2006.

Ess, Charles. *Digital Media Ethics*. Cambridge: Polity, 2009.

Foreman, Gene. *The Ethical Journalist: Making Responsible Decision in the Pursuit of News*. Malden, Mass.: Wiley-Blackwell, 2010.

Friend, Cecilia, and Singer, Jane B. *Online Journalism Ethics: Traditions and Transitions*. Armonk, N.Y.: M.E. Sharpe, 2007.

Johannesen, Richard; Valde, Kathleen; and Whedbee, Karen. *Ethics in Human Communication*, 6th edition. Long Grove, Ill.: Waveland Press, 2008

Kirtley, Jane, and Ison, Chris. *Media Ethics Today: Issues, Analysis, Solutions*. San Diego: Cognella, 2015.

Kovach, Bill, and Rosenstiel, Tom. *The Elements of Journalism: What Newspeople Should Know and the Public Should Expect*. New York: Three Rivers Press, 2001.

Kovach, Bill, and Rosenstiel, Tom. *Blur: How to Know What's True in the Age of Information Overload*. New York: Bloomsbury USA, 2010.

May, Steve; Cheney, George Edward; and Munshi, Debashish. *The Handbook of Communication Ethics*. New York: Routlege, 2011.

McBride, Kelly, and Rosenstiel, Tom. *The New Ethics of Journalism: Principles for the 21st Century*. Los Angeles: SAGE Publishing, 2013.

Meyer, Philip. *The Vanishing Newspaper: Saving Journalism in the Information Age*. Columbia: University of Missouri Press, 2004.

Meyers, Christopher. *Journalism Ethics: A Philosophical Approach*. Oxford University Press, 2010

Overholser, Geneva, and Jamieson, Kathleen Hall. *Institutions of American Democracy: The Press*. Oxford University Press, 2005.

Parsons, Patricia J. *Ethics in Public Relations*, 3rd edition. London: Kogan Page, 2016.

Patterson, Philip, and Wilkins, Lee. *Media Ethics: Issues and Cases*, 9th edition. Lanham, Md.: Rowman & Littlefield, 2018.

Peck, Lee Anne, and Reel, Guy S. *Media Ethics at Work: True Stories from Young Professionals*, 2nd edition. Los Angeles: SAGE Publishing, 2016.

Plaisance, Patrick. *Media Ethics: Key Principles for Responsible Practice*. Los Angeles: SAGE Publishing, 2009.

Seib, Philip. *The Al-Jazeera Effect: How the New Media Are Reshaping World Politics*. Dulles, Va.: Potomac Press, 2008.

Ward, Stephen J.A. *The Invention of Journalism Ethics: The Path to Objectivity and Beyond*. Montreal: McGill-Queen's University Press, 2005.

Ward, Stephen J.A. *Disrupting Journalism Ethics: Radical Change on the Frontier of Digital Media*. New York: Routledge Focus, 2018.

Willis, Jim. *The Mind of a Journalist: How Reporters View Themselves, Their World and Their Craft*. Los Angeles: SAGE Publications, 2010.

INDEX

ABC (broadcast network), 91-94, 102, 151-152, 218

Abduction, 109-112, 149-152

Abortion, 145, 223

Access (for news media), 25, 32, 52, 57-58, 90-91, 100, 143-144, 151-154, 163, 180, 205

Accountability, *xi*, *xii*, 10-13, 17, 18, 24, 26, 37, 41-45, 50, 54, 72, 90, 97-98, 106, 174, 207-231

Accuracy, *xi*, *xii*, 8-12, 18-23, 26, 53, 59-84, 123-133, 143, 162, 166, 177, 200, 205-206, 219, 223, 226, 228-230, 234-239

Acosta, Jim, 153-155

Adams, Brock, 32, 34, 36

Advertisers, 10, 50, 84, 117-122, 139, 160, 165, 205, 214, 223-226, 231

Agnir, Ron, 171

AIDS, 177

Ailes, Roger, 157

Allentown, Pennsylvania, *Morning Call*, 144-146

Alou, Moises, 74-75

Alpha Chi Omega, 126-128

Alter, Jonathan, 105-106

Ameri, Goli, 66

American Advertising Federation, 50, 84, 122, 160, 226, 231

American Editor, The, 208

American Journalism Review, 53, 220-221, 246

American Society of News Editors (ASNE), 41, 45, 57, 214, 233

Amsterdam, Netherlands, 152

Anderson County, Kentucky, 106-109

Anderson News, (Kentucky, 106-109

Anonymous sources, 8, 11, 16, 55, 60, 80-83, 115, 195-204, 216, 229, 239

Anthony, Casey, 151-152

Anthony, Caylee Marie, 151-152

Anthony, Cindy, 151

Anti-Defamation League, 133-135

Antolini, Carl, 171-173

Applied ethics, 3

Aristotle, 4-5

Arizona prison hostages, 62-63

Arizona Republic, 79, 82, 160

Asbury Park Press, 47, 79, 80, 162

Arrieta-Walden, Michael, 64-67

Asbury Park Press, New Jersey, 47, 79, 80, 162

Ashton, Jennifer, M.D., 102

Associated Press, 15, 46, 81, 82, 95, 96, 162, 171, 176, 186-187, 193, 198, 229

Associated Press Media Editors (APME), 40, 48, 83

Association of Health Care Journalists, 103

Association of Food Journalists, 161

Atlanta, Georgia, 14, 53; Atlanta Olympics 1996, 53

Atlanta Journal-Constitution, 53, 214

Austin (Texas) *American-Statesman*, 73

BALCO, 197-198

Baldo (comic strip), 27

Ballantine, Richard, 129

Bangkok, Thailand, 71

Baquet, Dean, 204

Barney, Ralph, xi, 91, 94, 106, 175, 200, 223, 243

Barry, John, 105

Barth, Laura, 215

Bartman, Steve, 74-75

Bay Guardian, San Francisco, 90

Baylor University, 89, 112, 170, 215, 219, 244

Bayonne, New Jersey, 186

Beaufort, Missouri, 110

Beckley, West Virginia, 171

Bennet, James, 203

Bentham, Jeremy, 6

Bergen County, New Jersey, *Record*, 186

Bernstein, Carl, 200-201

Besser, Richard, M.D., 102

Bianchi, Bruna, 147

Bianchi, Silvana, 149

Billboard magazine, 211-213

Black, Jay, xi, 2, 91, 94, 106, 175, 200, 223, 243, 248

Blair, Jayson, 215-217

Blasey Ford, Christine, 75-78

Blogs, *xiii*, 14, 31, 60-61, 79, 88, 147, 150, 211, 219, 229, 231

Bok, Sissela, 86

Bonds, Barry, 197-198

Boorda, Admiral Jeremy, 104-106

Border, United States, 117-119

Boston Globe, 215

Boulder, Colorado, 71-72, 128

Boyd, Gerald, 215-216

Bracamontes, Luis, 117

Bradlee, Ben, 200

Branzburg v. Hayes, 54-55

Brazil, 147-152

Brigham Young University, 243

Bring Sean Home Foundation, 148

Brooklyn, New York, 215

Brown, Fred, *xi*, 61, 73, 142, 146, 210, 243-244

Bryant, Jennings, 2

Bryant, Kobe, 31

"BTK" killer, 70

Buckeye, Arizona, 62-63

Bukro, Casey, 75, 234, 243

Burke, James, 74

Bush, George W., 117, 217-218

Bush, Jeb, 217

California, 71, 75-78, 117, 133, 173-174, 221

California First Amendment Coalition, 198

Cameras, xi, 33, 85, 87-93, 95, 167, 173-175; hidden, 85, 87, 90, 91-93, 95; in the courtroom, 165, 173-175

Cape Girardeau, Missouri, 156

Carlson, Ben, 109

Carlson, Carolyn, 243

Carter-Reagan presidential race, 1980, 218-219

Celebrity news, 4, 31, 61, 209-210

Central Intelligence Agency, 54-55, 220-223

Ceppos, Jerry, 175-177, 220-223

Charles Koch Foundation, 158-159

Charlottesville, Virginia, 181

Chavis, Benjamin, 131

"Checkbook journalism", 147-152

Chicago Cubs, 74-75

Chicago, Illinois, 74, 188, 190, 244

Chicago Sun-Times, 74

Chicago Tribune, 74, 190, 243

Cincinnati, Ohio, 157

Citizen journalists, 42

Clinton Administration, 117

Clinton, Hillary, 203

Closson, Troy, 191-192

Clooney, George, 169

CNN, 68, 84, 102, 105, 117-118, 133-134, 152, 153-155

Coeur d'Alene, Idaho, 110

Colbert, Stephen, 68

Colombia, 117, 220

Colorado, 55, 71-72, 128-131, 184, 197

Colorado Independent, 47, 156, 244

Colorado, University of, 71-72

Columbia Journalism Review, 208

Columbia University, 53, 180-181

Columbus Ledger-Inquirer, Ohio, 161, 164

Committee of Concerned Journalists, 214

Community journalism, 106-109, 112-117, 128-131, 171-173, 182-185

Confidential sources and confidentiality, 17-21, 32, 54-55, 63, 71-72, 75-78, 82-83, 195-199, 235, 238; Ethics codes on, 17-21, 235, 238

Conrad, Eric, 143

Conradt, Louis Jr., 87

Contempt of court, 54

Contra rebels, 220-223

Convention sponsorships, ethical issues, 158-159

Copyright, 208

Cornyn, Sen. John, 56

Corrections, 10, 12, 14, 19, 20, 74, 83, 84, 98, 99, 121, 207, 215-217, 226, 234, 236, 238, 241

Crack cocaine, 220-222

Crawford, Ethan, 244

Cupertino, California, 221

Daily Camera, Boulder, Colorado, 71

Daily Northwestern, 188-192

Dalek, Brian, 127

Daley, Mayor Richard, 74

Dallas Morning News, 95, 120, 161, 165, 193, 226

Dana, Will, 180-181

Daniels, Brittany, 170, 244

Dao, James, 204-205

Dark Alliance, newspaper series and book, 220-223

Dartmouth College, 27

"Dateline", 87-89

Davis, Richard Allen, 173-175

Day, Louis A., 27

De Blasio, Bill, 69

Deception, 1, 11, 20, 85-96, 167, 214, 224, 226

"Deep Throat", 200-202, 204

Defense, U.S. Department of, 142-144

Democratic Party, 56, 63, 73, 75-78, 107, 146, 221

Denver, Colorado, 75-78, 146-147

Denver Newspaper Guild, 146

Denver Post, 50, 71, 83, 163, 164, 205, 228, 229, 244

Denver, University of, 69, 101, 135, 209-210, 213, 244

Deontology, 4, 5, 134, 212-213

Deseret News, Salt Lake City, 226

Desert Storm, Operation, 89-91

Detroit, Michigan, 152

Detroit Free Press …47, 83, 95, 121, 136, 137, 163, 205

Dewey, John, 6

Diana, Princess of Wales, 209

Disney World, Orlando, 148

Dover Air Force Base, 89-91

Dow Jones & Co., 48, 49, 227

Duncan, Joseph, 110

Durango, Colorado 128-130

Durango Herald, Colorado, 128-131

Eagles (band), 146-1479

Eastern Kentucky University, 109, 244

Editor & Publisher, 70, 174

Embedded reporters, 143-144

Enforcement of ethics codes, xii, 10, 17, 34-36, 39-42, 51, 57-58, 116, 208, 234

Englewood, New Jersey, 185

Egalitarianism, 6-7, 29

Electronic News, 103

Ellerman, Troy, 197-198

Ensslin, John, Dedication page

Eramo, Nicole P., 181

Erdely, Sabrina, 179-181

Eshoo, U.S. Rep. Anna G., 77

Excellence in Journalism (EIJ) conference, 158-159

Facebook, 117, 119, 126-128

Fainaru-Wada, Mark, 197-198

"Fake news", 156

False light, 79

Fancher, Michael, 33

Farrell, Mike, Dedication page

Favre, Gregory, 174-175

FBI (Federal Bureau of Investigation), 76-77, 200-202

Feinstein, Sen. Diane, 76-77

Felt, Mark ("Deep Throat"), 200-202

Fiorina, Carly, 224

First Amendment, 10, 31-36, 44, 58, 83, 147, 154, 159, 198, 207-208

Fletcher, Paul, 51-58, 243

Florida and 2000 presidential race, 217-219

Florida Marlins, 74

Food Lion markets, 91-94

Fortune magazine, 102

Fox News, 55, 117-119, 155, 156-157, 159

Franklin, Jonathan, 89-91

Freedom of Information Act, 55, 57, 159, 165

Friedman, George, 201

Friedrich, Carl, 35

Gaines, James R., 131-132

Game of Shadows, 197

Gates, Jamilia, 126-128

Gay rights, 129-131, 144-146

Germany, 133-135
Gert, Bernard, 27
Golden Rule, 5, 49
Goldman, Bruna Bianchi, 148
Goldman, David, 148-152
Goldman, Sean, 148-150
Goldschmidt, Neil, 66
Goodhue County (Minnesota) Mental Health Center, 182, 184
"Good Morning America", 152
Gore, Al, 217-219
Gould, Bob, 132
Graphic images, 100-101, 133, 171-172, 174
Grassley, U.S. Sen. Charles, 54, 77
Gratz, Irwin, 144, 244
Groene, Dylan and Shasta, 110-111
Guardian Angels, 185-186
Guillaume, Kristine, 192
Gupta, Sanjay, M.D., 102, 104
Guttman, Jeannine, 143

Hackworth, David, 105
Haiti, 2010 earthquake in, 102-104
Hamilton, Jill, 135, 244
Hamilton Township, New Jersey, 185
Hannity, Sean, 156-157
Hansen, Chris, 87-89
Hansen, Elizabeth K., 223
Harvard Crimson, 192
Hazard, Geoffrey, 40
Hearst Newspapers, 230
Hentoff, Nat, 105
Herndon, Astead, 190-191
Hidden cameras, 85-93

Hilliard, Ardith, 146
Hilliard, Bill, 214
Hippocratic Oath, 103-104
Hoge, Patrick, 174
Holocaust, The, 133-135
Hoover, J. Edgar, 201
House of Representatives, U.S., 56
Hurricane Katrina, 141-142

Immigration, 117-119, 120, 192
Incest, 112-117
Indianapolis Colts, 169
International Child Abduction Prevention Act of 2009, 149
"Invasion" political ad, 117-119
Investigative Reporters and Editors, 70, 208
Iraq War, 143-144, 169-170
IRE Journal, 208
Irby, Kenneth, 124
iTunes, 211

Jackson, Michael, interview with mother, 152
Jersey Journal, 186-187
Jewell, Richard, 53
Johnson, Lyndon, 57
Jordan, Rep. Jim, 56
The Journalist and the Murderer, 195
Judeo-Christian ethic, 5
"Judge Judy", 209
Junkets, 160
Jurgensen, Karen, 215

Kanka, Megan, 185-188

Kant, Immanuel, 5-6
Karr, John Mark, 71-72
Kavanaugh, Justice Brett, 75-78
Keefe, Mike, 47, 156, 244
Kelley, Jack, 213-215
Kent, Thomas, 15
Kentucky, 106-109
King, Gayle, 69
King, Rodney, 33
Kirk, James T., 60
Kirtley, Jane, 248
Klass, Polly, 173-175
Knox, Olivier, 153
Koch brothers and conservative causes, 158-159
Kopel, David, 72
Kovach, Bill, 214, 248
Kuwait, 143

Lamz, Cory, 213, 244
Landman, Jonathan, 215
Lange, Lisa, 133
Las Vegas, Nevada, 100-101
Law in journalism, as compared with ethics, 34, 39, 51-58, 91-94
Letters to the Editor, 72, 128-131, 229
Levine, Cathie, 151-152
Lexington (Kentucky) *Herald-Leader*, 109
Libel, 43, 54-55, 91, 196, 208
Light for Life Foundation, 184
Linden, Tom, M.D., 103
Lorensen, Maria, 171-172
Los Angeles, California, 33, 220-221

Los Angeles Times, 78, 79, 83, 104, 161, 163, 169-170, 194, 198, 2057, 220, 228, 231
Louisiana State University, 27

Mahurin, Matt, 131-132
Main, Frank, 74
Maine National Guard, 143-144
Maine Public Radio, 143, 243
Major League Baseball, 143-144, 198
Malcolm, Janet, 195-196
Marin Independent Journal, 174
Marshall University, 125-128, 244
Martinsburg, West Virginia, *Journal*, 171
Maryland, University of, 216
Mason, Linda, 219
Masthead, 208
Mathews, Jay, 73
McBride, Kelly, 154-155
McCarthy, Brian, 118
McConachy, Selene, 69
McKenzie, Alyson Bethel, 243
McKerral, Gordon "Mac", 244
McLaughlin, Craig, 90
Medill School, Northwestern University, 188-192
"Megan's Law", 185-187
Merrifield, Chris, 141
Meta-ethics, 3
Mexico border, 117-119
Meyer, Philip, 39
Michigan in 2000 election, 217
Michigan State University, 115
Mill, John Stuart, 6
Miller, Judith, 54, 198

Minneapolis Star-Tribune, 199

Minnesota, 184, 199

Minnesota News Council, 112, 116-117

Mittelstadt, Mark, 186

Montana, 110

Moon, Craig, 214

Morals, moral reasoning, 1-7, 29, 31-37, 40, 43, 74, 86, 99, 100-101, 104, 128-131, 187-188, 195

Mothers Against Drunk Driving (MADD), 109

MSNBC, 88, 159

Muhammad, caricatures of, 27

Multichannel News, 150

MySpace, 128

NAACP, 33

National Football League, 118

National Press Photographers Association, code of ethics, 24-25; 132, 170

National Public Radio, code of ethics, 26; 80, 83, 96, 121, 124, 144, 243

NBC, 87-89, 102, 118, 147-151, 218

National Security News Service, 105

Navy, U.S., 104-106

Negative advertising, 223-225

Nemitz, Bill, 143-144

New Jersey, 147-149

Newkirk, Ingrid, 134

New Orleans, Louisiana, 141-142

News Photographer, 208

Newsweek magazine, 104-106, 131-132

New York City, 32, 55, 69, 147

New York Post, 152, 209

New York Times, 54, 55, 80, 96, 130, 157, 164, 181, 191, 198, 201-204, 215-217, 220-221

Nicaragua, 220-223

Nieman Reports, 208

Nixon, Richard, 55, 200-201

Normative ethics, 3

North Carolina, University of, 103, 133

North Jersey Herald & News, 186

Northwestern University, 188-192

Obama, Barack, 75

Objectivity, 18, 48, 79, 145, 166, 235, 237, 238

Obscenity, 137, 173-175, 208, 227

Ochberg, Dr. Frank, 115

Okrent, Daniel, 218

Oliver, John, 67-69

Ombudsman movement, 44, 208, 221

Online News Association, 14-16, 46

"Oprah Winfrey Show", 110

Orand, Amber, 112, 244

Oregonian, The (Portland), 29, 63-66

Orlando, Florida, 148, 150, 152

Orlando Sentinel, 243

Osama bin Laden, 214

Oswald, John, 186-187

Overholser, Geneva, 221

Ownby, Ben, 110

Packwood, Sen. Bob, 33, 66

PACs (Political Action Committees), 165, 223-225

Pakistan-Afghanistan border, 214

Panama, U.S. invasion of, 89-90

Parthenon, The, 126-128

Peabody Award, 68

Pease, Admiral Kendall, 105

Peer pressure, 3, 7, 182, 208

Pence, Mike, 56

Pennsylvania, 144, 152, 217

Pentagon, 89-90, 104

Persian Gulf War, 89-91

Personal relations and ethical conflicts, 140, 141, 161, 163, 190-205

Perverted-Justice.com, 87-89

PETA (People for the Ethical Treatment of Animals), 133-135

Petersburg, Virginia, 186

Phi Kappa Psi fraternity, 179-181

Philadelphia Inquirer, 163, 164, 230

Phillip Morris Co., 159

Photojournalism, 24, 101, 132, 167-175

Photoshop, 170

Physician-journalists, 102-104

Pirated music, 211-213

Pirro, Jeanine, 156-157

Plagiarism, 5, 9, 13, 14, 48, 51, 56, 84, 214, 238, 239

Plato, 4

Political activity and ethics, 9, 11, 12-15, 25, 26, 32, 73, 82, 84, 117-119, 120, 123, 137, 144-147, 153-157, 158-159, 162, 164-165, 194, 199-202, 205, 223-225, 235, 237, 240

Portland Press Herald/Maine Sunday Telegram, 143

Portyanko, Tanya, 171

Poynter Institute, *xi*, 52, 86, 88, 123, 124, 154-155, 188, 243

Pre-publication review (PPR), 72-73

Presidential election of 2000, 217-219

Press councils, 112-117, 208

"PrimeTime Live", 91-94

Prior restraint, 208

Privacy, right to and principles of, 13, 21, 31-32, 66, 75, 79, 90, 99, 111, 112, 117, 122, 167, 177-194, 196, 208, 236, 238, 240

Professional Rodeo Cowboys Association, 197-198

Project Censored, 90

Public Radio News Directors Inc., code of ethics, 26

Public relations, xi, 17-23, 27, 33, 40, 48, 84, 104, 118, 120, 133-135, 139, 162, 160, 223-225

Public Relations Society of America (PRSA) Code of Ethics, 17-23, 50, 84, 119, 160, 226

Pulitzer Prize, 169, 200, 213, 214, 244

Pumarlo, Jim, 116, 117, 182, 185, 243

Quill magazine, 142, 208

Rader, Dennis, 70

Radio Television Digital News Association (RTDNA), code of ethics, 11-13, 17, 158-159

Raines, Howell, 215-216

Rakoczy, Anthony, 152

Ramsey, JonBenét, 71-72

Ramirez, Deborah, 76-78

Ramos, Jorge, 68-70

Rape, 31, 32, 44, 76, 108, 179-181, 185-186, 193; "A Rape on Campus," 179-181

Raskin, Rep. Jamie, 56

Rawls, John, 7

Reagan-Carter presidential race, 1980, 218-219

Reason magazine, 188-189

Redbook, 133

Red Wing, Minnesota, *Republican Eagle*, 115-117, 182, 185, 244

Relativism, 6

Republican Party, 56, 63, 73, 117, 157, 199

Reuters Handbook of Journalism, 79, 121, 137, 165

Rhodes, Dawn, 190

Richards, Ann, 133

Rio de Janeiro, Brazil, 149-150

Ritt, Glen, 187

Ritter, Hal, 215

Roberts, Bill, 129-130

Roberts, Julia, 133

Rocky Mountain News, Denver, 71-72, 145-147

Rogers, Robbie, 89, 244

Rolling Stone, 179-181

Rossen, Jeff, 148

Route 91 Harvest Festival, 100-101

Rowe, Sandy, 65-66

Russell, Bertrand, 6

Rutenberg, Jim, 157

Rutten, Tim, 198

Sacramento Bee, 176

St. Louis Journalism Review, 210

St. Paul Pioneer Press, Minnesota, 82, 201

St. Petersburg, Florida, xi, 125

Salazar, Sen. Ken, 146

Salt Lake City, Utah, 108-110

San Antonio Express-News, Texas, 137

Sanders, Kerry, 141

Sanders, Sarah Huckabee, 153-155

San Diego, California, 133

Sanford, Bruce W., 40

San Francisco, California, 90, 198

San Francisco Chronicle, 174, 197-198

San Jose Mercury News, California, 49, 173-175, 194, 220-224

Satire as journalism, 67-69

Scheer, Peter, 198

Schofield Clark, Lynn, 244

Schotz, Andy, 78, 148-151, 243

Schuringa, Jasper, 151

Schwarzenegger, Arnold, 78

Sears Tower, Chicago, 214

Seattle Times, 32, 33, 36

Seidlin, Judge Larry, 209

Seigenthaler, John, 214

Sellers, Patricia, 102

Senate Judiciary Committee, 56, 75-77

Sexual assault, 29, 31, 32, 44, 62, 63-65, 75-77, 108, 109-112, 115-117, 179-181, 185-186, 193; "A Rape on Campus," 179-181

Shearn, Ian, 186

Shepherdstown, West Virginia, 171

Shepherd University, 171

Shield laws, 54-56, 80, 81

Siegal, Allan, 215

Sigma Alpha Epsilon, Marshall University, 126-128

Simpson, O.J., 131-133

Sinclair Broadcasting, 159

Singer, Isaac Bashevis, 133

Sioux Falls Argus Leader, South Dakota, 162, 205

Slate online magazine, 224

Slaughter, Chris, 141

Sliwa, Curtis, 185

Small-town journalism, 106-109, 112-117, 128-131, 140, 171-173

Smart, Elizabeth, and family, 109-112

Smith, Anna Nicole, 209

Smith, Rep. Chris, 149

Smith, Kevin, *xii*, 42, 150, 243

Smith, Michael, 116

Snowden, Edward, 68

Snyderman, Nancy, M.D., 102-104

Soave, Robby, 188-189

Society of Professional Journalists, *xi*, 14, 40, 41, 43, 45, 129, 153, 158, 243-244; Code of Ethics, *xii*, 8-10, 41-45, 51, 88, 100, 111, 118, 172, 189, 208, 233-241; Ethics Committee, *xiii*, 43; SPJ Foundation, 243

Socrates, 4

South Florida, University of, 243

Spears, Britney, 209-210

Sponsored content and ethical issues of sponsorship, 10, 12, 20, 56, 117-118, 158-159, 205, 226, 231

Stake-O-Meter, 29

Stanford University, 7, 63-64

Statesman-Journal, Salem, Oregon, 49

Stelter, Brian, 68

Steele, Bob, *xi*, 91, 94, 102, 106, 175, 200, 223, 243

Steroids and sports, 197-198

Stewart, Martha, 132

Stockholm Syndrome, 110

Stone, Sara, 88, 112, 170, 215, 219, 244

Stratfor.com, 201

Strupp, Joe, 70

Suggs, Elizabeth, 219, 244

Suicide, 87, 104-106, 107, 120, 182-185, 193, 222

Sullivan, Margaret, 190-191, 203

Sulzberger, Arthur, 203, 217

"Sunday Night Football", 118

Supreme Court, U.S., 54-55, 75-78, 83, 198, 199

Swetnick, Julie, 76-78

Tampa Bay Tribune, Florida, 136, 230

Tea Party, 157

Teleology, 5-6, 134, 213

Temple, John, 146-147

Texas, 73, 87, 133

Texas Monthly, 133

Thames, Rick, 70

Time magazine, 48, 100-101, 131-133

Ting Tings, The (band), 211

Tompkins, Al, 52, 88, 154-155

Tracey, Michael, 71-72

Trespass, 91-94

Trump, Donald, 68, 75, 117-119, 153-155, 156-157, 202-204

TV Guide, 133

UNESCO, 68

Uribarri, Adrian, 217, 243

USA Today, 54, 133, 141, 213-215

User-generated content, 16

Utilitarianism, 6

Van der Sloot, Joran, 152

Vieira, Meredith, 148

Virtue ethics, 4-5

Virginia, University of, 179-181

Virginian-Pilot, Norfolk, 193

Voter News Service, 217-219

Wabasha County Herald, Minnesota, 112-117

Walker, Yvette B., 244

Wall Street Journal, 49, 209, 227

Walsh, Lynn, 243

Walski, Brian, 169-170

Washington, D.C., 32, 74, 83, 105, 155, 201, 203, 215

Washington Post, 46, 48, 73, 76, 81, 84, 104, 179, 190-191, 200-202, 204, 215, 220-221

Washington state, 36; Washington News Council, 116

Waters, Maxine, 221

Webb, Gary, 220-223

Weblogs, *xiii*, 79, 147, 150, 211, 229, 231

Weinberg, Steve, 72-73

Westin, David, 218

Westminster, Colorado, 184

Whelan, Frank, 144-146

Whitaker, Charles, 188-192

White, Don, 106

White House, 125, 153-155, 202

White House Correspondents Association, 153-154

Wichita Eagle, Kansas, 70

Williams, Lance, 197-198

Williams, Monica, 243

Winfrey, Oprah, 110, 133

Wisconsin, University of, 170, 233

Wittman, Bob, 144-146

Woods, Keith, 124, 188

Woodward, Bob, 155, 200-202

Wrigley Field, Chicago, 74-75

Wu, David, 29, 63-67

WWL-TV, New Orleans, 141

Yale University, 76, 218

Yarnold, David, 174

Young, Nerissa, 128, 146, 173, 244

www.ingramcontent.com/pod-product-compliance
Lightning Source LLC
Chambersburg PA
CBHW071348290426
44108CB00014B/1477